Sixties Britain

Sixties Britain

CULTURE, SOCIETY AND POLITICS

Mark Donnelly

PEARSON
Longman

Harlow, England • London • New York • Boston • San Francisco • Toronto
Sydney • Tokyo • Singapore • Hong Kong • Seoul • Taipei • New Delhi
Cape Town • Madrid • Mexico City • Amsterdam • Munich • Paris • Milan

PEARSON EDUCATION LIMITED

Edinburgh Gate
Harlow CM20 2JE
United Kingdom
Tel: +44 (0)1279 623623
Fax: +44 (0)1279 431059
Website: www.pearsoned.co.uk

First edition published in Great Britain in 2005

© Pearson Education Limited 2005

The right of Mark Donnelly to be identified as author of this work has been
asserted by him in accordance with the Copyright, Designs and Patents Act 1988.

ISBN-10: 1-4058-0110-7
ISBN-13: 978-1-40580110-2

British Library Cataloguing in Publication Data
A CIP catalogue record for this book can be obtained from the British Library

Library of Congress Cataloging in Publication Data
Donnelly, Mark P.
    Sixties Britain : culture, society, and politics / Mark Donnelly.
        p. cm.
    Includes bibliographical references and index.
    ISBN 1–4058–0110–7
    1. Great Britain—Civilization—1945–   2. Great Britain—Politics and government—
1945–   3. Great Britain—Social life and customs—1945–   4. Nineteen sixties.   I. Title.

DA589.4.D66 2005
941.085′6—dc22

                                                                          2004051485

10   9   8   7   6   5   4   3   2
09   08   07   06

Set by 35 in 9.5/14pt Melior
Printed in Malaysia

The Publishers' policy is to use paper manufactured from sustainable forests.

*Dedicated to my wife, Clare,
and to the memory of my parents,
Joyce and Terry Donnelly*

Contents

List of tables and illustrations viii

Acknowledgements x

Publisher's acknowledgements xi

Preface xii

Introduction: reading the sixties 1

1 Post-war Britain, 1945–59 15

2 Consumerism, youth and sixties pop music 28

3 Anxieties, beliefs and intellectuals 48

4 Conservative crisis and Labour recovery, 1959–64 63

5 On screen 77

6 'Swinging London' and the 'long front of culture' 91

7 Labour's first term and the politics of race 104

8 Permissiveness and counter-culture 116

9 Poverty and devaluation 131

10 1968, cultural crisis and women's liberation 143

11 Powellism and nationalist politics 165

12 Labour crisis and Conservative recovery, 1968–70 180

Conclusion 193

Bibliography 198

Index 218

List of tables and illustrations

Tables

2.1	Top-selling singles artists in the UK, 1960–9	43
2.2	Top UK singles, 1960–9	43
4.1	Results of the General Election, 15 October 1964	76
7.1	Results of the General Election, 31 March 1966	111
12.1	Results of the General Election, 18 June 1970	192

Illustrations

(*In central plate section*)

1   British Prime Minister Harold Wilson and President Johnson take time out from talks on Vietnam to pose for pictures in Johnson's office at the White House, February 8, 1968.

2   23 April 1968: Demonstrating dock workers, holding banners in support of Conservative politician Enoch Powell, march past Monument in the City of London, on their way to the House of Commons.

3   Anti-Vietnamese War Demonstration, London, 1968.

4   British soldiers patrol the streets of Belfast during the period of civil unrest in July 1970.

5   Carnaby Street, the 'Mod' Scene.

6   29 August 1970: Isle of Wight Pop Festival. From the hillside, camping pop fans look down on the jammed area behind the fence.

7   The Beatles, 'All You Need is Love'. L–R: George Harrison, Paul McCartney (front), Ringo Starr, John Lennon, 1967.

8   Barclaycard advertisement.

9   General Charles de Gaulle, French statesman and President of the Fifth French Republic, speaks in Paris in 1967 about the United Kingdom's entry into the European Economic Community.

10   31 October 1969: The Queen's Buildings housing estate in Southwark, London.

11   Family hugging outside home, 1960s.

12   16 November 1967: Members of the Scottish National Party and Plaid Cymru (the Welsh National Party) during a joint conference at Caxton Hall in London, celebrating Scottish Nationalist Winifred Ewing MP taking her seat at the House of Commons.

13   Cilla Black at Chappell Studios, London, recording 'Step Inside Love', composed for her by Paul McCartney (background).

14   The Kray twins at home after having been questioned by police about the murder of George Cornell in 1966.

15   Richard Hamilton, *My Marilyn*, 1965.

16   Mick Jagger, singer of British pop group The Rolling Stones, is driven to Brixton prison to begin a three-month sentence for drug offences. He was released pending an appeal the next day.

Acknowledgements

My first debt of thanks is to Heather McCallum at Pearson Longman for commissioning this book. She provided valuable support and advice along the way, and showed great patience when the original deadline was missed by a mile. Casey Mein, Melanie Carter and Helen Marsden gave me expert advice on preparing the manuscript. Elizabeth Harrison and Fiona Kinnear helped with the finishing touches. British Library staff were constantly helpful and generous with their time. Participants at the Institute of Contemporary British History's 2001 summer conference, 'The Permissive Society and Its Enemies', provided insights into the sixties that have found their way into the text. I apologise for the fact that, because these often resulted from the discussions that followed the papers, it has proved impossible to attribute the sources of these ideas properly. My colleagues in the History Programme at St Mary's College have been a source of encouragement and inspiration. Stuart Oliver read part of the manuscript and made some very useful comments. Steve Fox helped in the search for pictures. Lawrence Black provided the inspiration for one of the chapter sub-headings. I would like to thank the anonymous reader of the original proposal for this book whose comments persuaded me (eventually) to change the way that the discussion was structured. The anonymous academic reader of the manuscript helped me to refine parts of the discussion. Finally, I owe a great debt to those writers whose earlier work on the sixties has proved such a rich source of information and interpretation. I hope they agree that I have endeavoured at all times to treat their work fairly.

Paul and Sue Donnelly, Jane, John, Michael and Daniel Butler were supportive as ever. John and Lesley Chapman were always on hand to tell me 'what it was really like' in the sixties. My wife, Clare, has helped me to appreciate – in keeping with the more self-indulgent aspects of sixties culture – that there are more important things in life than deadlines. I dedicate this book to her.

Publisher's acknowledgements

We are grateful to the following for permission to reproduce copyright material:

Tables 2.1 and 2.2 from Dave McAleer, *The Warner Guide to UK & US Hit Singles* (1994), originally published by Carlton Books Ltd; tables 4.1, 7.1 and 12.1 from Butler, D. and Butler, G., *British Political Facts, 1900–1994* (1994), reproduced with permission of Palgrave Macmillan.

Plates 1, 5 and 6 © Bettman/Corbis; plates 2 and 10 by Evening Standard/ Getty Images; plates 3, 4, 7, 9, 11, 13 and 14 © Hulton-Deutsch Collection/ CORBIS (plate 4 photo by M. Stroud); plate 8 by The Advertising Archive, Ltd; plate 12 by Wesley/Keystone/Getty Images; plate 15 © Richard Hamilton 2004, all rights reserved, DACS, photo © Tate, London 2004; plate 16 by Keystone/Getty Images.

In some instances we have been unable to trace the owners of copyright material, and we would appreciate any information that would enable us to do so.

Preface

This book makes no attempt to celebrate, defend or condemn sixties Britain. Categorising decades into 'good' or 'bad' ones is an irrelevance. Nor is this book a pseudo-memoir from 'one who was there': I was born in 1967, too late for any conscious recall of the times discussed here. Instead the book's principal aim is to survey the main contemporary and subsequent literature on Britain's sixties experiences and to make connections in a way that – to my knowledge – has not been done anywhere else. Unlike most previous writings on the period that focus solely on politics or on social and cultural themes, the starting point of planning this book was to produce a work that combined discussion of all of these overlapping and inter-related categories. Thus, after a brief contextual discussion of post-war Britain, there are eleven chapters, each of which examines related themes. The sequence of these chapters should provide some sense of the narrative of events across the decade. Of course, in a book of this size, difficult choices had to be made about what to include and what to leave out. The final shape and scope of the text could have been handled in a limitless number of ways, but my hope is that the coverage of subjects here represents a sensible – if not ideal – compromise between the available choices and the word limit agreed with the publisher.

The book's secondary aim is to map into the synthesis some of the contradictory impulses that can be seen to have shaped sixties Britain and to consider how – if at all – these contradictions were apparently resolved as Britain entered the seventies. It is not a polemic. The debate about the legacy of the sixties has long been overheated, with the result that the ambiguities and complexities of the period have too often disappeared from view. So what reading of the past is offered here? As will be explained in greater length in the introduction, sixties Britain was shaped above all by the social and cultural legacy of the Second World

War and the ongoing pressures of the Cold War (we can include under either of these headings the politics of welfarism and full employment) and the economic consequences of post-war reconstruction. Instead of viewing the decade as a definitive turning-point that produced clear lines of development (whether welcome or unwelcome) which reached into the seventies and beyond, we should see the sixties as a time when British society and culture were in a constant state of flux. Traditional certainties were challenged, new ways of conceptualising individual identity became apparent, and social relations were in some respects transformed. But the effects of this were uneven, with the impact varying across boundaries of class, gender, generation, region and ethnicity (notwithstanding the fact that the validity of these identifying categories were themselves called into question in the sixties). In some respects – for example in its laws on personal morality, levels of Christian church attendance, the place of pop music in the wider culture, the size of its black and South Asian population – Britain in 1970 was a profoundly different country from the one that had watched the Queen's coronation in 1953. We should not forget, however, that many aspects of sixties change were fiercely contested at the time, culminating in an authoritarian back- lash on behalf of the so-called 'silent majority' towards the end of the decade. We can also cite other features – its political infrastructure and governing culture, the gender division of labour, popular assumptions about the nature of marriage and the family, the ancient universities' dominance of public life – as examples of a striking degree of continuity across this period. As the autobiographical material suggests, many individuals in the sixties had their lives transformed by new experiences, opportunities and freedoms – particularly among the metropolitan young. In contrast, millions more saw little difference in the ways that they experienced or imagined their daily lives, beyond perhaps having a little more money to spend and enjoying a greater degree of consumer choice than before. For millions of Britons the sixties – or at least the media version of the sixties – was a party that was happening somewhere else, one that they could watch only via people whose lives were more socially privileged. Moreover there were parts of Britain – the old indus- trial heartlands of the North-East, North-West, Central Scotland and South Wales, the poorer districts of London – where millions of people were left behind in the economic advances of the 'golden age'. Similarly, while cultural 'classlessness' and a weakening of traditional deference were undoubtedly features of a period that saw all forms of authority questioned, there was no fundamental redistribution of income and wealth across social classes – despite six years of Labour government – nor was there a shift of power away from the sources of authority that were known collectively as the 'Establishment'.

By the early seventies some developments that had seemed so portentous just a few years earlier now appeared to be no more than passing curiosities. The optimistic assumptions of Labour's 'National Plan' seemed to belong to another age. The invasion of the US record charts by British beat groups in 1965 had not produced the predicted shift in power in the international music industry. And it was scarcely credible that Soho had been regarded as a centre of international filmmaking as recently as 1966–8. But this is not to lose sight of other developments of more lasting consequence. From the vantage point of the early twenty-first century there are perhaps four which merit particular attention. Firstly, the modern consumer economy was established in the sixties, reaching across the social and generational divides as never before and transforming popular culture in the process. Second, the period saw an increasing preoccupation with personal autonomy. This had implications for the ways in which individual and civil rights were conceived, and it undermined long-held assumptions about the relevance of a moral code that was derived from Christianity. Third, it was in the sixties that the country felt the full impact of immigration from the New Commonwealth, making way for the arrival of multicultural Britain in the late twentieth century. Finally, British foreign policy was reoriented towards Europe and the nation's global role was diminished. Former colonial territories in Asia and Africa were relinquished and Britain's military presence east of the Suez Canal was withdrawn. The fact that this reordering of Britain's diplomatic priorities, culminating in entry to the European Economic Community in 1973, remains controversial with a sceptical public forty years on suggests that Britain's sense of itself is conditioned more by its memory of the Second World War – and more specifically the heroics of 1940 – than the 1960s.

As we will see, much of what is popularly associated with the sixties has its roots in the post-war period or earlier. Moreover, many manifestations of sixties change – the Women's Liberation Movement, gay rights activism, the post-material politics of the ecology movement – only became prominent in the 1970s. In other words, in order to make sense of the sixties we need to view the decade in a wider context. Thus the first main chapter of this book examines Britain in the aftermath of the 1939–45 conflict, while the conclusion takes the discussion into the 1970s. But before this, the introduction reviews the historiography of sixties Britain.

Introduction: reading the sixties

What was it that transformed 1960s Britain – in many respects just another decade in the country's history – into 'sixties Britain', a heavily edited and reworked concept that is saturated in symbolism, meanings and myth? The obvious response is that sixties Britain was a composite part of the wider international phenomenon of 'the sixties'. As such it was subject to many of the same forces that produced cultural liberation, social change and political upheaval at various points and times across the globe during that period. Highly affluent western consumers, Latin American revolutionaries and Vietcong fighters battling against colonialism in South-East Asia were all within reach of these explosive forces. With its network of partnerships within Europe, the Commonwealth and with the United States, sixties Britain caught the rippling effects of change in other parts of the world. The agents that drove this widely felt change, and which were to make the sixties the most richly mythic decade of the twentieth century, were complex and in some respects amorphous. They defy precise itemisation. But as a starting point we might identify the following as shaping international influences. The 'baby boom' generation, born in the mid- to late 1940s, came of age in the sixties. Unlike earlier generations, whose lives were forged during the hard times of war or the depression years of the twenties and thirties, many of these baby boomers grew up in what Eric Hobsbawm has called the 'golden years' of post-war economic growth among the industrialised nations (1994: 257–286). In outlook, values and expectations the baby boomers were to show themselves to be less like their parents than any previous generation in modern times. In place of the 'ethic of scarcity' that their forbears had so often endured, the sixties children were more likely to have unrestrained appetites. A 'now' mentality developed as the young calculated that postponing pleasure as their parents had done was a pointless trade, not least as there was a declining faith in the promise of an afterlife. Theirs was a secular world in which there was a hunger for instantaneity (MacDonald 1995: 18–19). This sense of heightened contrast between generations owed something to the living memories of a World War that had ended some fifteen years earlier. True, the sixties generational revolt was multi-faceted, but in Britain and the United States at least part of it was self-consciously targeted at the nostalgic 'pleasure culture' of revisiting the lighter, or more heroic, moments of the Second World War that developed in the late 1940s and 1950s. Technological innovation – whether in the form of contraceptive pills, colour television, moon rockets or computers – played a part in shaping the new times, creating unprecedented opportunities and making possible new modes of behaviour and expression. So too did the intellectual challenge to two hundred years of Enlightenment rationalism that characterised the new 'post-modernist' way of comprehending and representing the world. This intellectual revolution – seen most clearly in the academies of France and North America – opened up previously unexplored spaces in which received wisdoms and traditional notions of authority were challenged. Meanwhile, across the globe, nationalist movements fought to shake off European imperialism, only to find in some cases that a subsequent struggle was required to prevent its replacement by a new form of US-imposed colonialism. Finally, we might add that the nature of capitalism changed in the post-war era. What drove it forward now was an emphasis on the needs of consumption (in other words spending) rather than production (which required saving and investment). In consequence came a culture across the west that repeatedly privileged hedonism over self-discipline, play over work and sexual gratification over restraint. Thus the sixties were to witness in some quarters at least a revival of eighteenth- and nineteenth-century Romanticism and a fascination with the realms of the imagination and the senses. But the striking irony of this revived Romantic spirit in its mid-twentieth century incarnation was that so often it came to be seen as something that was best expressed via personal consumption of material goods.

So where did this leave sixties Britain? As the preface explained, the following chapters will argue that sixties Britain was characterised by competing discourses and shaped by a mass of contradictory impulses, some of which were historical in origin, some of which were driven by simple demographics, some of which were the product of international trends. These discourses and impulses made sixties Britain a site of contest, one in which dynamic forces of change were seen to be locked in a recurring struggle with the forces of resistance. The contradictions took a number of forms. Sixties Britain was a place that worshipped the new and the modern but in which a discourse of anxiety about the future was repeatedly heard. It was a time of renewed national self-confidence, coupled with a sense of foreboding at the country's international decline and waning world power. Sixties Britain was obsessed with youth and the icons of youth culture, yet it continually categorised the 'youth question' as a social problem that threatened established modes of behaviour and moral norms. The unprecedented rises in living standards and consumer conveniences that accompanied the decade coincided both with the 'rediscovery of poverty' in its middle years and the anti-materialism of the counter-culture towards its end. It was an era, too, of often striking political idealism, yet by 1970 the Conservatives had returned to power on a self-consciously 'right-wing' programme. These kinds of oppositions do not by themselves make the sixties unique – the past is full of periods that experienced similarly powerful dynamic contradictions. What makes the sixties special is that *as an entity* they attract more attention than any comparable decade. They have become a totem, something that people are either 'for' or 'against'. They are the historical equivalent of a brand identity, representing a set of meanings, values and attitudes. Now that they have passed, they are summoned as imagined territory to be fought over, malleable material to be constructed, analysed, critiqued and pulled apart again. Also, they left a legacy that refuses to go away. The semiotics of the sixties, the fashions, the music, the flower-power aesthetic, have never been far from the surface of contemporary culture. Books, magazines, newspaper supplements, adverts, television, radio and other electronic media continually revisit the sixties. In 1996 The Beatles sold more records than they managed in any year while they were still recording. In the early years of the new millennium the *Austin Powers* films continued to make impressive profits by affectionately parodying media clichés about the 'swinging sixties', while the Rolling Stones played to sold-out stadiums on another 'farewell' world tour. ITV remade the classic sixties serial *The Forsyte Saga* for a modern audience, the BBC repeated *The Great War* (first broadcast in the infant days of BBC2) and Tate Britain hosted a 2004 retrospective on sixties British art called *This Was Tomorrow*. The sixties loomed large over everything that came after. As Jonathon Green's recent popular history of the sixties counter-culture observed:

> *We live in the shadow of the Sixties. Of all the artificial constructs by which we delineate our immediate past, 'the Sixties' have the greatest purchase on the mass imagination. They stand, rightly or not, as the dominant myth of the modern era. That one might have been too old or too young to enjoy them, indeed, that one might not even have been born, is of marginal importance. Rightly or wrongly again, the great edifice casts its shadow and everything must seek its light within it.*
>
> (Green 1998b: ix)

But why the fuss? Green suggests an answer from the vantage point of the late twentieth century.

> *As the century draws to a close, it is hard not to see the Sixties as the pivotal decade. It was not the only momentous period and its perceived importance now may be ascribed to the current domination of the media by those whose youth was played out against its gaudy wallpaper, but for all the importance of the Twenties and Thirties, the years of the two World Wars, and the grim destructive Eighties, the Sixties seem to stand in the centre of it all, sucking in the influences of the past, creating the touchstones of the future. Certainly what has come since is consistently measured against the era – whether in the nostalgia it evokes or its demonisation.*
>
> (Green 1998b: xiii)

Narratives like this written since 1960 tell us that for good or ill *something* important happened in the sixties, marking the decade off from anything that had gone before or happened since. But how should we imagine and conceptualise the changes that occurred? Even to ask the question raises a problem, because it implies the possibility of establishing a 'true' holistic notion of the sixties and thus assuming some kind of proprietorship over how the decade should be represented. No one can claim 'ownership' of the sixties, implicitly or otherwise, nor can any writer hope to show 'what really happened'. There is no essential 'one-ness' to sixties Britain that can be recovered, whatever methods or sources are mobilised. Perhaps the best that we can do at this stage is to think in terms of recurrent overarching themes in the literature on the period. This would show, for example, that the sixties are viewed as the years when the world remade itself after the two World Wars, and not just in Western Europe and the United States. Castro's rule in Cuba, Mao's Cultural Revolution in China and the success of African nationalist movements in shaking off European colonialism were all regarded as ruptures in the old world order. The hydrogen bomb and the space race made questions of peace, disarmament and international cooperation ever more urgent and interesting to a wider range of people. Moreover, improvements in mass communications such as satellite broadcasting and faster travel by air led commentators to talk seriously for the first time about a 'global village' in which there was increasing recognition of the interdependence of nations. Britain contributed to, and in turn was affected by, these wider developments. But it was also seen to have its own more specific experiences of the decade. Numerous attempts have been made to impose particular readings on these experiences and to fix a position on how sixties Britain should be imagined. These can be clustered around a series of alternative perspectives.

One set of readings contends that sixties social and cultural change was mostly unwelcome and in some respects damaging in the longer term. Viewed from this negative perspective sixties Britain saw the beginnings of a breakdown of order and authority, a prioritising of self-indulgence over personal responsibility, a fashionable but dangerous acceptance of moral relativism, a vacuous preoccupation with cultural trivia rather than cultural self-improvement and an uncritical elevation of the new above the established. This is the sixties presented as 'the end of civilisation as we knew it'. It is a politically-charged commentary that typically comes from the conservative right. More important, perhaps, it makes its onslaught on the sixties from a distinctly Victorian viewpoint, regretting the fading power of values such as self-discipline, sexual restraint and the belief in moral certainties. Such attacks began early. In 1969 in *The Neophiliacs: a study of the revolution in English life in the Fifties and Sixties* the journalist Christopher Booker wrote that Britain had just suffered a kind of collective nervous breakdown, brought on by people's inability to cope psychologically with the unprecedented riches of the post-war economic boom. In his view Britain lived through a dream in the late fifties and early sixties, beginning with a 'gigantic "vitality-fantasy"' around 1956 and ending in 1965 (for him the pivotal year of 'Swinging London') by which time all that remained was the 'nightmarish blanket of unreality' (1969: 79, 273). Booker explained:

> In the closing years of the Sixties, the extent to which the years between 1955 and 1966 could be looked back on as a distinct episode in England's social and political history became increasingly clear. From time to time in the years that followed there were eruptions and echoes of the hysteria of earlier years, notably in the scandals which in 1967–8 marked the apogee of the teenage drugs craze, and in the student unrest which in 1968 came to its head in Britain's universities. But by and large in these years, as the particular collective fantasy which had so dominated English life between 1955 and 1966 continued to subside, the climate was one of aftermath, disillusionment, exhaustion, even of reaction . . . by 1967–8, many people were beginning to feel to a more or less conscious degree that, in the previous ten years, they had come through some kind of shattering experience.
>
> (Booker 1969: 292)

This dream's origins, said Booker, lay in the early twentieth century. Its power was malign, he continued, because it consumed people with false hopes of fulfilment and progress, leading them to worship the false gods of materialism, scientific advance, celebrity icons and instant self-gratification. He attributed much of the blame for this to the combined workings of the avant-garde and the trendy intelligentsia and their fatal conjunction with the media.

> For what has happened in the Fifties and Sixties is that, on all sides, the twentieth century dream has taken a step towards fulfillment on a scale dwarfing everything that went before. The coming of the space age, of the H-bomb and the intercontinental missile, the rise of modern technology in its new and more impersonal guise to the point where it has come to invade and overshadow almost every aspect of life, the establishment at the heart of social and political life of the unreal glare of television, the revolt of the young and the overthrow of the last vestiges of Victorian

propriety, the reaching of new boundaries of sensationalism in the arts and the widespread merging of popular and avant-garde culture – all this has marked not only a tremendous acceleration of the process which has been underway since 1900, but also a major installment in the toppling of those barriers which kept the dream out of reach and therefore intact. The dream has come true – and the real fruit of the Fifties and Sixties lies in the fact that, as never before, its hollowness has been exposed.

(Booker 1969: 299)

Bernard Levin in *The Pendulum Years* wrote in a less mystical but equally elegiac tone about the sixties as 'shaken and ambiguous years' (1970: 332). He saw that an old Britain had given way to the new, but this new country was weighed down with economic problems, political failure and international decline. The traditional forces of religion, authority and buttoned-up sexual morality were lost, and Britain became a place where students went on the march and celebrity status was given to criminals like the Great Train Robbers and the Kray twins. The country, he argued, had lost its way, leaving charlatans to fill the void.

It was a credulous age, perhaps the most credulous ever, and the more rational, the less gullible, the decade claimed to be, the less rational, the more gullible it showed itself. Never was it easier to gain a reputation as a seer, never was a following so rapidly and readily acquired. . . .

There was a restlessness in the time that communicated itself everywhere and to everyone, that communicated itself to the very sounds in Britain's air, the stones beneath Britain's feet. These stones shifted as she walked ahead with her once-purposeful stride, so that she began to stumble, then to stagger, then to fall down. Eventually she had fallen down so often that she was not only covered in mud but the laughing-stock of passers-by.

(Levin 1970: 9–10)

This negative verdict on the sixties was shared and articulated by the British New Right in the 1970s and 1980s. Above all they were appalled by the liberal law reforms of the sixties, blaming these for what they saw as the social ills of late-twentieth century Britain – the breakdown of traditional family forms, rising rates of teenage pregnancy, a spiralling drugs culture, personal irresponsibility and growing rates of crime and juvenile delinquency. Margaret Thatcher argued in 1982 that: 'We are reaping what was sown in the sixties . . . fashionable theories and permissive claptrap set the scene for a society in which the old virtues of discipline and restraint were denigrated' (cited in Masters 1985: 14). Norman Tebbit similarly railed against sixties permissiveness three years later: 'Family life was derided as an outdated bourgeois concept. Criminals deserved as much sympathy as their victims. Many homes and classrooms became disorderly – if there was neither right nor wrong there could be no basis for punishment or reward. Violence and soft pornography became accepted in the media. Thus was sown the wind; and we are reaping the whirlwind' (cited in Masters 1985: 15). More recently Peter Hitchens has lamented the loss of pre-1960s social values in *The Abolition of Britain* (2000). The country was a better place, he argues, before the toxic effects of the 'cultural revolution' that was launched in the sixties became apparent. In the years that followed Winston Churchill's death in 1965, writes Hitchens, just about every feature of British life worsened. The national culture became infected with pornography, foul language, a decline in religious faith, sexual licence (of all kinds) and 'political correctness'. But according to Ian MacDonald (1995) the irony of such critiques is that it was the very materialism and individualism celebrated by Thatcher's Conservatives – and which first became universalised in the sixties – that caused the social fragmentation about which they complained. It was not the New Left, counter-cultural hippies or liberal progressives that were the problem in the sixties. The truly corrosive influence came from those who worshipped the unexamined life of modern consumerism.

> So far as anything in the Sixties can be blamed for the demise of the compound entity of society it was the natural desire of the 'masses' to lead easier, pleasanter lives, own their own homes, follow their own fancies and, as far as possible, move out of the communal collective completely . . . Indeed the very labour-saving domestic appliances launched onto the market by the Sixties' consumer boom speeded the melt-down of communality by allowing people to function in a private world, segregated from each other by TVs, telephones, hi-fi systems, washing machines and home cookers . . . What mass society unconsciously began in the Sixties, Thatcher and Reagan raised to

*the level of ideology in the Eighties: the complete materialistic
individualization – and total fragmentation – of Western society.*

(MacDonald 1995: 29–30)

A more positive set of readings holds that the sixties were a time of
social and economic progress and cultural reinvigoration. On this analysis
the drab, grey austerity of the fifties was replaced by a day-glo wonder-
land of new opportunities. These commentaries share the view that a
'cultural revolution' fused together naive idealism, post-war materialism,
youthful rebellion, sexual freedom, social mobility, limitless possibilities
and artistic innovation. Brian Masters in *The Swinging Sixties* (1985)
acknowledged that Britain had its share of problems in the decade, and
he makes much of what he believes was a strong sense of national resentment that the country had been denied the rewards it deserved for its
'finest hour' in the Second World War. But his concluding perspective on
the decade was resolutely upbeat, if perhaps overly nationalistic.

*If pride was the leitmotif of the sixties, then one can see how all of the
achievements of that period grew out of the affirmation of what was best
in the British character. Tolerance was our forte; well then we should
demonstrate its civilizing power, not meekly acknowledge its presence,
and earn the world's admiration. . . . Tolerance extended to all kinds of
private emotional or lustful activity, and homosexuals finally ceased to
be criminals. Even the noise of popular music, far louder than it had
ever been before, was tolerated along with outrageous dress. Dissident
political views, especially concerning the control of nuclear weapons,
were freely entertained and widely discussed. . . .*

*It is significant that this sounds and reads like a congratulatory
hymn rather than a conclusion. That is because it has become the
fashion to denigrate the advances made in the sixties and deplore their
consequences. Those who want more muscle, dynamism, greatness, are
usually hostile to the gentler virtues which flourished at the time, and
which must continue to be applauded if the essential British character
is to endure.*

(Masters 1985: 222–3)

Shawn Levy offers a less patriotic verdict than Masters in *Ready,
Steady, Go! Swinging London and the Invention of Cool* (2002), but he is

equally upbeat. In his popular account, 'Swinging London' stands as an emblem of the wider social and cultural loosenings of the sixties, leaving a legacy that continues to reverberate. If the fifties belonged to Paris and Rome, he opens, and the seventies to California, Miami and New York, then the sixties were Swinging London, 'the place where our modern world began'. Here it was, he argues, that in 'those few evanescent years it all came together: youth, pop music, fashion, celebrity, satire, crime, fine art, sexuality, scandal, theatre, cinema, drugs, media – the whole mad modern stew' (2002: 6). And what did it all add up to?

> *A group of people living in one place found one another and the thing they always wanted, and they lived it and became it and let it go or got left by it, and the ones who lived through it – and some who didn't – could rest satisfied that they had had their time.*
> *Maybe their only time, yes, but maybe our only time, too.*
> *The party of all parties; the time of all times; the granddaddy of all golden moments; the seed of everything we're about: Swinging London.*
> *You hadda be there.*
> *You are.*
>
> (Levy 2002: 363)

Bart Moore-Gilbert and John Seed in *Cultural Revolution? The challenge of the arts in the 1960s* (1992) share much of the optimism transmitted by Masters and Levy, even if their analysis is ultimately very different. In their introduction to a scholarly collection of essays which set out to critique some of the orthodoxies about sixties Britain, Moore-Gilbert and Seed argue that the decade's main cultural currents were outward looking and internationally respected. Far from being easily contained, oppositional culture was challenging to the 'establishment', varied in its point of attack on established values, and genuinely inclusive and democratic. The 'amorphous utopias of the counter-culture' may not have been realised, and they also concede that 'in many ways it was precisely the groups who seemed to be finding a voice in the 1960s – young people, women, blacks – who have suffered the worst effects of economic recession and political reaction during the 1970s and 1980s'. Nevertheless, they maintain, 'in all kinds of ways, the political ramifications of cultural change in the 1960s were undeniably significant' (1992: 1–12).

Arguably the most important recent British work on the sixties is Arthur Marwick's *The Sixties: Cultural Revolution in Britain, France, Italy and the United States, c.1958–c.1974* (1998). As the title makes clear, Marwick is interested in the sixties as an international experience. Nevertheless, a series of earlier writings on British social and cultural history allows us to disentangle from his overarching thesis his reading of what the sixties meant for Britain. There may have been 'no political or economic revolution, no fundamental redistribution of economic power' in the sixties, he argues, but what did take place was a 'cultural revolution' which transformed 'material conditions, lifestyles, family relationships, and personal freedoms for the vast majority of ordinary people' (1991: 67–8; 1998: 15). For Marwick, the consequences of this 'cultural revolution' were overwhelmingly beneficial. But what did it involve? In *The Sixties* he offers a useful sixteen-point conceptualisation. In summary Marwick argues that the sixties saw the formation of new subcultures and movements, generally critical of, or in opposition to, established society; an outburst of entrepreneurialism, individualism, doing your own thing; the rise to positions of unprecedented influence of young people; important advances in technology; the advent of 'spectacle' as an integral part of the interface between life and leisure; unprecedented international cultural exchange; upheavals in class, race and family relationships; general sexual liberation; new modes of self-presentation; a vibrant popular culture; striking developments in elite thought; the expansion of a liberal, progressive presence within the institutions of authority; the continued existence of elements of extreme reaction – particularly in police forces; new concerns for civil and personal rights; and the first intimations of the challenges and opportunities presented by multiculturalism (1998: 19–20).

The Sixties is relentlessly hostile to what Marwick terms the 'Great Marxisant Fallacy', the notion pushed by leftist cultural theorists that bourgeois society was on the point of collapse in the sixties, and that the revolutionary task was to destroy its very language, culture, values and ideology. The book is full of hostile references to the 'avant-garde academics' of the Parisian Left Bank and North American universities, whose post-structuralist and post-modernist theories began to reshape intellectual activity in the sixties: Marcuse, Lévi-Strauss, Barthes, Lacan, Althusser, Foucault and Derrida are the main writers charged. And yet as Callum Brown notes, an alternative reading of the sixties is provided by those contemporary cultural theorists who 'argue that the 1960s was a key decade in ending "the Enlightenment project" and modernity'. The view that the sixties marked the end of modernity is one that Brown evidently shares.

> In its place the era of post-modernity started to mature. Structural 'realities' of social class eroded, and there was a repudiation of self-evident 'truths' (concerning the role of women, the veracity of Christianity, and the structure of social and moral authority), a new scepticism about the science-derived nature of 'progress', and the disappearance of an agreed 'reality'. Science, social science and Christianity were equally victims in the making in the 1960s. They started to be undermined by the 'linguistic turn' – the deconstruction of the role of language, signification and discourse which had constructed the Enlightenment narrative of history, rationality and progress.
>
> (Brown 2001: 176)

The increased sensitivity to the use of language that accompanied the 'linguistic turn' and the repudiation of what had previously been regarded as self-evident 'truths' helped to revitalise the left in the sixties. Some of the key memoirs from the period focus on the sixties as a time of student rebellion, anti-capitalist protests and demonstrations against the neo-colonial powers of Europe and the United States. These are highly situated and personalised accounts, but they are significant because they have helped to shape some media perceptions of the period. Tariq Ali, whose name became a shorthand signifier of student militancy in 1968, sought to defend sixties left activists from the condescension of history in *Street Fighting Years* (1987) by defiantly reasserting the integrity of the cause.

> Mocking the sixties became a European pastime in the late seventies and eighties. That was a small price to pay for our defeats. Many in the flambé soixante huitards of France felt so betrayed by history that they renounced their pasts. . . . Many mistakes were made by individuals (including myself) and collectives. There was a great deal about that period that was shrouded in mysticism and fantasy. The dominant theme, however, was a passionate belief that we needed a new world.
>
> (Ali 1987: 258, 268)

Sheila Rowbotham, one of Tariq Ali's co-activists on the left, described her developing consciousness both as a radical socialist and as a feminist in *Promise of a Dream: Remembering the Sixties* (2000). Throughout this memoir the intense conviction and moral earnestness of the revolutionary left shine through. However, much to Rowbotham's increasing disillusion, the revolution they pursued in 1968 and 1969 was exposed as a Leninist one in the making, to be led by a vanguard of intellectuals from the International Socialists and International Marxist Group who would tell the inert 'masses' what to think and what to do. Her response in 1969 was to switch her energies from left activism to the Women's Liberation Movement. As she looked back on the period the sense of defeat remained strong. The promise had been betrayed.

> *We looked backwards and forwards, forwards and backwards as the world spun around. Our sense of crisis, our intensity, our conviction that time was running out, these did not simply derive from a youthful self-importance. We faced the very real problem that capitalism was changing very much faster than we were . . . 'The personal is political' declared the American New Left, and the slogan passed into the women's movement. They might have added, 'The personal is also big money'. Ironically, openings created by social movements were to present market opportunities – the slogans transmogrified into designer labels and some quick-footed 'alternative' capitalists emerged from the mêlée. Yet the radical dream of the sixties was to be stillborn, for we were not to move towards the cooperative egalitarian society we had imagined. Instead the sixties ushered in an order which was more competitive and less equal than the one we had protested against.*
>
> (Rowbotham 2000: xiv–xv)

Part of the problem was that subsequent decades failed to live up to the rich promises of the 'high' sixties (roughly late 1964 to mid-1967). The hike in oil prices in 1973 signalled the end of economic good times and the arrival of recession induced political and industrial strife, culminating in the 'winter of discontent' of 1978–9. This in turn opened up space for the Thatcherite backlash against union power and liberal social policies of the eighties. In *Too Much: Art and Society in the Sixties, 1960–75* (1986) Robert Hewison argued that the sixties failed to halt long-term cultural decline in Britain, a process that had been underway since

1939. There may have been temporary high points, like the celebratory and ultimately democratic aesthetic of Pop Art, which helped to break down the barriers between 'high' and 'popular' culture. Also, the cultural politics of feminism and gay rights in the seventies and eighties were the beneficiaries of the liberalising drive of the sixties. But ultimately, Hewison argued, the short-lived optimism of the sixties gave way to disillusion.

> In the 1960s the consciousness and the tempo was one of change: Pop was affirmative and celebratory, the long front of culture offered the possibility of greater choice for a wider range of people. But it was also a fantasy, since it was based on the illusion of unending economic expansion. The counter-culture released a great deal of potential – and some monsters of violence and self-destruction as well – but dissipated it almost as quickly, as bohemias tend to do. The combination of economic recession and cultural reaction has, in the place of change, substituted decay.
>
> (Hewison 1986: 303)

CHAPTER 1

Post-war Britain, 1945–59

The return of peace

The price of victory in 1945 was high. In addition to almost 500,000 Britons who died in the conflict, the Second World War cost Britain about one-quarter of its national wealth. With overseas trade disrupted and Britain's economic effort focused on war production, exports had fallen to one-third of their pre-war level. Some valuable overseas markets had been lost to the trading superpower of the United States and it was unlikely that they would be regained. The national debt had trebled by 1945, making Britain the world's largest debtor nation. As peace resumed the country was living beyond its means by some £2 billion per annum. Much of Britain's industrial plant and machinery was worn out after nearly six years at war. Throughout the country's towns and cities millions of homes, schools and other buildings had been damaged or destroyed by the Luftwaffe. Repairing the damage to the national infrastructure would take time, as well as more money than the Exchequer had available. There were also problems abroad to consider. Victory had seen the return of Britain's captured colonies, making it once more the head of the largest empire in history. This brought challenges and dangers alongside (for many people) enhanced national pride. Moreover, the global reach of the conflict had left Britain with a military presence in more than 40 countries by the time the guns stopped, including a shared occupation of Germany alongside the Soviet Union, the United States and France. As the US scholar William Fox had pointed out in 1944 Britain could rightly regard itself as a 'superpower', one of the 'Big Three' (with the US and USSR) who were soon to win the war (1944: 21). The problem here of course was that any meaningful claim to world power had to be supported by a degree of economic strength that Britain simply lacked. Towards the end of 1945, John Maynard Keynes joined a delegation which negotiated a huge loan from Washington so that Britain could escape from the looming catastrophe of a 'financial Dunkirk'. It was not the last time that Britain was to go to the United States for help with paying the bills. In essence the post-war transatlantic 'special relationship' was a deal that gave Britain financial assistance from the US in return for its (usually) unequivocal support for American foreign policy. Britain may have fought from September 1939 to safeguard its independence, but the unintended consequence of the struggle was that it left the country ever more reliant on the United States from 1945 onwards.

Successive British governments would struggle to cope with the domestic and international legacies of the war effort for decades. For most British people, however, the problem of how the country would adjust in a changed post-war world was a far-off issue. After all, it was popularly assumed, the war had provided a striking vindication both of the British way of doing things and the character of its people. Britain (together with its imperial partners) was the only power to endure six full years of war, including a year in 1940–1 when it had stood virtually alone in Europe against the dictators. No doubt those same qualities that saw it through the test of conflict would come to the fore in peacetime. The glow of victory was expected to burn long after the victory parades, and few doubted that the country would retain its ranking among the top nations. It was hardly surprising, therefore, that in the years that followed many would look back on wartime with a mixture of nostalgia, pride and affection. It was understandable too that a 'pleasure culture' of war should take hold in Britain like nowhere else, with the war constantly re-enacted through films, television programmes, books, memorabilia, children's comics and replica toys. The British, it appeared, had shown the best of themselves between 1939 and 1945 and they were determined to keep the memories of the wartime experience alive. Within a decade or so, however, a younger generation would begin to chafe against their parents' tales of the 'Spitfire summer' or watching the Blitz from the rooftops. For those who grew up in the shadow of the atomic raids on Hiroshima and Nagasaki, and who lived with the very real threat of Cold

War tension escalating into nuclear annihilation, the concept of war took on a very different meaning. The sixties generational clash, in part at least, was to be played out in the space between memories of the 'good war' and anticipation of an impending nuclear apocalypse.

In terms of national politics, what most people wanted in 1945 was rewards from the state for their wartime efforts. Politicians could hardly complain if this public mood put them under pressure to deliver high returns. Throughout the conflict they had continually inflated expectations about what could be achieved once victory was secured. The Labour Party, in particular, captured the public imagination about the possibilities of a 'New Jerusalem', making ambitious promises from the earliest stages of the war about jobs, houses, a national health service and first-class public services for all citizens. The energy and strategic positioning of this campaign carried them to a landslide victory in the 1945 election against a Conservative Party led by Winston Churchill, the 'man who had won the war'. With a Commons majority of 146, Clement Attlee's post-war government was able to carry through its legislative programme, deservedly gaining a reputation as perhaps the greatest reforming administration in British political history. The National Insurance Act (1946), the National Health Service Act (1946) and the National Assistance Act (1948) were the building blocks of the modern welfare state. Full employment remained a priority, and the Bank of England, fuel, power and inland transport industries were nationalised. But while the government was able to control its programme, its management of the economy – particularly the vulnerable position of Britain's balance of payments – was a different matter. In a pattern that was to haunt governments throughout the fifties and sixties, in the immediate aftermath of the war Britain spent collectively more on imported goods than it earned in foreign exchange through exports. The resulting imbalance caused a major currency crisis in 1947, a year that ended in the resignation of the Chancellor, Hugh Dalton. In 1949 the government (in which a youthful Harold Wilson served in Cabinet) was forced to devalue sterling. As the currency functioned among other things as a symbol of the nation's international economic status, devaluation marked a humiliating retreat by the Labour government. In real terms for British consumers it meant higher prices, smaller rations (certain goods were even more scarce than they had been in wartime) and public spending cuts, all of which added up to lower living standards. Far from enjoying the fruits of wartime victory Britain was now living through the so-called 'age of austerity'. Dalton's replacement as Chancellor, the ascetic Stafford Cripps, called for yet more resources to be diverted from home consumption to the export drive. Casting the drive for national economic recovery in ethical and moral terms, Cripps urged the population towards new levels of material self-denial. Whether it was for cars, clothes or pianos, British consumers faced lengthening waiting lists as the government put limits on what manufacturers could sell on the home market while the rest of their stock was sold overseas. The damaging political consequences for Labour soon followed. Partly because of a 'housewives revolt' among women who were weary of struggling to make domestic ends meet, Labour lost support from key groups of female and middle-class voters before they had even served a full term in office. This drift of support away from the government from 1947 onwards meant that in the 1950 election Labour's commanding majority was reduced to a mere five seats. The following year Attlee called another election in search of a more decisive mandate. Perhaps if he had waited for one more year the government's popularity would have benefited from economic recovery. But in 1951 the swing of popular opinion against Labour in key constituencies continued and they were pushed out of office, despite having won the highest aggregate vote of all the parties. Few within Labour's ranks would have predicted that the party was about to embark on a thirteen-year period in opposition, ending only when Harold Wilson led them back into government with another knife-edge majority in 1964.

Before it fell from power the post-war Labour government made one telling contribution to the gaiety of the nation. In May 1951, exactly a century after the Victorian Great Exhibition showcased Britain's world power status, the Festival of Britain opened on London's South Bank. It was a civic celebration that drew a line under the hardships of the previous ten years and pumped up national pride as the country faced what was predicted to be the long-drawn-out threat of the Cold War. For Herbert Morrison, who was responsible to the Cabinet for organising this event, the Festival was about 'the people giving themselves a pat on the back' (Lewis 1978: 11). It was also a foreign tourist attraction, pulling in visitors at a time when tourism remained one of the country's most important dollar earners. Despite the fact that, as Michael Frayn argued,

'Festival Britain was the Britain of the radical middle class – the do-gooders; the readers of the *News Chronicle*, the *Guardian*, and the *Observer*; the signers of petitions; the backbone of the BBC' (1986: 307–8), the event was a popular triumph. Over eight million people came to the South Bank to see the Festival, and in towns and cities across the country millions more attended the mini-celebrations – carnivals, sports events, historical pageants, firework displays, bonfires – that were organised to complement activities in the capital. The event was designed to offer something to everyone. For those who wanted their national pride affirmed the Festival sang a stirring hymn to Britain's manufacturing prowess and industrial heritage, with coal and shipbuilding venerated alongside a spectrum of inventions that stretched from the vital to the eccentric. For those who wanted to see and hear the 'best' of British high culture, King George VI's opening of the Royal Festival Hall was a high point in the celebrations (even though the opening night offered a concert of purely *English* music). For everyone else there were the Festival Pleasure Gardens at Battersea Park. Here fun-seekers braved lengthy queues to enjoy fairground rides like the 'Big Dipper' and the 'Dragon Ride', except on Sundays when the country's moral guardians ensured that the Gardens remained closed (Hylton 1998: 15, 18). For cynics who saw the £11 million spent on the Festival as a waste of public money at a time when the government had more serious problems to tackle (not least the Korean War), there was a perverse satisfaction to be gained from the event's organisational shortcomings. When the Festival opened it put such pressure on the capital's power supply that other parts of London were plunged into darkness. The Pleasure Gardens, meanwhile, opened behind schedule and over budget because of strikes, go-slows and work-to-rules by construction workers who demanded to be paid a special 'exhibition money' rate for their labour. The Conservative opposition, who were at best unenthusiastic about the Festival, saw these problems as further examples of socialist mismanagement and misjudgement. As far as they were concerned it was not the government's job to tell free citizens in a free society how to enjoy themselves. When they returned to power shortly after the Festival closed in September 1951 they left most of its infrastructure to fall into disrepair: thus it was that a site of 27 acres lay unused and derelict in the heart of London, waiting to be transformed a decade later into an ugly commercial office block and car park (Frayn 1986: 326).

'Setting the people free': Conservative government, 1951–57

Churchill's Conservatives returned to government in October 1951 on a promise to restore consumer prosperity and 'set the people free' from socialist bureaucracy and controls. But the free-market consumer paradise that they projected in their election literature took the best part of a decade to arrive. In the meantime, early 1950s Britain remained, in the words of Andrew Graham-Dixon, the place of the 'tightened belt, the ration book and Spam' (1996: 226). It was a country where food rationing (of meat, butter and bacon) remained part of everyday life until 1954 and where queues and restrictions were the norm. Backyard privies were common, while across much of urban Britain, cleared bombsites awaiting redevelopment were children's playgrounds for years. Even Cabinet ministers reluctantly obeyed Churchill's instruction to take a pay cut in 1951 because of the ailing condition of the economy. Compared with the inter-war years of periodic and widespread (if regionally-specific) depression and the sacrifices of wartime, the hangover of austerity into the fifties was an inconvenience rather than real hardship. Many adults could endure the dullness of early-fifties Britain because it was accompanied by unprecedented domestic security. This was in some respects a comforting time, a period when social relations were underpinned by a new consensus between people and state, the twin pillars of which were full employment and a properly-funded welfare system. True, the shiny materialism of fifties America depicted in advertisements and Hollywood films suggested that the British were lagging behind their richer wartime ally. But at least there were jobs, stable prices and pensions.

Despite opposing most of the Attlee government's reforms when they were out of power, Churchill's Conservatives never intended to overhaul the 'post-war settlement' once they were back in government. Welfare capitalism was the shared governing assumption of the time. Hence denationalisation was kept to a minimum: only road haulage and iron and steel were returned to private ownership (both in 1953). The emollient Walter Monckton (nicknamed 'the oilcan') at the Ministry of Labour maintained cordial relations with the trade unions, consulting them on strategic questions of economic management and quietly dropping plans made in opposition to reform trade union law. Rab Butler as Chancellor ensured that there were real-terms spending increases on the welfare state and made full employment a priority consideration in macro-economic policy, even though the effect of both was to stoke up inflationary pressures. Harold Macmillan, meanwhile, poured energy and resources into his 'Grand Design for Housing', aided by Churchill, who judged that 'housing and red meat' were the two domestic issues closest to voters' hearts (Weiler 2000; Seldon 1987: 71). Macmillan's success in building houses at a faster rate than his Labour predecessors, eventually hitting his target of 300,000 a year in December 1953, was a major boost to his national profile – even though he obviously sacrificed build quality for speed of construction. The sole female Cabinet minister (and no favourite of Churchill), Florence Horsburgh, focused her efforts at the Ministry of Education on the non-partisan tasks of building more schools and recruiting more teachers. Unfortunately for her, Churchill preferred building houses. By the time she was replaced by David Eccles there was little evidence that a specific Conservative philosophy on education had guided her policy decisions. Churchill's domestic policies, in other words, were a triumph of pragmatism. Social and political controversies were largely avoided, but the down side of this cautious approach was that the 1951–5 government was subsequently criticised for ducking out of 'necessary' but difficult measures. Depending on the perspective of the critic these 'lost opportunities' would include immigration controls, trade union legislation, a more targeted approach to welfare, and the failure to create what was later referred to as a 'property-owning democracy' (Seldon 1987: 85–7).

Perhaps pragmatism was to be expected from an administration led by Churchill, the wartime colossus and national figurehead whose best days were obviously in the past. Churchill suffered a stroke in June 1953 – just weeks after the Queen's coronation was presented by commentators as the start of a new Elizabethan age – and by the last six months of his premiership he was wholly unfit for office. He was fortunate that a deferential press colluded in playing down the gravity of his ailing health, allowing him to remain in post until April 1955 when he finally resigned at the age of 80. His successor was Anthony Eden, the Tory heir-apparent since 1941, whose own serious medical problems had kept him out of action for much of 1953. Eden announced a general election almost immediately and led the Conservatives to an increased majority of

58 seats. 'Conservative Freedom Works' had been their campaign slogan. Millions of voters had no compelling reason to disagree. The commanding political position that Eden inherited as Prime Minister, however, was destroyed within a year by a misjudged foreign expedition. The defining moment of what turned out to be Eden's brief premiership was the Suez crisis of 1956, when Britain and France (with Israeli assistance) invaded Egypt in an attempt to regain control of the Suez Canal from Colonel Nasser's government. Eden, wounded by press coverage that dismissed him as an ineffectual successor to Churchill, had hoped to prove that he was a resolute defender of Britain's imperial interests. But his attempt to humiliate Nasser rebounded disastrously. The United Nations condemned Anglo-French aggression, demanded a ceasefire and debated whether to use their own troops to restore peace. The United States, alarmed at the revival of 'old' European imperialism operating without American permission, threatened to use their vast foreign currency reserves to engineer a sterling crisis unless Britain withdrew. In the largest example of popular protest since the 1930s, thousands of anti-war demonstrators gathered in Trafalgar Square to signal their opposition to western aggression and to demand Eden's resignation. Faced with opposition on all sides, not least from the Egyptians who blocked the Suez Canal, Eden was forced to evacuate British forces. It was a humiliating climbdown, and the sharpest indication up to that point of the limits of post-war British power. The other lesson that the British political class learned was that the approval of the United States was required for all major foreign policy decisions. The price of Eden's failure to anticipate the risks of invading Egypt was soon apparent. His already fragile health was ruined by the strain of the Suez crisis and he resigned in January 1957.

'Never had it so good?': the late-fifties affluent society

A new Prime Minister whose party had been in government for almost six years could be expected to exaggerate a little about how the country had improved in recent times. But when Harold Macmillan declared that most people in the country had 'never had it so good' in July 1957, he identified what for many was a reality. The deep social divisions of the thirties, the strains of war and the dull ache of post-war shortages gave way to a more comfortable age in the mid-fifties. A booming economy, soaring stock market values, low unemployment, a wealth of accessible consumer choice and improved welfare services were the defining features of a new age of affluence. Rationing and austerity measures no longer applied. Average weekly earnings (including overtime payments) rose by 34 per cent between 1955 and 1960, a rate that comfortably out-paced the rise in the cost of living (Marwick 1990: 114). As a result most Britons were healthier, better-educated, better-housed and more prosperous than ever before (Porter 1993: 13). The country was at last enjoying the kind of boom conditions that characterised post-war America – indeed, the 'never had it so good' phrase was provided by a US trade union leader who had used it two years earlier. In a less frequently quoted part of Macmillan's speech in July 1957 the Prime Minister had correctly warned that economic growth and a tight labour market were likely to produce inflation. Action would have to be taken, he counselled, to maintain price stability. Such caution, however, was lost amidst a long-suppressed release of pent-up consumer demand. Even Macmillan proved reluctant to heed his own warnings about inflationary pressures when, in January 1958, he preferred to accept the resignation of his Chancellor, Peter Thorneycroft, and two other Treasury Ministers, Nigel Birch and Enoch Powell, rather than agree to their proposals to cut £50 million from public spending. The Prime Minister dismissed the resigna-tions as 'little local difficulties' and expansion was allowed to continue.

Across the country people spent their rising real incomes on cars, homes and domestic appliances. Refrigerators and washing machines began to appear in people's kitchens and helped to transform everyday household routines. Television sets became commonplace, their popular-ity heightened by the arrival of commercial television in 1955. Fashion was no longer the preserve of the wealthy. The development of cheaper synthetic materials that could be mass-produced, dyed in different colours and turned into off-the-peg outfits made the latest designs more accessible – even though the joke at the time was that male outfitters such as Burton's offered customers a choice of only three styles: small, medium and large. Personal spending surged as the range of consumer products widened dramatically in the late fifties. The easing of credit controls in 1958, and the £300 million worth of tax cuts that Chancellor

Heathcoat Amory gave away in his pre-election budget of April 1959, further fuelled demand. The first indications that this economic prosperity would come to be equated with a new cultural liberation were evident in the colour magazines which told readers how to fill their increased leisure time and live the fashionable life. Self-fulfilment through consumption was the fantasy that drove post-war capitalism forwards. Poverty, it seemed, was a slain giant, a term that was due to be expunged from the political lexicon or at least updated for new times to mean the non-ownership of a television set. Such prosperity, it should be recognised, was not unique to Britain. Western economies boomed after the Korean War, so much so that affluence became a cultural weapon to wield against communist states in the Cold War – material proof, it seemed, of the benefits of capitalism. But many in Britain had no interest in the external reasons for the economic good times. As far as they were concerned the new-found prosperity of the fifties was a national phenomenon, and they gratefully re-elected the Conservative government that had presided over the boom years with another comfortable majority in 1959.

The celebration of post-war affluence was widespread, but it was not universal. Some refused to be seduced by promises of consumer luxuries and an inexorable rise in living standards. Many within the Labour Party, for example, regarded the 'affluent society' as an 'acquisitive society'. One activist from Hornchurch Constituency Labour Party, interviewed by the author in the 1990s, recalled his anxieties that people's priorities were becoming confused in the Macmillan era.

> *We could see British society changing and we were desperate to put a halt to that element of Conservatism that was coming in – the get-rich-quick society of Harold Macmillan, the first signs of me first and greed. Outside the Labour Party it was obvious that people were beginning to get more concerned with their own affairs and improving their own position, and the wonderful spirit that was around in 1945 had dissipated. . . . I remember the horror my wife and I felt when we saw a young family from the East End at Stratford Co-op – the children obviously needed some decent footwear, the mother was rather shabbily dressed – discussing the merits of various television sets.*

(cited in Donnelly 1994: 230)

The idea that there was a growing disjunction between private affluence and poorly-funded public services found its most forceful advocate in American economist J.K. Galbraith. His book *The Affluent Society* (1958) reinforced Tony Crosland's warnings in *The Future of Socialism* (1956) about the need to re-balance social spending and individual consumption. Further criticism came from the so-called 'Angry Young Men', a group of writers whose common identity owed more to the media's habit of putting people into groups than it did to any genuine collaboration between the writers themselves. The closest they came to representing a cohesive force was when publisher Tom Maschler collected some of their work in a volume called *Declaration* in 1957. In fact certain members of the 'group' hated each other's work, but they could at least agree about the need to attack what they regarded as the lazy decadence, stifling social mores and rigid class structures of their time. As Ian MacDonald explained, the 'braying upper-class voices on newsreels, the odour of unearned privilege in parliament and the courts, the tired nostalgia for war', all combined in the fifties to produce a sense of revolt among the aspirant young who perceived themselves to be locked out from influence and alienated from the bland cultural mainstream. The Angry Young Men were at the forefront of rejecting 'the genteel, class-segregated staidness of fifties British society' (MacDonald 1995: 7). Unlike the Oxbridge-educated, ex-public-schoolboys who formed the core of the 'Establishment', the Angry Young Men typically came out of the post-war grammar schools and redbrick provincial universities. John Osborne, who wrote the plays *Look Back in Anger* (1956) and *The Entertainer* (1957), Colin Wilson, whose book *The Outsider* (1956) was a best-selling 'Angry' philosophical tract, and John Braine, author of *Room At The Top* (1957), were among the most celebrated names in this new literary trend. Kingsley Amis, whose novel *Lucky Jim* was published in 1954, was also retrospectively labelled an Angry Young Man by the media. By definition, of course, women were excluded from this new literary clique, but Joan Littlewood's Theatre Workshop should be bracketed alongside the Angry writers as another outlet of class-based cultural criticism during this period. It was a neat coincidence of timing that a collective label was applied to this otherwise disparate group around the time of the Suez fiasco. After all, the affair was a sharply-defined symbol of what it was about Britain that made these writers angry. Suez provided critics with a licence to attack Britain's ruling elite, both for its arrogance in launching the operation against Nasser and for its ineptitude in being forced to back down. But as Macmillan skilfully led his government away from Suez, the media's brief infatuation with the Angry Young Men drew to a close. It was left to the satirists of the early sixties to carry forward artistic assaults on the Establishment. Meanwhile the portrayal of working-class (usually masculine) alienation in the provinces was left to writers like Alan Sillitoe and David Storey, and the social realist 'kitchen-sink' New Wave films and *Armchair Theatre* dramas on ITV. Viewed from a distance the Angry Young Men works lacked the creative energy of their 'beat' equivalents in the United States – led by Jack Kerouac, Allen Ginsberg and William Burroughs. Also, most of these Angry writers were born in the 1920s. To teenagers who came of age in the sixties, therefore, they were yesterday's angry men. But for a while they at least provided a focus for those who wanted social change and who were unlikely to be consoled by the promise of a quick material fix.

Although the Angry Young Men were hardly adolescents in the mid-fifties (most were nearer thirty), their courtship by the media can be seen as part of a more general fascination with post-war youth. The 'baby boomers' and those born a little earlier were subject to scrutiny like no previous generation. The word 'teenager' came into general usage in the fifties and fixed the conceptualisation of this age cohort as a separate social category. Their habits, spending patterns, cultural pursuits and attitudes were continually studied by social researchers. Among the most striking findings of this research was the amount of boredom and alienation experienced by the nation's youth. Herein lay the central irony: despite its intense interest in covering the 'youth question', the mass media offered little specifically for teenagers. To many young people the fifties were predominantly a grey, drab space: a cultural desert where there was little or nothing to do on a Sunday and where – at least until Elvis Presley arrived – adolescents listened to the same music as their parents and dressed much like them too. The 'slumberous tranquillity' of Fifties crooners like Perry Como and Michael Holliday dominated the charts (MacDonald 1995: 19). BBC radio and television were unadventurous. Perhaps this suited middle-aged audiences in the Home Counties, but it left teenagers unfulfilled. British film-makers similarly failed to cater for the youth audience, preferring instead to make solid war films,

Norman Wisdom comedies and middle-of-the-road pictures like Rank's *Doctor in the House* (1954), a film which spawned several sequels and a long-running TV series. It was no surprise, therefore, that British teenagers looked to the United States to provide the role models for (always male) adolescent angst. In the cinema they found it in the brooding screen personas of Marlon Brando (in *The Wild One*, 1954) and James Dean (in *Rebel Without a Cause*, 1955). In literature they found it in Holden Caulfield, the narrator of J.D. Salinger's *The Catcher in the Rye* (1951). The recognition that there were widening cultural differences between young people and their parents provoked much earnest discussion about the 'generation gap' by commentators and youth workers. The National Union of Teachers was so alarmed by the phenomenon they held a special conference on 'Popular Culture and Personal Responsibility' to investigate its implications in 1960. The one British writer who made an attempt to understand the generational divide as a potentially positive development was the journalist and novelist Colin MacInnes. In his essay 'Young England, Half English' (1957) he recognised the importance of the 'teenage revolution' and the growing cultural force of adolescent pop stars like Tommy Steele: 'Today', he wrote, 'youth has money and teenagers have become a power' (cited in Gould 1985: 67). MacInnes despaired, however, at the Labour Party's failure to interest, much less inspire, this new generation. Alienated from traditional forms of authority and organisation, the culture gap was to widen in the sixties as the post-war babies grew up and sought ways to distance themselves further from their elders. Courted by a new breed of film-makers, advertisers and pop entrepreneurs, the baby boomers were to live the sixties in important respects as a conscious reaction against the social and cultural assumptions of the previous decade.

CHAPTER 2

. . . .

Consumerism, youth and sixties pop music

Affluence, materialism and the consumer society

Fifties prosperity was carried to new heights in the sixties, driving social and cultural change as it climbed. Beatlemania, King's Road boutiques, Pop Art, student activists, hippies and most other emblems of sixties culture either depended on the wealth generated by a buoyant mixed economy, or emerged in dynamic relation to it. Never before had the products of the culture industries been consumed on such a scale, never before had cultural entrepreneurs been faced with such favourable market opportunities, and never before had the critics of materialism been able to voice their objections from such a comfortable economic position. The sixties offered wider cultural choice and more money to spend on what was available than ever before. When Viv Nicholson won £152,000 on the Littlewoods pools in 1961 she knew what the spirit of the times demanded she do with it – 'spend, spend, spend'. Surplus cash fuelled the growth of industries such as pop music, film, fashion, television and publishing. Professional sports were also transformed by the economic and social effects of affluence. The abolition of the maximum wage in football in 1961 allowed the top players to push their earnings at least closer to their true market value. The replacement of the old 'retain and transfer' system in 1964 (under which clubs held the registration of their players even after their contract had expired) with a new system of contractual relations was a further improvement in footballers' rights over their employers. In cricket the distinction between amateurs and professionals (by which the professionals were relegated to subordinate positions within clubs and teams) was scrapped in 1963. Five years later the first 'open' Wimbledon tennis championships allowed professionals to compete in the tournament. Earning good money, it seemed, was no longer to be viewed with quite such patrician distaste. Even those who stole it acquired a certain status. When, in August 1963, a postal train was robbed in the Midlands of £2.5 million in used banknotes, the legend of the 'Great Train Robbers' was born. Despite causing a fatality the robbers were turned (in some eyes at least) into modern day Robin Hoods, feeding off a gangster chic that also helped the East-End Kray twins and the south London Richardson gang to enjoy a degree of celebrity cachet. New patterns of consumption, and the ways in which these interacted with broader social and cultural change, were evident in a wide range of fields and activities from the early sixties onwards. Not everybody felt the transforming power of prosperity and consumerism, but most did.

In fact for some people the wider availability of consumer goods and services that were previously regarded as luxuries was the decade's defining characteristic. Their 'cultural revolution' was less about sexual freedom and psychedelia and more about high-street spending. If the sixties was the age when people were preoccupied with the self – self-fulfilment, the autonomous self, the contemplative self, integrity of the self, self-adulation – then consumption was important because it offered more people than ever before the chance to buy themselves identities and lifestyles. These identities may have been more imagined than real, but the implications were profound. Advanced capitalism generated profits by persuading people that the route to personal fulfilment lay in buying the latest 'must-have' consumer item. Now, as average real wages rose in the early sixties, even the working classes could express their sense of self in terms of what they bought. As Peter York remembered, the sixties was a great time to be a consumer:

My own sixties memories seem to be about things *– having them and wanting them. Early on my parents acquire a kind of washing machine called the Hoover Keymatic, which claims to be programmed. I am fascinated because of the allusion to computers. A bit later I get a*

gramophone (pre-stereo) called Bush, which has won a kind of award.
It looks slick. . . . At no time do I: take LSD, protest (I hardly know or
care about Vietnam), join a pop group, meet a Beatle. I like Hair *for the*
same reason I like the Archies – good tunes . . .

   For student protest and hippies, substitute Engelbert Humperdinck,
a first taste of prawn cocktails at the Batley variety club, holidays in
Spain, real cream, not having to have an Army-issue haircut, Wrighton
Californian kitchens. A cornucopia of consumer goodies – only
contemptible to those who'd got them already.

(York 1980: 182–3)

As a style commentator for *Harper's and Queen* in the 1970s and 1980s, York could be expected to attach more meaning than most to material possessions. Nevertheless, his recollections contain some useful insights. The ending of National Service in 1960 meant that York and his youthful contemporaries were not required to sacrifice their early adult years to the regimentation and routine of the military, policing what remained of the empire (the final cohort of conscripts left the services in 1962). Student rebellions in the late sixties held no appeal – indeed, protesting students tended to provoke indifference or outright hostility. Moreover, much of the extra income available in the sixties was either spent on the home or on home-centred activities. Spending patterns that were established at the beginning of the decade helped to transform Britain by the 1970s. Consumer durables, which were previously reserved for a wealthy minority, now became commonplace, thanks to a combination of technological advance, improved production techniques and easier consumer credit in the form of hire purchase. By the 1970s, almost every household in the country had a television, most households had labour-saving devices such as vacuum cleaners, washing machines and refrigerators, and about half of all households had a telephone. The share of the household goods and services market taken by electrical appliance retailers increased steadily in the 1960s – Currys, the Co-op, Civic Stores and the showrooms of the old electricity and gas boards led the way – and their turnover was to grow by more than 70 per cent in 1966–71 (Critchley 1973: 40). In the earlier part of the decade there had been spectacular opportunities for entrepreneurs to make profits in unsaturated markets for durable goods. John Bloom, the 'cut-price king', was emblematic here, selling washing-machines at a price that undercut his rivals by some £30. His strategy was to rely on mass sales to offset a narrow profit margin, chasing the market with such heavy advertising that his company had the biggest advertising spend in the country in 1963. Bloom eventually overstretched himself and his company collapsed in 1964. But in the meantime he made a fortune and revolutionised selling and advertising methods. Aggressive competition on price became a normal feature of the consumer goods market, benefiting the customer and squeezing the margins of producers (Sampson 1965: 558–61).

Outside the home there was a growth in car ownership, particularly among the more affluent professional classes. It was these consumers who could afford to buy cars like the Ford Cortina Mk 1, launched in 1962 and priced at £639. In 1961 less than one-third of all households owned a car, but by 1966 this had risen to 49.2 per cent of English and Welsh households, with ownership among the professional and managerial classes as high as 75 per cent (Halsey 1972: 551). Overall in Britain the number of car owners doubled from 5,650,000 in 1960 to 11,802,000 in 1970 (Wheen 1982: 165). This growth was reflected in the increased turnover of the motor trade more generally, rising from £2,962 million in 1962 to £4,198 million in 1967. A surge in motorcycle registrations in 1959 also meant that there were 1.75 million of these on the roads until the number declined in the late sixties (Clarke 1996: 255). The road network expanded to meet the increase in vehicle ownership, including a rapid increase in the motorway network following the opening of the first section of the M1 in 1959. Increased car use helped to promote changes in shopping habits, with consumers increasingly preferring 'one-stop shopping' in self-service supermarkets that offered wide choice, discounts and plenty of car-parking spaces. In 1958 there were about 300 supermarkets in Britain. By 1972 there were about 5,000 – with a corresponding closure of some 60,000 smaller grocers (Critchley 1973: 2–5). The character of Britain's high streets was thus transformed. Supermarkets such as the Co-op, Sainsbury's, Tesco, Fine Fare and Marks and Spencer were most popular in London and the South-East and least popular in Wales and Scotland, where the independents continued to resist the market penetration of the big retailers. As shopping habits changed, the larger supermarkets extended their own brand ranges: Sainsbury's, for example, added some 1,000 of their own-brand products during the sixties, and by 1970 these accounted for over 50 per cent of the company's turnover (Williams 1994: 144, 147). Increasingly consumers also wanted products that were as simple to use as the supermarkets themselves. Consumption of convenience foods such as frozen or processed vegetables, fish fingers, soups, cakes and biscuits rose steadily, enabling people to put meals together in minutes rather than hours (Burnett 1989: 309–10). Despite the popularity of the supermarkets and other larger stores throughout the sixties, however, infrequent bulk-buying had yet to gain a significant hold on British shopping culture. A survey in the early 1970s found that only 2 per cent of households favoured this type of shopping, while over half of all households did some form of shopping at least four days a week – Friday was the most popular day, with some major supermarkets closed on Mondays as well as Sundays (Critchley 1973: 17; Williams 1994: 153–4). In the battle to capture the supermarket consumer, advertising budgets soared. By the end of the decade Kellogg's Corn Flakes and Weetabix, Maxwell House coffee, milk and the soap powders Radiant, Persil, Ariel and Daz all featured among the ten most heavily advertised products, annually spending around £1 million each on advertising, and tempting customers with snappy slogans such as 'Omo adds Brightness to Cleanness and Whiteness' or 'Drinka Pinta Milka Day'. Despite the efforts of the Consumers' Association magazine *Which?* to help shoppers find best value, heavily-promoted brands comfortably outsold their less well publicised competitors (Sampson 1971: 413–4, 418, 420).

Rising real incomes and the arrival of cheaper air travel opened up opportunities for travel and holidays abroad, with new resorts on the Costa Brava and Costa del Sol becoming the favourite destinations for those Britons who holidayed overseas. According to the Passport Office, the number of new passports issued in the United Kingdom each year rose from approximately 580,000 in 1956 to 980,000 in 1966. The British Travel Association estimated that the number of Britons who holidayed abroad doubled from 2 million in 1955 to 4 million in 1961 (Halsey 1972: 549–550). By 1971, this figure had climbed to nearly 8 million. In the sixties, however, holidaying abroad was largely confined to the middle classes. The real dawn of mass overseas travel was delayed until deeper into the 1970s. Perhaps one reason why the foreign travel boom was delayed was the government's insistence in July 1966 that holidaymakers could take no more than £50 worth of sterling in foreign exchange out of the country. But those Britons who did manage to sample culture overseas at least helped to ensure that others shared some of their experiences, if only at second hand, on their return. They bought cookbooks by Elizabeth David (for example, *Italian Food* and *French Provincial Cooking*) and cooked Mediterranean dishes such as *quiche lorraine* and *boeuf en daube* for middle-class dinner parties. The proliferation of French, Italian and Greek restaurants in the country's high streets also catered for increasingly adventurous metropolitan tastes. People, at least some of the time, wanted more than the scampi-in-the-basket, fish and chips or meat and potatoes that were served in the nation's steakhouse chains (Wheen 1982: 167). As restaurateur Alvaro Maccioni observed of the English customers who ate pasta and pizza in the new trattorias, the old puritan functionalist approach to eating was giving way in the early sixties to a new theatricality: 'Before, food was like gas or electricity: then it became another form of entertainment' (Levy 2002: 52). Of course the variables of class and generation operated here. Much of the trade for restaurants consisted of business customers buying meals on expense accounts. Meanwhile, a 1975 survey confirmed that the wealthiest were comfortably outspending the poorest – including many pensioners – in the weekly food budget: £5.89 per head compared with £4.30. As wealth and social status increased, so did consumption of fruit, fresh green vegetables, fresh meat and milk. The less wealthy working classes ate more potatoes, cereal products, sugar and convenience foods, preferring to divert their earnings to consumer durables and holidays (Driver 1983: 66). Exacerbating the class divide still further, it was the broadsheet newspapers and upmarket magazines such as *Harper's Bazaar* that carried recipes and restaurant reviews, enabling the middle classes to see themselves as pioneers of new tastes and changes in food consumption patterns.

Changes in consumer habits had wider cultural ramifications. As people stocked refrigerators and cupboards with supermarket goods, filled their homes with electrical appliances, and spent money on carpets, decorating and better heating systems, the family home became the principal site of most leisure time in Britain. Instead of spending their free time on communal activities in public spaces, people increasingly preferred home-centred leisure activities. Television viewing was by far the most popular of these, accounting for 23 per cent of male and female leisure time by 1969. Predictably the figure was highest among married middle-aged men with children and lowest for young single adults, but even with these variations, watching television was popular for all social groups (Central Statistical Office 1970: 78). As Anthony Sampson remarked: 'in the last twenty years the small screen has become the central factor in most people's spare time. . . . British families on average watch television for eighteen hours a week – far more than any other European country, and twice as much as Belgium, Italy or Sweden' (1971: 442). The next most popular leisure activity for males was gardening, particularly in new towns, accounting for 12 per cent of leisure time. Almost 80 per cent of British households had a garden (only Luxembourg among European nations had a higher proportion), and there was a sizeable market for lawn mowers, plants, sheds and all the other paraphernalia of the keen amateur gardener. Females, meanwhile, devoted 17 per cent of their free time to crafts and hobbies, usually knitting (Sampson 1971: 426–7). The pull of the world beyond the home and garden was only experienced forcefully, it seems, by the under-25s. Contradicting the stereotype of sixties youth, however, by no means all of them sought their escape in coffee bars, dance halls or bookshop-basement poetry readings. Instead, physical recreation took up about 25 per cent of the leisure time of young males and females at the end of the sixties (Central Statistical Office 1970: 78). In his survey updated in 1971, *The New Anatomy of Britain*, Anthony Sampson could barely conceal his disapproval of the British taste for mundane leisure pursuits:

> *Britain is the greatest nation in Europe for handymen and potterers-*
> *about; it has the highest proportion of people who do their own*
> *wallpapering, painting, drilling, and plumbing, and the highest*
> *proportion who buy second-hand cars. A broad picture unfolds of the*
> *British living a withdrawn and inarticulate life, rather like Harold*
> *Pinter's people, mowing lawns and painting walls, pampering pets,*
> *listening to music, knitting and watching television. If one wanted*
> *a symbol of what distinguishes contemporary British life from that*
> *of other countries it might well be a potting shed.*

(Sampson 1971: 427)

Youth cultures, moral panics and pop music

Older Britons might have spent their surplus income on new television sets and do-it-yourself, but the nation's youth had different spending patterns. As a social group they were to become the arch consumers of the sixties, spending some £800 million on themselves each year in the early part of the decade. Mark Abrams' research probably exaggerated the reach of affluence among young Britons at the time (1959 and 1961), but their growing economic power was undeniable and it was to become one of the decade's key cultural determinants. Not only were young people more wealthy, there were simply more of them. The post-war baby boom of 1945–8 meant that a bulge of teenagers appeared in the population in the late fifties. And it was as good a time as any to be young. Elvis Presley was the symbol of a newly energised (and sexualised) youth culture that was blowing in from the United States, and, as we have seen, the ending of conscription in November 1960 meant that young men no longer had to endure two years of National Service and having their hair cut off. In the short term, the main beneficiaries of this favourable climate for youth were working-class teenagers. Unlike their middle-class counterparts, who were more likely to stay in education until they were 21, working-class youths tended to leave school at 15 and take advantage of the high demand for unskilled and semi-skilled labour. Few of these teenagers had significant fixed financial commitments like a mortgage, nor did they buy 'white goods' like fridges, cookers or washing machines. Instead they spent their disposable income on leisure, luxury items and cultural markers, a point that the culture industries were quick to grasp. Magazine publishing, fashion, film and cosmetics responded to the growing youth market with new products and integrated marketing strategies. Advertisers fought to attract young consumers and popular papers such as the *Daily Mirror* actively sought a more youthful readership through their coverage of pop, fashion and teen issues. The most important field of all, in terms of how it allowed young people to shape their own environment, was pop music. Teenagers bought cheap, portable, plastic Dansette record players for their bedrooms, along with the records to play and posters of the groups and singers. In effect they turned their part of the family home into shrines that celebrated their favourite pop stars (Rees 1986: 36).

This distinctive leisure market for youth was hardly a new phenomenon: something resembling one had begun to take shape in Britain
as far back as the mid-nineteenth century (Osgerby 1997: 6). But what
was novel in the post-war period was the amount of attention focused on
young people as a specific social category, whether in the form of the
teenager (usually working-class) in the fifties, or youth (which was seen
to transcend class and other cultural attachments) in the sixties. This
attention was partly the result of public anxiety about increased juvenile
delinquency in the fifties and sixties, continuing an upwards trend in
youth petty crime that had been evident since the war years (Muncie
1984: 59). At the centre of rising juvenile crime rates were working-class
male youths who drifted in and out of delinquent behaviour. Organised
mobs of delinquent youth were rare, and although there were several
style tribes among the nation's young there was as yet no evidence that a
British gang culture had evolved. The crimes committed by these juven-
iles were relatively minor. The main offence was petty theft which,
according to studies such as Mays' in Liverpool (1954) and Wilmott's in
Bethnal Green (1966), had become accepted as a cultural norm among
young people (Muncie 1984: 62–4).

The other reason for society's obsession with youth was young
people's growing predilection for forming highly visible subcultural
groups. Youth, it appeared, had developed a rebellious autonomy by the
early sixties which it expressed through leisure pursuits. The result was
a generalised moral panic about impending social breakdown. For a time,
the 'youth question' became a metaphor for wider post-war social change
and an index of social anxiety (Hall *et al*: 1978: 234). By no means all
youths, it should be emphasised, had a close affiliation with subcultures
or saw themselves as rebellious. In fact, surveys suggested that young
people in this period were usually quite conservative in their attitudes
to sex, morality and social values. Most of them believed that they had
an investment in the social system as it stood and responded to it either
deferentially or aspirationally (Eppels and Eppels 1960; Schofield 1965;
Veness 1962; Brake 1985: 60, 72). Moreover Pearl Jephcott's survey of
youth in Glasgow and West Lothian, which she carried out in 1964–6,
contradicted the stereotype of rebellious teenage trendsetters, finding
instead youngsters who lived rather humdrum and limited lives in their
leisure time. Boys liked to kick a football around, girls liked to visit

friends, and overall the mood was one of vague dissatisfaction. Earnings were not particularly high amongst her sample of 15–19 year olds, and in any case, most of what these teenagers earned was passed straight to their parents (1967: 55–6). Minorities, however, lend tone and colour to the society they inhabit. Also, cultural radicalism can be seen as the leading edge of deeper-lying tensions and changes within the time and place in which it is produced. It was significant, therefore, that from the early sixties onwards a number of youth subcultures emerged that stood in opposition to adult and normative ('bourgeois') values, sparking off periodic media scares about the 'youth of today' and dragging wider cultural change in their wake. Furthermore, it was this phenomenon that made British youth distinctive from its international counterparts. More so than anywhere else, British youth subcultures identified themselves by their dress, musical preferences, speech patterns and behaviour, and by what Lévi-Strauss called 'bricolage', a process in which signs and symbols were reordered and recontextualised to communicate coded meanings (for example, the way that Mods appropriated the RAF target symbol on their clothing, or dressed up Lambretta scooters with shiny chrome). These subcultures tended to be male dominated – female youth culture was more of a private, domestic affair (Rees 1986: 42) – and almost exclusively white, with membership stratified into a hierarchy. The subcultural vanguard consisted of 'full-time', righteous members who reacted against their personal material experience by creating their own culture from below. These were the few who dictated styles, fashions and codes. Most of the rest were part-timers, content with buying some of the trappings of subcultures pre-packaged from high-street retailers who had carefully tracked the latest changes in youth fashion.

The starting point for this formation of post-war youth subcultures were the Teddy boys, who caught the public's attention when one of them murdered a youth on Clapham Common in 1953, and after gangs of Teds fought at St Mary Cray railway station in a south London suburb in 1954. Two years later they jived in the aisles and tore up cinemas during the rock and roll movie *Rock Around the Clock*, after which the media built a full-scale moral panic around them. Teddy boy violence – often between local groups fighting over dilapidated inner-city territory, but also targeted at immigrants during the Notting Hill riots of 1958 – was a tribal means of celebration and signature (Nuttall 1968: 30). It was also guaranteed to capture headlines, exaggerating the size of the numbers involved and setting the tone for the press coverage of subsequent youth cults. Delinquency and youth increasingly became synonymous terms for journalists. For example, the Teds' immediate descendants, the motorcycling Rockers – leather-clad and aggressively masculine, style cousins of the Californian 'Hell's Angels' – were pilloried in the popular press as inarticulate working-class morons (Leech 1973: 4). The media could find no redeeming features in a group whose members were primarily interested in showing off their motorcycling skills – those who reached 100 mph gloried in the label 'ton-up boy' – and meeting at petrol station cafes to swap stories of adrenalin-pumping rides. Media hostility to Rockers was partly a matter of aesthetics. The homoerotic uniform of leather jacket, tight blue jeans, studs and peaked cap might have worked for Marlon Brando in *The Wild One*, but most bikers fell some way short of this ideal. Instead the popular view of Rockers was that their dishevelled appearance betrayed both a suspect temperament and a lack of self-respect.

In contrast to Rockers, the fastidiously well-groomed, style-obsessed Mods favoured Church's hand-made brogues, silk ties and mohair suits. These youthful dandies were British by birth but Italian at heart, picking up sartorial influences from Italian immigrants and films including *Roman Holiday* (1953) and *La Dolce Vita* (1960). Mods arrived in east London in the late fifties with an interest in modern jazz (hence the Mod title), continental fashions and some aspects of urban black immigrant culture (Hebdige 1979: 87–94). The tribe spread to the London suburbs of Shepherd's Bush and Richmond in the early sixties and eventually reached the provinces, making Mods the dominant youth style of the time. Despite their association with amphetamine drugs (known as 'purple hearts' and 'French blues'), Mods were considered safe enough to have their own programme on the offshore commercial station Radio Luxembourg. They were similarly courted by fashion retailers and magazine publishers who recognised the commercial value of Mods as upwardly-mobile consumers. The sub-culture cross-fertilised with art students, providing the basis for pop groups such as The Rolling Stones, The Beatles, The Who and The Kinks. But typically Mods were employed in routine white-collar occupations such as messenger, clerk or office boy, husbanding their wages carefully in order to buy themselves style

– and thereby status – for night-time and weekend display. As the *Sunday Times* magazine discovered in 1964 in this – obviously exaggerated – account of typical London Mod life, drawn from an interview with seventeen-year-old Denzil, the primary purpose of the subculture was a hedonistic pursuit of pleasure:

> *Monday night meant dancing at the Mecca, the Hammersmith Palais, the Purley Orchard, or the Streatham Locarno. Tuesday meant Soho and the Scene club. Wednesday was Marquee night. Thursday was reserved for the ritual washing of the hair. Friday meant the Scene again. Saturday afternoon usually meant shopping for clothes and records, Saturday night was spent dancing and rarely finished before 9.00 or 10.00 Sunday morning. Sunday evening meant the Flamingo or, perhaps, if one showed signs of weakening, could be spent sleeping.*
>
> (cited in Hebdige 1979: 90)

The hedonistic rituals were not to last much longer and, by the middle of the decade, the Mod scene was all but finished. Carnaby Street, where the original Mods had bought continental suits in John Stephen's 'His Clothes', was a tacky tourist trap by 1965. Mod fashions were increasingly manufactured from above by profit-seeking entrepreneurs rather than developed organically from below. And after Mods skirmished with Rockers at the southern seaside resorts of Clacton, Margate, Brighton and Hastings on successive Bank holidays in 1964, media coverage switched to portraying them primarily as folk devils rather than style darlings. The legacy of the Mods' involvement in group violence was picked up by the more overtly working class and aggressively masculinised Skinhead subculture, whose image of shaven heads, braces and Dr. Marten boots was a conscious rejection of the late-sixties hippie aesthetic. Group violence was also the favoured activity of football hooligans, who featured regularly in the national press from the 1966–7 season onwards. Indeed, as seasonal attendances at football league matches fell from 33 million to 25 million across the decade, grounds increasingly became the preserve of younger fans, a trend that continued throughout the seventies as football violence and gangs of youths rampaging through British Rail Football Special trains became a national scourge.

Distinctive middle-class youth cultures tended to be associated more with political protest and alternative lifestyles than with fashion or tribal allegiance. More likely to prolong their education through to university, the young alienated bourgeoisie had greater opportunity to intellectualise their sense of distance from mainstream society and, assisted by what in retrospect were generous state maintenance grants, the freedom to question the work ethic that Mods at least accepted as a requirement to fund their lifestyle. The formation of CND in 1958 provided a cause and a vehicle for thousands of youthful idealists who became moral crusaders against the bomb. Disengaged from party- or class-based politics, the youngsters who made up an estimated 90 per cent of CND Aldermaston marchers in 1962 were drawn to a movement which favoured the march and the demonstration over the committee room. More important still, their cause could be seen in part as a crusade against the moral bankruptcy of an older generation. On the annual Aldermaston to London Easter marches, during the sit-down protest outside the Ministry of Defence in February 1961 and on 'Battle of Britain Sunday', when 12,000 peace campaigners crowded into Trafalgar Square in September 1961 for a demonstration that led to 1,300 arrests, young people wearing donkey jackets, duffel coats and peace badges were to the fore. They never managed to ban the bomb, but they developed a taste for protest and learned valuable lessons about organisation that later resurfaced in anti-racism groups, the Women's Liberation Movement and the broad church that was the counter-culture. As Jeff Nuttall recalled, it was through CND that the young moral crusaders first joined forces with the beat bohemians:

> On the march you got pacifists, you got Quakers in large numbers,
> conscientious objectors, mostly from the middle class. You got
> contingents from trade unions. And you had the beatniks who suddenly
> emerged – and nobody had known about them outside their own
> favourite haunts – Soho coffee bars and jazz clubs. And they appeared in
> the standard uniform at the time which was tattered jeans and dirty old
> donkey jackets.

(Green 1998a: 7)

The beat bohemians – or beatniks – embraced a form of cultural radicalism that saw them retreat from what they perceived to be the philistinism, materialism, and impersonality of modern society. Their immediate cultural influences were American: modern jazz music and beat writers such as Jack Kerouac, Allen Ginsberg and William Burroughs, who had criss-crossed the USA in the late forties and early fifties, fuelled by drugs, alcohol and the zealous pursuit of a new artistic vision. More distantly, they also looked back to the Bohemianism that had emerged in Paris in the 1840s and which flowered again in European capitals in the 1890s and 1920s. Whereas the middle-class students who formed the core of the moral crusaders were motivated by an idealistic political agenda, overlaid with disillusion at what they saw as the stasis of the old left, bohemians looked towards a more personal model of liberation. Theirs was a decisive turn towards the self. Instead of hoping to change society, they opted to remain on its outside, free from the constraints of moral norms and bourgeois ambition. They were prepared to join with others to campaign against nuclear weapons, but once they saw that CND was doomed to failure in 1962, they focused on more passive forms of resistance – such as dropping out and avoiding paid work – and living for the immediate sensations that could be found in drugs and sex. It was an inward-looking and alternative lifestyle that would later become known as the counter-culture. The use of drugs in the search for self-fulfilment was also, as Jeff Nuttall rationalised in *Bomb Culture*, a response to Cold War anxiety and the impending horror of nuclear catastrophe:

> *Clearly in a way of life devoted to the sensation of the moment, drugs were of considerable use and began to be used. That they may be addictive or lethal was comparatively irrelevant because such dangers belonged to the future and the future was, to say the least of it, not a safe bet, too improbable to be taken seriously into account.*

> (Nuttall 1968: 114)

At the start of the sixties there was obvious mutual antagonism between different youth groups, heightened by class distinctions. To more respectable contemporaries, Rockers seemed violent and tasteless. In some eyes, Mods were the shallow dupes of fashion retailers and leisure outlets. The earnest middle-class protesters who carried their banners on the CND marches looked like dull, naive squares to the less politically committed. Beat bohemians, meanwhile, could be dismissed as self-indulgent, pretentious poseurs. But as the decade wore on bridges were built between these formerly disparate groups, and the most important bridge of all was constructed around popular music. Whereas youth groups had previously used their musical preferences as a cultural boundary, a new form of rock music which emerged around 1964–5 had a more universal youthful appeal. Rock music fused together elements of modern jazz, folk protest songs and rock and roll in a way that offered something to everybody. Beat poetry was also incorporated into the mix as performers increasingly wrote their own songs, inspired perhaps by beat poets who gave readings of their work at bookshops or clubs accompanied by a music soundtrack. Rock music now provided a common reference point for previously antagonistic youth groups, all of whom found they could connect with artists like The Beatles or Bob Dylan (who left folk behind for electric music in 1965). The breaking-down of these boundaries helped to make youth, for a time at least, a more homogenous phenomenon, rather than one that was continually divided along class lines. This is not to claim that all previous differences were buried indefinitely. In the late sixties, for example, class antagonism underpinned the skinheads' hatred of bourgeois hippies. None the less, the opening up of shared space for youth groups was to become an important feature of the middle and later sixties.

Sixties pop music

A more homogenous youth identity, held together by shared consumption of popular music, found a voice in the mainstream music press and the pop station BBC Radio One (broadcast from 1967). Offshore pirate pop stations, including Radio London and Radio Caroline, were another common reference point for youth. For most hours of the day, the pirates were the only source of pop for British listeners, until the authorities closed down these unlicensed stations shortly before Radio One arrived. Television programmes like *Ready, Steady, Go!* (first broadcast in 1963), *Top of the Pops* (first broadcast in 1964) and *The Beat Room* (1964–5) showed pop music cross-fertilising with other media. Films, fashion and magazines similarly drew on pop music's energy and elevated it into *the* driver of sixties youth culture. In short, British pop music matured in the sixties. Manufactured fifties teen idols like Tommy Steele and Adam Faith – who mostly sang other people's songs – were superseded by the do-it-yourself ethos of the guitar bands and singer–songwriters. In the fifties most of the UK's favourite singles artists came from the United

States – albeit with the qualification that the weekly singles charts were not taken completely seriously before 1969, as they were open to manipulation by record companies (Harker 1980: 94). During the sixties the majority of the most popular chart acts were home-grown, and some of these went on to export their success across the Atlantic.

TABLE 2.1 ◆ *Top-selling singles artists in the UK, 1960–9*

Rank	Artist	Nationality	Record label
1	Cliff Richard	UK	Columbia
2	The Beatles	UK	Parlophone/Apple
3	Elvis Presley	US	RCA
4	The Shadows	UK	Columbia
5	The Rolling Stones	UK	Decca
6	The Hollies	UK	Parlophone
7	Manfred Mann	UK	HMV/Fontana
8	Roy Orbison	US	London American
9	Adam Faith	UK	Parlophone
10	The Kinks	UK	Pye
11	The Everly Brothers	US	London/Warner
12	Tom Jones	UK	Decca
13	Billy Fury	UK	Decca
14	The Beach Boys	US	Capitol
15	Herman's Hermits	UK	Columbia
16	Cilla Black	UK	Parlophone
17	Englebert Humperdinck	UK	Decca
18	The Supremes	US	Tamla Motown
19	Dusty Springfield	UK	Philips
20	The Searchers	UK	Pye

TABLE 2.2 ◆ *Top UK singles, 1960–9*

Rank	Title	Artist(s)
1	She Loves You	The Beatles
2	Wonderful Land	The Shadows
3	I Remember You	Frank Ifield
4	Sugar Sugar	The Archies
5	It's Now Or Never	Elvis Presley
6	Cathy's Clown	The Everly Brothers
7	You've Lost That Lovin' Feelin'	The Righteous Brothers
8	Tears	Ken Dodd
9	Green Green Grass of Home	Tom Jones
10	Telstar	The Tornados

Source: McAleer, D. (1994) *The Warner Guide to UK & US Hit Singles*, London: Carlton / Little, Brown, p. 65.

A high point came in May 1965 when British recordings held an un-precedented nine of the top ten places in the US singles chart. At the start of the sixties the upper reaches of the UK singles chart typically con-tained at least one US artist: Elvis Presley in particular was a towering force, selling millions of units and holding a virtual monopoly on the international male singer and personality awards in the *New Musical Express* readers' polls in the sixties. A symbolic moment arrived in August 1961 when the domestic industry's confidence was boosted by the first all-British top three (Helen Shapiro, Eden Kane and John Leyton). Even if we accept the doubts about the way they were compiled, the charts remained important because they determined both radio playlists and which acts were booked to appear on TV pop shows. The most consistent British chart performers in the early sixties were Billy Fury, Cliff Richard (who was voted best British male singer by *NME* readers every year from 1960–6, and indeed best male singer in the *world* in 1963) and The Shadows (who after several false starts had their first instrumental hit with *Apache* in August 1960). Instrumentals in fact were big business in Britain around 1960, with tracks by The Shadows, The Tornados, Johnny and the Hurricanes, Duane Eddy and similar artists sometimes account-ing for one-third of top twenty hits. The early sixties also saw a trad jazz boom (based around traditional New Orleans jazz) led by Acker Bilk, Kenny Ball and Chris Barber. But above all, perhaps, these years are famous for the emergence of British R&B and the Merseybeat sound, both of which fused US rhythm and blues and native art-school sensibilities in ways that reached far beyond the initial core Mod audience. The new scene was dominated by guitar groups, including The Beatles (who released their first single in October 1962), Gerry and the Pacemakers (whose first hit was in March 1963), Freddie and The Dreamers (first hit June 1963), Brian Poole and The Tremeloes (first hit July 1963), Dave Clark Five (first hit December 1963) The Rolling Stones (first hit Decem-ber 1963), and several others whose success confirmed, among other things, that UK audiences liked to consume 'black' music that had been anglicised and repackaged for them by white artists.

By March 1964 several of these acts featured in the first British top ten consisting of purely local artists, led by Cilla Black's debut number one, *Anyone Who Had A Heart*. Fellow female artists like Shirley Bassey, Brenda Lee and Helen Shapiro made an impact on what was an otherwise male-dominated singles chart in the sixties. But Cilla Black was one of only three female acts who made the list of the twenty top-selling singles artists in the UK across the whole decade: the other two were The Supremes and Dusty Springfield. True, each of the four main UK labels had its own female star who was marketed to the public as a 'girl next door'. Springfield (Philips), Black (EMI Parlophone), Sandie Shaw (Pye) and Lulu (Decca) were all major successes. And, in the longer format, Julie Andrews deserved as much credit as anyone for making the *Sound of Music* soundtrack the top-selling UK album of the sixties. But in terms of studio time, attention paid to production quality and the size of the marketing budgets, even the biggest female stars continually lost out to their male counterparts. Nor were there any successful all-female bands in the sixties – notwithstanding the popularity of female *vocal* groups. That much-prized asset of popular music – the authenticity of the truly expressive artist – was held to be a masculine quality in the sixties.

Many of the most popular (male) chart acts at this time wrote their own material. Initially the dominant discourse was teen romance. As one writer has observed, for example, the lyrics of all 49 songs copyrighted by The Beatles during 1963–4 were about boy–girl romance (Brown 2001: 178). Self-expression through rock music, which helped to articulate a new sensibility for youth, arrived a little later in the decade. The resulting body of 'serious' work earned sixties popular music its high reputation. One of the features of this period was a growing tendency among fans and critics to differentiate between 'pop' music (pure entertainment) and 'rock' music (artistically authentic). The terms themselves were loosely defined, but the split was taken to be important. As popular music began to be taken more seriously as an art form, albums became more important for critics than hit singles. No group was more successful in either format than The Beatles, whose cultural impact on the period is impossible to overstate. At no point in the sixties were The Beatles seen to be out of step with the times – notwithstanding the bemused public reaction to the Boxing Day television screening of *Magical Mystery Tour* in 1967. Certainly from 1965 onwards the music weeklies treated the group with a reverence that was quite unlike anything their predecessors – or indeed contemporaries – inspired. Even classical music critics took them seriously. In retrospect some of the group's work appears overrated, but we should not forget that The Beatles' output was prolific (an album a year for the best part of the decade) and that their artistic ambition set new standards – lyrically, musically and in the use of studio technology – for others to emulate. *A Hard Day's Night* (1964) broke new ground because the group wrote every track on the album. *Rubber Soul* (1965), *Revolver* (1966) and *Sgt. Pepper's Lonely Hearts Club Band* (1967) saw The Beatles at the peak of their creative powers before self-indulgence and paranoia took their toll towards the end of the decade. Only The Rolling Stones rivalled The Beatles' commercial strength and iconic status – but even they needed Lennon and McCartney to write them their first major hit, *I Wanna Be Your Man*. Among the second tier of UK artists who wrote their own material were The Who, The Kinks, Small Faces and Cream, and solo performers such as Van Morrison and Donovan. Given that the counter-culture's lead guitarist, Jimi Hendrix, had to come to London to find a recording deal, and that his group was completed by Noel Redding and Mitch Mitchell, perhaps the UK can also lay some claim to ownership of the Jimi Hendrix Experience.

In fact the cross-Atlantic traffic of performers and recorded output makes the concept of a purely indigenous UK music industry in the sixties largely redundant. Artists on either side of the ocean listened to each other and were influenced by the same root sources. US and UK acts competed for success in both countries' charts. British artists The Who, Joe Cocker and Graham Nash played at the Woodstock Festival in 1969. In the other direction, Bob Dylan headlined at the Isle of Wight Festival of the same year. US performers the Doors, Joni Mitchell, Leonard Cohen, Sly and the Family Stone and Joan Baez were all included in the 1970 Isle of Wight line-up, together with Hendrix, who was to die three weeks after the event. Brian Wilson's song-writing for The Beach Boys influenced his British counterparts, not least The Beatles. And most singer-songwriters of the period owed a debt to Bob Dylan, who did as much as anyone to explore the potential of the three-minute song and, in the process, wrote himself into popular music's DNA. Towards the end of the decade, the US bands The Velvet Underground and The MC5 laid down the roots for the punk rock explosion that hit both the United States and Britain in the mid-seventies.

The United States was not the only outside influence on the UK music scene. New Commonwealth immigration brought with it the sounds of Jamaican ska – a fusion of Jamaican and American R&B and the 'jump' beat that was played on the black radio stations of Miami and New Orleans. Ska was at its height in Jamaica in 1961–7, recorded by the pioneer producer Coxsone Dodd and consumed in the UK by the first wave of young Jamaican émigrés. The form was known as Blue Beat in the UK – after the label that carried most of the tracks – and had a following among the country's Mods (Larkin 1998: 4946). The availability of Jamaican music in Britain also became more widespread after Chris Blackwell moved his Island Record label from Jamaica to London in 1962. Although ska did not have a major impact on the charts there were hits for Millie (*My Boy Lollipop* and *Sweet William*, both 1964), the Skatalites (*Guns of Navarone*, 1967) and Prince Buster (*Al Capone*, 1967). Jamaican artists were popular performers in Wardour Street's Flamingo club and the Ram Jam in Brixton. Sonny Roberts' Planetone label, which shared premises with Island Records in London, also provided an opportunity for Jamaicans who had settled in the UK to record their own music. By 1967 ska was giving way to rocksteady. This had a slower, more refined sound that was best captured by vocalists like the Wailers or Ken Boothe. In 1968 reggae arrived in Jamaica and soon had a UK following. In addition to its fan base among Britain's Jamaican-born population, reggae was popular with the new Skinhead sub-culture. This combined support enabled several reggae artists to enjoy chart success in the late sixties and early seventies – among them were Desmond Dekker, Jimmy Cliff and Bob and Marcia. When Island Records recorded the Wailers' album *Catch a Fire* (1973) with a rock audience specifically in mind, reggae became a global musical form. Throughout the 1970s reggae became the favoured musical expression of rastafari politics in the UK and a form through which Britain's black communities could articulate their dissatisfaction with white society.

CHAPTER 3

Anxieties, beliefs and intellectuals

What's wrong with Britain?

Post-war prosperity had produced sufficient contentment among voters to see the Conservatives re-elected in 1955 and 1959, each time with almost 50 per cent of the vote. At another level, however, attitudes towards the new age of affluence were more ambiguous. By the early sixties, commentators and intellectuals were expressing their anxieties about the state of the nation. *What's Wrong With Britain?* was the introspective title of a series of Penguin books that explored this theme. The sense of unease that pulsed through this elite discourse centred above all on Britain's continued lack of international competitiveness, something which had been a growing source of concern since at least the turn of the century. By the early sixties the long narrative of relative economic decline had arrived at the point where Britain was being left behind in what amounted to a third industrial revolution, this time based around space-age technologies, automation and advanced methods of communication. Britain, it seemed, was about to squander finally its post-war inheritance as one of the principal victor nations: winning the war had apparently bred complacency, leaving not just the United States but defeated nations like Germany and Japan to surge ahead economically through the 1950s. According to one contemporary assessment of Britain's economic standing in Europe, whereas West Germany was doubling its production every 10 years, and France every 17, Britain required

32 years to achieve a similar increase. Returning from a meeting of the International Monetary Fund in 1961, economist Sir Roy Harrod told Macmillan that Britain was universally regarded as a country of 'very low growth' (Porter 1993: 19). As a result, while domestic prosperity levels were undoubtedly high, they were below where they could have been; worse still, home consumers continually preferred foreign-made goods such as Japanese transistor radios, German record players, American cars and Italian clothes to British products. An OECD survey in March 1962 reported that poor levels of exports, balance of payments difficulties and inflationary pressures were the main shortcomings in Britain's economic performance (Porter 1993: 13). What caused these shortcomings? The Duke of Edinburgh offered a typically blunt and simple assessment, telling his fellow Britons in 1961 that 'it was about time we pulled our fingers out' (Sampson 1962: 37). Michael Shanks in *The Stagnant Society* (1961), one of the first 'state-of-the-nation' books, blamed the 'British disease' on a combination of middle-class individualism and trade union obstructionism, the type of low-level class antagonism that was satirised in the Boulting brothers' film *I'm All Right Jack* in 1959. Nicholas Davenport's book *The Split Society* (1964) took a different view, arguing that a City-based moneyed ruling elite continually damaged the national economy by putting the interests of finance capital above those of the working class.

More fundamentally, Anthony Sampson's *Anatomy of Britain* (1962) described a widespread sense of malaise in the country, commenting that '[A] loss of dynamic and purpose, and a general bewilderment, are felt by many people, both at the top and the bottom in Britain today' (1962: xiii). At the heart of the problem, according to Sampson, was a systemic failure of leadership, caused principally by the dominance of self-reinforcing elites in the country's public, cultural and commercial life. Despite a century of democratic reform, two world wars and occasional Labour governments 'the Establishment' was alive and well, centred around a few aristocratic families, the top public schools and the domination of Oxbridge. Its continued power had a stultifying effect, preventing Britain from mobilising the dynamism of its brightest and best among the wider population. Sampson's analysis found a receptive audience, with commentators increasingly willing to believe and circulate the thesis that an 'old-school-tie' network at the top of British society was holding the country back. This led to calls for change, usually based around the somewhat vague but fashionable concepts of 'modernisation' and 'meritocracy', both of which were taken up successfully by the Labour opposition at the time. Ironically, Labour's shadow cabinet was full of Oxbridge fellows and ex-public-schoolboys, but fortunately for them the term anti-Establishment was increasingly taken to mean anti-Conservative. Pressure for change came from artists as well as socio-political commentators. The playwrights John Osborne, Arnold Wesker and John Arden contributed to state-of-the-nation soul-searching. The 'radical' Royal Court Theatre productions and the democratic aesthetic of Joan Littlewood's Theatre Workshop attacked the stasis of British social relations – in front of audiences, it should be said, of mainly middle-class graduates. Working-class empowerment, they all agreed, was essential for national renewal. The supposedly malign influence of the Establishment also sustained a satire boom in the early sixties, led (again ironically) by a group of young writers and performers who were themselves the beneficiaries of an Oxbridge education. In 1960 two Cambridge Footlights performers, Peter Cook and Jonathan Miller, joined two Oxford graduates, Dudley Moore and Alan Bennett, in a revue called *Beyond the Fringe*, which began life at the Edinburgh Festival before moving to London in 1961. The revue offered surreal humour and topical, politically-grounded comedy. Later in 1961 Cook opened a Soho nightclub, *The Establishment*, which evoked at least the spirit of political cabaret in Weimar Germany (although as Cook commented with a wry sarcasm, look at how that had stopped the rise of Hitler!). Around the same time, the magazine *Private Eye* was founded by Richard Ingrams, Christopher Booker and William Rushton, providing further space for expressions of cynicism towards and dissatisfaction with the twin targets of leadership and power in Britain. But it was television that brought satire fully into the public domain and popularised the perception that the country's leaders were a bunch of faintly ridiculous, if on the whole benign, out-of-touch incompetents. *That Was The Week That Was* (*TW3*) led the way from its first broadcast in November 1962. With a mixture of sketches, impressions and slick observations on the oddities of the week just passed, *TW3* devoted at least part of each programme to showing people that it was no longer obligatory for them to respect their political leaders. It was a major hit for the BBC and made stars of its mainly young presenters, who included David Frost, Roy Kinnear and Lance Percival. Macmillan was fairly relaxed about the satiric treatment of his govern-ment and told colleagues to leave *TW3* alone. Being laughed at was a good thing, he said, and anyway it was better than being ignored (Sinclair 1994: 34). Perhaps it helped that the jokes were made by middle-class chaps from good universities. Certainly the humour lacked genuine anger, but none the less the satire was part of the political mood music of the early sixties and contributed to the sense that it was time for a change of direction. Macmillan and Alec Douglas-Home, his successor as Prime Minister, were pilloried as dullards. Fortunately for Labour, nobody made the same joke about Harold Wilson.

As well as concerns about Britain's economy and the power of the Establishment, the 'what's wrong with Britain?' theme of the early sixties also diagnosed that the country was suffering from a wider cultural malaise. This malaise was multi-faceted, but at its heart was a concern about the apparent 'Americanisation' of British popular culture, reflected in its growing obsession with celebrity, consumerism and trivia. Pop artists liberally quoted American influences in their work, but not every-one shared their tastes. Glossy, American-style mass media images were particularly noxious for the high-minded left, who were convinced that the working classes were being distracted from the repressive nature of capitalism by trashy 'spectacle' – the modern equivalent of the way Roman emperors had used circuses to keep the mob happy. Taking a lead from Richard Hoggart's *The Uses of Literacy* (1957), they were also scornful of the ways in which organic working-class culture was being corrupted by the mass media. Raymond Williams, who warned that Britain was fast becoming culturally an American colony, carried the argument forward in *Communications* (1962). He offered this reflection on what popular culture had too often come to mean:

> *In the worst cultural products of our time, we find little that is genuinely popular, developed from the life of actual communities. We find instead a synthetic culture, or anti-culture, which is alien to almost everybody, persistently hostile to art and intellectual activity, which it spends much of its time misrepresenting, and given over to exploiting indifference, lack of feeling, frustration, and hatred. It finds such common human interests as sex, and turns them into crude caricatures or glossy*

facsimiles. . . . In Britain, we have to notice that much of this bad work is American in origin.

(Williams 1962: 74–5)

Unfortunately for the intellectual left, the British working class could hardly get enough of this 'synthetic culture'. They watched ITV game shows like *Double Your Money* in their millions, they read the scandal and titillation of the popular newspapers and they flocked to the bingo halls each week. The left's strategy for curing this addiction was to bring the 'best' in the arts to a wider public. It was in this spirit of cultural renewal that the radical playwright Arnold Wesker launched the Centre 42 project in July 1961. The project took its name from resolution 42, which was submitted by the television engineers' union to the TUC Conference in 1960. This called on the trade union movement to recognise its responsibility for promoting the arts among workers. Initially Centre 42 took art to the people via a rolling series of festivals in 1962 across cities and towns like Leicester, Nottingham, Birmingham, Bristol and Southall. In an attempt to establish a permanent base for the project Wesker acquired the Round House in Camden in 1964, but for the rest of the decade he struggled to raise the finances to convert the building into an arts centre until he finally abandoned the whole Centre 42 project in 1970. Without a subsidy from local or national government, it seemed, even modest arts projects struggled to survive. The onus was therefore on the state to reverse its traditional neglect of the arts. But as Anthony Sampson noted:

> *The social philosophy of the industrial revolution – the doctrines of self-help, hard work and profit concealing the undergrowth of poverty and drunkenness – still lingers to promote austere notions of leisure: material prosperity and full employment have undermined their basis, but little has come up to replace the old puritanism, shown for instance in the State's attitude to the arts. . . . The total annual government grant to the arts in 1963 was £11 million – one 200th of the defence budget – which included £5.5 million for the upkeep of art galleries and £1.5 million for preserving stately homes.*

(Sampson 1965: 623)

At least in the eyes of the intelligentsia, therefore, Britain was a long way from being a nation at ease with itself in the early sixties. But pressure for change was growing and the territory that was to be fought over was being mapped out. On one reading, Britain was a backward, complacent and philistine place, in urgent need of renewal – culturally and politically. The problem for those who advocated a change of course was that the forces of inertia, both at the institutional and structural level, were powerful. Britain was a place of peace and relative freedom. More important still, affluence was a social fact and a culture of contentment had settled over much of the country.

Secularisation, the New Left, post-structuralism and fiction

While shopping, television, pop music and to a lesser extent cinema functioned as important common reference points in early sixties Britain, traditional Christianity lost much of its cultural power. Sixties Britain was a secular place. According to Callum Brown, following a remarkable growth in institutional religion between 1945 and 1956, all indices of Christian religiosity in Britain then went into decline. By 1963, most of these indices were in 'free fall'. To take one example, the number of Anglican churchgoers over the age of 15 fell from 9.9 million in 1961 to 5.4 million in 1966 (see Wilson 1969: 22–5; Bédarida 1991: 263–9). There was only one possible conclusion about what this meant. 'Across the board, the British people started to reject the role of religion in their lives – in their marriage, as a place to baptise their children, as an institution to send their children for Sunday school and church recruitment, and as a place for affiliation' (Brown 2001: 188). Also, what seemed to be occurring was not simply a rejection of institutional expressions of Christianity, it was the beginning of an accelerated decline in faith itself. No longer was it the norm for people to look towards Christianity either for a moral compass or for a guide to making sense of the world around them. Why had this happened? Brown's argument is that secularisation occurred not as a gradual process but as a violent rupture around 1963 after the discursive power of Christianity waned. What happened was that the old institutional structures of cultural traditionalism crumbled. Censorship was relaxed after the 1960 *Lady Chatterley's Lover* trial. Liberal law reforms allowed more personal moral latitude over issues such as homosexuality, abortion and divorce. The Women's Liberation

Movement emerged in the late sixties, students rebelled, and a vibrant youth culture developed which incorporated a range of cultural pursuits and identities (Brown 2001: 176). The effect was to liberate young people (young females in particular) from conventional discourses that had previously persuaded them that it was 'natural' to attend church and to believe in the basic tenets of Christianity. Arguably the implications of this were self-reinforcing: as cultural traditionalism weakened, so Christianity lost much of its force, and so in turn people were encouraged to challenge still further cultural traditions and long-established conceptions of moral priorities. Added to this was the fact that the kind of ethical concerns that had resonance in the sixties and beyond – gender and racial equality, nuclear weapons and power, environmentalism, vegetarianism, the well-being of body and mind – largely bypassed the Christian churches. In terms of attitudes towards Christianity, therefore, the early sixties saw the beginning of a massive generational shift. 'The result has been that the generation that grew up in the sixties was more dissimilar to the generation of its parents than in any previous century' (Brown 2001: 190). Attempts by the Christian churches to move with the times, whether in the form of the Bishop of Woolwich's call to reorient the language of the Anglican Church towards a more personal conception of 'God as love' in *Honest to God* (1963), or the *aggiornamento* (bringing up to date) of the Catholic Church with Vatican II (1962–5), did not stop the flow of people away from Christianity. True, the decline of the official churches did not necessarily mean that there was a lack of yearning for the 'divine'. The period witnessed a growth in Christian sects, such as Jehovah's Witnesses, Plymouth Brethren, and Seventh-Day Adventists. Similarly there was increasing interest – mostly among university students – in the oriental spiritualism of Zen, Yoga, Sufism and Transcendental Meditation (Bédarida 1991: 269). But for most people the main Christian churches were no more than occasional venues for the ceremonies of birth, marriage and death, and perhaps a site to visit during the main public holidays of Christmas and Easter.

The declining adherence to traditional Christian beliefs and practices undermined an important set of certainties about how and for what purpose people should live their lives. By itself this was of great significance. But what made the 'death of Christian Britain' an even more noteworthy phenomenon was that it was accompanied by secular equivalents. Other beliefs which had formerly been regarded as fundamental certainties – intellectual, political and moral – were similarly challenged and found wanting in the fifties and sixties, creating the conditions for change across a number of fronts. The first of these challenges shook the revolutionary left. British Marxism's uneasy accord with the Soviet Union and international communism, already reeling from President Khrushchev's denunciation of Stalin's abuses in February 1956, was finally shattered when Red Army tanks rolled into Hungary to crush a popular uprising the following October. The Communist Party of Great Britain suffered an exodus of 10,000 from what was already a small membership base. In 1957 some of these dissidents coalesced as a 'New Left' and announced their intention to find an alternative path between the rigidities of Soviet communism and the timid orthodoxies of the Labour left. They set themselves the task of adapting the traditional Marxist concern with class and power to the new conditions of the affluent society and the Cold War. Thus, in place of the old left's authoritarianism, they sought to embrace libertarianism. Instead of the old left's commitment to a centralised party structure they favoured decentralisation, diversity and internal democracy. And in place of the old left's obsession with economic relations they were interested in the cultural practices through which people actually lived their lives – inspired in part by the earlier humanist writings of a younger Marx in *The Economic and Philosophical Manuscripts of 1844*, which had been published in the 1930s. They took a lead here from writers like Lukács and Gramsci who had sought to renew Marxist theory in the mid-twentieth century. As part of their overarching project to reconcile revolutionary theory and praxis, these writers had argued that all cultural activities could be seen as part of an ideological superstructure that was largely (but not wholly) conditioned by society's economic base (Kearney 1994: 136–50; 169–89). Thus the New Left resolved to supplement their analysis of the relations of production with discussions about television, advertising, films, jazz and youth culture. Reflections on contemporary culture were published in journals like *The New Reasoner* and the *Universities and Left Review*, the two of which merged to form the *New Left Review* in 1960. The New Left even had its own coffee bar, the Partisan in Soho, which helped it to connect with the more earnest manifestations of youth culture (Black 2003: 67). Another significant feature of the New Left between 1958 and 1962 was that it was a driving force within CND. Unfortunately for its followers, much of the New Left's energies were eventually dissipated by internal disputes, not least between the rival cliques which formed around Perry Anderson, editor of the *New Left Review* from 1962, and the man he ousted from the *NLR* editorial board that year, historian E.P. Thompson. Under Anderson, the *NLR* became a more rigorously theoretical journal, publishing long analyses of modern European Marxism and bringing to the attention of British intellectuals the ideas of Antonio Gramsci, Jean-Paul Sartre, Louis Althusser, Claude Lévi-Strauss and others. To its select readership, *NLR* was a valuable translator and interpreter of continental Marxism, and in the absence of a native Marxist theoretical tradition, the nearest thing that Britain had to the French *Temps Modernes*. To its many critics, however, who bemoaned the *NLR*'s obsession with theory and its failure to establish any contact with the life experience of ordinary people, *NLR* eventually 'degenerated into a convoluted and jargon-ridden never-never land of Marxian scholasticism' (Young 1977: 148). Nevertheless, the forces which had initially propelled the creation of the New Left continued to reverberate. Indeed, it was on the terrain between a discredited Communist Party and a beleaguered Labour government after 1966, that the student movement of 1968 appeared, as did the Women's Liberation Movement, black struggles, gay rights protests, libertarian groups and direct action campaigners who fought with the authorities on the issues of squatting, rents and evictions. In a further debt to the New Left, most of these groups or movements drew on the insights that had been opened up by the *NLR*'s early analysis of cultural politics.

New Left Review's provision of house room to the leading contemporary thinkers in the fields of critical theory, structuralism and post-structuralism pointed towards a rupture more profound than that implied by the fragmentation of Britain's revolutionary left. These writers were among the first to articulate the new theories of knowledge whose outlines could be glimpsed in the early sixties. What they offered readers were new models of thinking and new ways of comprehending the world around them. Although these theories had their most immediate impact in the fields of linguistics and literary criticism, they also had wider sociological implications. Structuralism, for example, interpreted social phenomena in the context of a system of signs whose significance lay solely in the interrelationships among them. Developing out of this was the conviction that individual human beings functioned solely as elements of the (often hidden) social networks to which they belonged. In this sense structuralism was a synthesis of Marxist economics, Freudian psychoanalysis and Ferdinand Saussure's study of language. Unlike existentialism, which claimed that individuals were condemned to make and remake themselves, structuralism argued that each individual was shaped by sociological, psychological and linguistic structures over which they had no control. Post-structuralism refined this analysis one stage further by arguing that the deep underlying 'truths' or structures in society had no unifying essence, but were in fact themselves constructions. The key structuralist and post-structuralist works were translated into English, usually within a few years of their original publication. They included Roland Barthes (*Mythologies*, 1972), Michel Foucault (*Madness and Civilisation*, 1965; *The Order of Things*, 1970; *The Archaeology of Knowledge*, 1972), Claude Lévi-Strauss (*The Savage Mind*, 1966; *The Raw and the Cooked*, 1969), Louis Althusser (*For Marx*, 1972; *Lenin and Philosophy*, 1971; *Reading Capital*, 1970), Jacques Lacan (*The Language of the Self: The Function of Language in Psychoanalysis*, 1968; *The Four Fundamental Concepts of Psychoanalysis*, 1977) and Jacques Derrida (*Speech and Phenomena*, 1973; *Writing and Difference*, 1978; *Of Grammatology*, 1977). These writings ranged widely across subjects and academic disciplines, but, in terms of political activism, one of the immediate lessons they offered was that meaningful social and political change could not be brought about simply by manning the barricades – even though intellectuals such as Foucault did eventually take to the streets in Paris in May 1968. Instead, they seemed to show, revolution had to be preceded by changes in the very culture, customs, habits and language that led people to believe that things were as they were because it was 'natural' for them to be that way.

The full implications of these theoretical developments were to become apparent in subsequent decades. It was in the seventies and eighties that what we now call post-modernism developed out of post-structuralism, becoming an increasingly common theoretical approach in the academies of Europe and North America. By the early twenty-first century it had become a critical orthodoxy. In essence post-modernism was significant because it challenged some of the founding assumptions of modern Western European culture across epistemological fields – in linguistics, philosophy, the arts, science, politics, sociology. It was controversial because it was seen as a dark, nihilistic force that threatened centuries of intellectual 'progress', and one that might sweep away the very structure of social and moral authority in western societies. Although the term itself refers to a multi-dimensional concept, postmodernism can be seen to rest on two assumptions. First, there is no transcendental signifier – whether that is 'God', or 'nature' or 'the truth' – that guarantees the essential 'oneness' of the world or the possibility of a universal objective truth that could be uncovered and which would hold the answers to the questions posed by the human condition. Second, all human systems (starting with language) are reflexive rather than referential; thus meanings and values are constructed rather than being innate properties (Ermarth 1998). According to post-modern theorists, objective knowledge becomes impossible; rather, objectivity is seen as a disguise for power within the academy, functioning perhaps as the last fortress of white male authority. Reason is seen as little more than a particular historical form on which time has now been called. The implications of all this were to be far-reaching, not least at the levels of culture, ethics and aesthetics. Moreover, early traces of the impact that post-modernism was to make were at least visible in the sixties.

In the cultural field, post-modernism was distinguished by what Susan Sontag was to call a 'new sensibility' – a new pluralism that developed out of the collapse of the traditional distinction between high and popular culture (Storey 1993: 155). This in turn was a reaction against the absorbtion of modernism into the bourgeois prison of universities, art galleries and 'classic texts'. Where once the works of Picasso, Eliot, Joyce and other modernists were seen as threatening and outrageous, now they formed the canon of bourgeois culture and as such they had to be rejected by those whose goal was to change society. Because modernists had championed a rigorously intellectual and demanding elite culture, postmodernists reacted against this by seeking to rescue popular culture from the long years of condescension. Hence the stage was set for Andy Warhol's celebration of everyday consumer iconography (Campbell's soup tins, Brillo pads) in Pop Art and the elevation of film, pop music, advertising and fashion into 'serious' cultural forms in the sixties. Arising naturally out of the New Left's concern with ideological superstructures, the study of popular culture entered the academy with the founding of the post-graduate Centre for Contemporary Cultural Studies at Birmingham University in 1960. The attack on the Enlightenment's privileging of reason also opened the way for the various sixties manifestations of irrationality, spontaneity and playfulness in culture. This occurred at a time when capitalism was changing, characterised by a shift from a society that was organised around the needs of production to one that was driven by consumption – encouraging hedonism, display, gratification and new habits and lifestyles. As *Oz* editor Richard Neville argued in *Play Power* (1970) 'play' had become as important as work. Drawing on ideas that had appeared several years earlier in Herbert Marcuse's *One Dimensional Man* (1964), *Play Power* was a manifesto for the counter-cultural rejection both of the work ethic and the tedious practicalities of 'straight' political organisation – in Neville's words the contrast was between the 'sober, violent, puritan New Left extremists' and the 'laughing, loving, lazy, fun-powder plotters' (cited in Hewison 1986: 168). But the book's celebration of play also serves as a reminder of how capital adapted to the changed conditions of private affluence and increased leisure time in the sixties. Intellectually, post-modernism meant the rejection of the modern Enlightenment project – the belief that universal human progress could be engineered by the application of reason, science and technology. It meant also a mistrust of totalising explanations of western society's development, the kind of 'metanarratives' found in the writings of Kant, Hegel or Marx. In the aftermath of Auschwitz, Hiroshima and the Soviet gulags, many had simply lost faith in the idea that the modern story of humankind was one of progress towards rational, material and moral ideals. Morally and aesthetically, in fact, post-modernity implied the adoption of a continual relativism in place of absolute thresholds. Thus post-modernism came to be characterised by fragmentation and decentering of forms, understandings, narratives and authority.

Beyond a small self-referential community who could engage with the complexities of the literature, the full implications of post-modernism's assault on the foundations of western culture were only half understood: in most cases, even within the universities, they were ignored until the 1970s and 1980s. But as the counter-cultural challenge to bourgeois materialism and political hegemony gained force in the second half of the sixties, post-modernist insights became a useful weapon, even in their half-understood form, because in their trickle-down essence they opened up a space in which old certainties and self-evident 'truths' could be held up to the light and exposed as ideologically powerful fictions. In the prevailing intellectual and cultural climate of the sixties the growing influence of French structuralism and post-structuralism laid down a challenge to British intellectuals, whose task it was to breathe in that rarefied air. In the theatre Harold Pinter and Tom Stoppard were the leading British practitioners of the 'Absurd', a form that explored a 'post-God' world in which older religious and philosophical explanations of the human condition no longer held. Pinter's plays, *The Caretaker* (1960), *The Lover* (1963) and *The Homecoming* (1965) employed abstraction, non-naturalistic settings and conversational non sequiturs in ways that recalled Samuel Beckett's existentialist meditation *Waiting for Godot* (first English staging 1955). Unlike Pinter, whose work was soaked with class antagonism and violent menace, Stoppard fused comedy and absurdism to produce critically-acclaimed but more accessible plays such as *Rosencrantz and Guildenstern Are Dead* (1967). Nicolas Roeg and Donald Cammell's *Performance* (1970) is an example of a British 'postmodern' film – in the sense that it makes reference to high art and popular culture, deals with the issue of interchangeable identities in the characters of Turner (Mick Jagger) and Chas (James Fox) and employs fractured narrative in a way that denied the audience access to easy meanings (Street 1997: 167). In France, Roland Barthes and others used the novel to explore the new ways of seeing implied by the 'linguistic turn' of post-structuralism, but it was a challenge that remained beyond most established British fiction writers. Instead, their work in the sixties was often derided as dull, middlebrow and uncomfortably middle-class. British novelists, it seemed, were hidebound by their continuing attachment to naturalistic narrative forms and parochial themes. Set against the range, formal innovation and intellectual quality of the best writing overseas, British novels of the late fifties and sixties were frequently dismissed as mediocre, effete and unexciting. The decline of British fiction was seen to mirror the post-Suez decline of British world power, with novelists such as William Cooper, Angus Wilson and C.P. Snow often cited as exemplars of the malaise. The 'Angry Young Men' who had briefly revitalised fiction in the fifties with their working-class provincial anti-heroes had burnt themselves out by the sixties. What seemed to be left after their departure were country-house novels, nostalgic recreations of the past and dull meditations on the manners, morals and political dilemmas of the British middle classes. This is not to deny that naturalistic fiction could reach occasional high points. Anthony Powell's twelve volumes, *A Dance to the Music of Time* (1951–75), a sequence that was set between the end of the Great War and the late sixties, has been described by Randall Stevenson as 'the most substantial English account of social life and manners in the twentieth century' (1986: 141). Paul Scott's *Raj Quartet*, the first two of which appeared in the sixties, *The Jewel in the Crown* (1966) and *The Day of the Scorpion* (1968), showed the possibilities of using Britain's colonial retreat as a theme. But in less imaginative hands the traditional form of the novel was seen to be treading water. Part of the problem was that at a time when the market for novels was shrinking for all but the biggest names, writers were under pressure to appeal to the proven tastes of a solidly bourgeois readership. Compounding this problem, Arts Council subsidies were insufficiently generous to support writers who wanted to produce experimental, non-commercial fiction. The 1964 Public Libraries and Museums Act, which heralded a major expansion of the public lending libraries (by far the main purchasers of new novels) provided some relief, but still the commercial environment for the novel encouraged middle-of-the-road conformity. Thus it was that in his survey of the contemporary novel in 1970, Bernard Bergonzi offered this negative overview:

> *For complex historical and cultural reasons, English (sic) literature*
> *in the fifties and sixties has been both backward- and inward-looking,*
> *with rather little to say that can be instantly translated into universal*
> *statements about the human condition . . . [I]n literary terms, as in*
> *political ones, Britain is not a very important part of the world today.*
>
> (Bergonzi 1970: 56–7)

Perhaps this was why between Winston Churchill's success in 1953 and William Golding's thirty years later no British writer won the Nobel Prize for literature. Within this bleak landscape, however, there were some occasional interesting peaks. Samuel Selvon's *The Lonely Londoners* (1956) was one of the first novels of the period to explore the lives of New Commonwealth immigrants. Experimentalism had its place, with writers such as Doris Lessing (*The Golden Notebook*, 1962),

B.S. Johnson (*Albert Angelo*, 1964), and towards the end of the decade, John Fowles (*The French Lieutenant's Woman*, 1969) and Alan Burns (*Babel*, 1969), employing a range of innovative narrative forms or stylistic improvisations that reflected both the influence of European and American fiction and the contemporary debate about the future of the novel in the wake of the structuralist proclamation of the 'death of the author' (McHale 1987; Stevenson 1986). Anthony Burgess's creation of a polyglot, pun-riddled teenage slang in *A Clockwork Orange* (1962) was at least one rejoinder to the claim that British writers' use of language lacked vitality and invention (Bergonzi 1970: 68–9). Perhaps reflecting the post-modernist elevation of popular culture to the same plane as elite culture, the period also saw what Bart Moore-Gilbert has characterised as 'a sharply accelerated cross-fertilization between "popular" and "serious" narrative forms' (Moore-Gilbert and Seed 1992: 181). Kingsley Amis, Brian Aldiss, J.G. Ballard and Michael Moorcock explored the possibilities of science fiction. Len Deighton and John Le Carré brought critical 'respectability' to spy fiction. Meanwhile, Iris Murdoch, Muriel Spark and Angela Carter were among a number of writers who reworked the gothic novel genre. The use of these popular forms helped to democratise notions of what constituted 'good' literature (Moore-Gilbert and Seed 1992: 196–7). Novels, it appeared, had been brought within what came to be called the 'long front' of culture.

CHAPTER 4

Conservative crisis and Labour recovery, 1959–64

The 'low ebb' of Conservative rule

In October 1959 Harold Macmillan's Conservative Party won a third successive election victory and handed Labour its worst defeat since 1935. The ease with which the Conservatives secured a 100-seat majority led some commentators to write off Labour as a party of government and look towards a future of permanent Tory hegemony. Peace abroad and prosperity at home were the unifying themes of the Conservatives' electoral appeal, particularly the latter, as the party reaped the political rewards of tax cuts, full employment, buoyant consumerism and relative price stability. 'Life's better with the Conservatives, don't let Labour ruin it', was a slogan that captured the pragmatic simplicity of the party's strategy in 1959. 'We were beaten by *prosperity*', observed Labour's own inquiry into their defeat, arguing that the spread of affluence had hardened middle-class opinion against Labour and cut into the party's traditional base of working-class support. The inquiry was half-correct. Prosperity itself was not the problem, it was Labour's political response to it that failed to attract key groups of voters. For the government, of course, the question was whether favourable economic circumstances could be relied upon indefinitely to underpin its popularity. As Britain moved into the sixties the Conservatives' narrow reliance on being able to satisfy voters' material ambitions became increasingly exposed.

The warning signs were there to be seen. British consumer spending had sucked in imports and only a fortuitous movement in the terms of trade had prevented a balance-of-payments crisis. Any adverse movement in the terms of trade would force the government to restrict consumption and break its promise of continued rising prosperity. The decision to cut taxes by £300 million in Heathcoat Amory's 1959 pre-election budget had paid off in the short term. But in the longer term it fed inflationary pressures and raised popular expectations about sustainable economic growth to unrealistic levels, both of which were problems that soon required attention. Moreover, it was increasingly clear by the early sixties that Britain's economic performance was relatively unimpressive in comparison with its international competitors. This was the paradox that helped to unseat a Conservative – and later a Labour – government in the period. Viewed from a domestic perspective the economy was continually overheating, but viewed from an international perspective its growth was stubbornly sluggish. In April 1960 Amory had wanted to ease inflationary pressures by putting up taxes. Macmillan, however, was anxious to avoid the charge that the government had bribed voters the previous year with irresponsible tax cuts and so forced his Chancellor to publish a neutral budget. It was left to Amory's successor at the Treasury, Selwyn Lloyd, to face economic realities with an emergency 'little budget' in July 1961 that introduced tough counter-inflationary measures. Lloyd put in place a credit squeeze, projected cuts in public spending and announced a 'pay pause' for public sector workers, the aims of which were to close the gap between productivity growth and wage rises and set down a marker for private sector pay settlements. This was the painful 'stop' phase of what was called 'stop-go economics': periods of growth followed by deflationary measures to check rising prices. The political cost was high. Borrowers faced higher repayments and the pay pause hit millions of middle- and low-income state employees, many of whom had voted Conservative in the 1950s. Rab Butler, who was Macmillan's deputy as well as Conservative party Chairman, noted that the morale of party workers declined after the emergency measures. Labour, meanwhile, saw an upturn in its fortunes, moving into an opinion poll lead which it kept until after the 1964 election.

In 1959 there had been no compelling reason to remove the government from office. Within a year or two it was difficult to find reasons why they should be allowed to stay there. Macmillan sensed that voters were bored with the Conservatives and searched around for a mission that would give his party a renewed sense of purpose and direction. There were two broad opportunities. The first involved Britain's changing international role, an issue which had been at the forefront of government minds ever since Suez had shown up the limits of Britain's world power in 1956. The days of imperial grandeur were numbered, if not yet finished, by the early sixties. Countries within the old empire or new Commonwealth had become less important as trading partners for Britain, and it was increasingly apparent that the imperial network was a less than impressive vehicle for Britain's influence in global diplomacy. So it was that Macmillan bowed to a combination of economic realities, geopolitical calculations and the ending of conscription into Britain's armed forces by accelerating a process of post-war decolonisation. At Cape Town in February 1960 the Prime Minister had referred to the growing power of African national consciousness as a 'wind of change' that was transforming the continent. As France and Belgium relinquished their African colonial territories, Britain had little choice but to manage similar transfers of power, aiming always to minimise the danger that newly-independent African states might align themselves with the communist bloc rather than the west. Nigeria, Uganda, Tanganyika and Kenya all became independent within the next few years, meanwhile the apartheid state of South Africa became an independent republic outside the Commonwealth in 1961. This withdrawal from Africa in the early sixties saw Britain transformed from being a global power with an overseas empire into a regional power. Its potential to exert independent influence on the world stage was severely limited, and measured by the hard test of national self-interest its remaining overseas possessions were a drain on resources rather than meaningful assets. Britain's hopes of retaining informal influence in Africa via economic ties and defence agreements with its former colonies were largely disappointed, although cultural ties remained with those states choosing to remain members of the Commonwealth. African decolonisation was at least achieved relatively peacefully – there was no British equivalent of France's Algerian problem – and without serious political difficulties at home. But what did it imply for Britain's world role? As an imperial power on the wane it signalled that Britain's geopolitical preoccupation had swung further towards Asia. More significant for the longer term, it was in part a recognition that Britain's future lay in becoming a leading member of the European Economic Community that had been formed in 1957.

The Conservative government overcame its initial reluctance to join the EEC and agreed in 1960 that it would seek entry, a decision that marked perhaps the most profound change in British foreign policy in the twentieth century. The reasoning was straightforward. The EEC was a club that benefited its members, proof of which was confirmed by the impressive economic growth rates of the six founding members since 1957. The fastest growing markets in the post-war years were in the rich industrialised western nations rather than in the primary producing countries, a trend that gave Britain's trading links with Europe primacy over Commonwealth trade: by 1962 British exports to Western Europe would exceed those to the sterling area. It was ever more vital that Britain enjoyed the same terms of access as its main competitors on the continent to a European customs union which contained some 250 million relatively affluent consumers – not least as the Treaty of Rome foresaw the eventual free movement of capital, goods and labour within the EEC. Moreover the United States (always an important consideration in London) favoured British entry, reasoning that it would strengthen the EEC as a barrier against European communism. British policy-makers were therefore anxious to avoid undermining what they saw as the transatlantic 'special relationship' and have Washington look to Paris and Bonn for its main European allies. A more immediate political driver towards entry was Macmillan's calculation that an approach to join the EEC would be an energising project for his government, a 'big idea' to counter the accusation that the Conservatives were drifting aimlessly. The formal application was made in August 1961. Edward Heath led the British negotiating team that was charged with resolving the terms and conditions of Britain's entry. Macmillan met with the French President de Gaulle in June and December 1962 in an attempt to settle outstanding issues, but his diplomatic efforts met a cold response. De Gaulle vetoed Britain's application in January 1963, partly because it threatened French dominance of the EEC and partly because the two countries had different attitudes towards the United States. Britain had resolved after Suez that it would never again be on the wrong side of the US. The French at the same time decided never again to put their full trust in the US. So when

Britain entered a deal to obtain US Polaris submarines as the launch platform of its nuclear missiles, it simply reinforced de Gaulle's belief that the British would act as a 'Trojan horse' for American interests inside the EEC. If Britain joined the EEC, he calculated, they would always seek advice from Washington about what they should say in advance of any meetings of the Community. Determined to avoid a US influence over the EEC by proxy, de Gaulle blocked Britain's entry to the Community (he was to do the same again in 1967).

The second opportunity for revitalising the Tory government's fortunes lay in its adoption of economic 'modernisation' as a priority, which in effect meant searching for a solution to Britain's relative economic decline. The forming of the Robbins Committee on higher education in 1961 gave the government an eye-catching opening for a plan to improve the workforce's skills base. When the Robbins Report was published in October 1963, shortly before an election was due, it recommended a 50 per cent increase in higher education students by 1967, and a 250 per cent increase by 1980. The Conservatives accepted these targets and committed Britain to a massive expansion of university places. In fact, Robbins' targets were eventually exceeded. Between 1963 and 1971 the number of students in full-time higher education more than doubled, from 216,000 to 457,000 (Halsey 1988: 270–1). In terms of the strategic management of the economy, the main institutional expression of the modernising drive was the National Economic Development Council (NEDC), a tripartite body with representatives from government, leading employers and trade unions which met for the first time in March 1962. It was followed by a National Incomes Commission, an organisation that aimed to discourage workers from submitting large pay claims and employers from paying them out. 'Modernisation', however, was more a rhetorical trope than a set of worked-out policies, failing to enthuse even government ministers, much less the electorate (Tomlinson 1997: 32–3). By the time that the Conservatives left office inflation was rising omin-ously, company profitability was lower than it had been in the 1950s and, most damaging of all, there was a serious balance of payments prob-lem (Woodward 1993: 73–8). In any case modernisation was a difficult theme to pursue for a government that had been in power for more than a decade: after all, voters were entitled to ask, who had presided over decline in the first place? A week after the initial meeting of the NEDC the Conservatives lost one of their safest suburban commuter seats at the Orpington by-election, next door to Macmillan's own Bromley constituency. The Liberals captured the seat on the largest by-election swing in British political history, more than doubling their share of the vote from the 1959 election. According to the Gallup polls, support for the Conservatives in the country dropped to its lowest level since 1946 (Porter 1993: 18). In June Labour made their first by-election gain since the general election at Middlesbrough West. The following month the Conservatives were pushed into third place at Leicester North East. Iain Macleod, who had taken over from Butler as party Chairman, urged the Prime Minister to respond to the Liberal resurgence and to the mounting signals that Labour for the first time in a decade had made itself electable.

Harold Macmillan – the 'Supermac' of the popular press – had long been an electoral asset for his party. A master politician who *looked* by the late 1950s as if he was born to lead, Macmillan cultivated an image of old-world, effortless superiority. At home he had presided with quiet competence over the 'never had it so good' consumerist society, abroad he dealt easily with Eisenhower, Khrushchev and de Gaulle (at least up until the veto) as fellow statesmen and former wartime allies. But as his government lost its way Macmillan increasingly looked like a tired reminder of a world that had passed, his gentlemanly nonchalance embarrassingly out-of-date when set against the youthful dynamism of John F. Kennedy, the United States' President who took office in 1960. In an attempt to create a younger ministerial team and connect his government with modern times, Macmillan sacked Selwyn Lloyd as Chancellor together with six other Cabinet ministers on 12–13 July 1962 in the so-called 'Night of the Long Knives'. Further moves followed in a reconstruction of the government that most contemporary observers saw as an ill-judged and panic-driven measure. *The Times* read it as an indication of the electoral malaise into which the government had fallen and the *Daily Telegraph* compared it to a Stalinist purge. Macmillan's approval ratings slumped to the lowest of any Prime Minister since Chamberlain in 1940 and speculation intensified about a leadership challenge within the party. By the end of the year, Labour had added Dorset South and Glasgow Woodside to its by-election gains and seen its lead in the opinion polls climb to around 10 per cent.

If an uncharacteristic loss of nerve and a sluggish economy had called the competence of the Prime Minister and his government into doubt in 1962, the following year raised even more damaging questions about the moral worth of their national leadership. With the government already wounded by the rejection of Britain's application to join the EEC in January, the final months of Macmillan's premiership were played out against the backdrop of the Profumo affair – a tale of sex, decadence and deceit at the heart of Britain's establishment. It was an irresistible story for press and public, centering on a sexual relationship between a War Minister, John Profumo, and an eighteen-year-old call-girl, Christine Keeler, and featuring a sprawling associated cast of pimps, hustlers, a Russian diplomat and the aristocratic 'Cliveden Set'. Ultimately, in terms of the wider issues of governance, it was a trivial episode, despite the indignant froth of newspaper editorials following Profumo's admission that he had lied to Parliament about his relationship with Keeler. Nor was there any breach of national security, as Lord Denning's subsequent inquiry into the episode confirmed. But the Profumo affair was significant because of what it was taken to symbolise – the hypocrisy and moral degeneracy of the governing classes – and because of the way it fused with the pre-existing discourse about national decline. Popular memory tends to recall the sixties as a time of optimism and renewed national self-confidence. Perhaps there are good reasons for this, but at best the celebratory mood applied only to the middle of the decade, around the time of 'swinging London' magazine articles and the 1966 World Cup victory. In the earlier part of the decade, notwithstanding the undoubted material benefits of affluence, Britain was increasingly viewed as a stifling, moribund place, held back by class prejudice and nostalgic complacency about its imperial past. This was why the Profumo affair was interpreted immediately as a crisis for Conservative Britain, a point that was made in *The Times*' editorial of 11 June 1963;

> *Eleven years of Conservative rule have brought the nation*
> *psychologically and spiritually to a low ebb . . . The Prime Minister and*
> *his colleagues can cling together and be still there a year hence . . . They*
> *will have to do more than that to justify themselves.*

When Macmillan resigned because of ill-health in October 1963 it was hoped in some quarters that the Conservatives would choose a much younger replacement to renew the party's moral and political purpose – perhaps Iain Macleod, Reginald Maudling or Edward Heath. Instead, in the days before Conservative leaders were elected on a formal ballot, the choice came down to three candidates from the same generation as Macmillan: Rab Butler, Lord Hailsham and Lord Home. Despite his illness, Macmillan was determined to control the succession and prevent Butler from taking over, largely because he doubted his deputy's strength of character. Hailsham, the popular choice of the party outside parliament, ruined his own chances with a vulgar display of self-promotion at the Conservatives' Blackpool Conference. This left Home to 'emerge' in soundings among Tory parliamentarians as the least divisive candidate and most MPs' second preference. The sixty-year-old Home (pronounced Hume), who was a landowner, former Etonian and student of Christ Church Oxford, renounced his peerage and became Sir Alec Douglas-Home, finding a seat in the Commons at a hastily-engineered by-election at Kinross and West Perthshire. Tony Benn had predicted in his diary on 14 October that Home would 'be a dud when it comes to exciting the electorate', and that Labour's own recently elected leader, Harold Wilson 'will make rings round him' (1987: 70). Home was by no means the liability for the Tories that some expected, but he was a gift to the satirists of *Private Eye* and *That Was The Week That Was*, not least when he admitted that he used matchsticks to help him count. Home also faced simmering resentment from frustrated senior colleagues and their allies at the way the succession had been handled, highlighted by the refusal of Enoch Powell and Iain Macleod to serve under him and Macleod's public criticism of how Macmillan and a 'magic circle' of Old Etonians had manipulated the arcane consultation process to thwart Rab Butler (Macleod 1964). To make matters worse, he also had only a year in which to make an impression on the wider public and find a compelling response to Labour's charge that after 'twelve wasted years' the Conservatives were no longer fit for office. The new Prime Minister's area of expertise was foreign affairs, but his government urgently required some eye-catching domestic measures. Unfortunately, the only significant policy initiative implemented during Home's brief premiership was Heath's plan to abolish Resale Price Maintenance (RPM), a new measure that compelled manufacturers to abandon their right to control the retail price of their goods. Heath's intention was to stimulate competition among retailers as part of an overall drive towards economic modernisation, but politically the policy backfired as thousands of Conservative-supporting small traders and shopkeepers protested against the measure, assisted by some 40 Tory rebels on the backbenches (Findley 2001: 327–353). With an election due in 1964 the prospects of a fourth consecutive triumph for the Conservatives depended heavily on whether Labour could manage to throw away their best opportunity for taking office since 1951.

Old Labour, 'New Britain' and the 1964 election

Labour's political recovery from the continual defeats of the 1950s was long and difficult. It was a process that was complicated by personality clashes at a senior level, damaging disputes over policy and a falling party membership. Much of Labour's energy was spent on an internal 'fight for the soul' of the party between traditionalists and revisionists (sometimes called modernisers), which centred in particular on the place of public ownership in the party's programme. The reforms of the wartime coalition and the post-war Attlee government had delivered to ministers the tools of macro-economic management and the superstructure of the modern welfare state, enabling them apparently to consign the mass unemployment and poverty of the inter-war years to the past. What was to be the next stage of the British socialist project? Traditionalists called for an expanded programme of public ownership and further state economic 'planning', remaining committed to a class-based analysis of society in which Labour was the defender of working-class interests. Revisionists, however, believed that cloth-capped socialism was no longer relevant in the changed conditions of affluent post-war Britain, not least because social researchers told them that working-class identity was being eroded by a combination of rising living standards and structural changes in the economy (Abrams 1960; Zweig 1961). Articulated most coherently in Tony Crosland's *The Future of Socialism* (1956), the revisionists' case was that the control of industry by a salaried managerial class and the growing power of trade unions had made the question of ownership of capital less important than government's ability to redistribute its returns. Instead of a programme of public ownership, the priorities for a future Labour administration should be greater social equality – which in effect meant redistribution of income and wealth and a fairer education system – together with improved public services and extensions of personal freedom.

So convinced were some revisionists after the 1959 defeat that Labour's working-class identity was a liability, they suggested a radical makeover for the party. The 'Hampstead Set' revisionists, which included party leader Hugh Gaitskell, Roy Jenkins, Tony Crosland, Douglas Jay, and Patrick Gordon Walker floated ideas such as a name change – perhaps to 'Labour and Radical' or 'Labour and Reform' – cutting the party's link with the trade unions, abandoning the constitutional commitment to public ownership and exploring a progressive association with the Liberals. In the end the wilder ideas were abandoned and the leadership focused its attention on removing from Labour's constitution Clause Four, the principled commitment to common ownership which had served as the party's socialist myth since 1918. Gaitskell opened up the issue at the party's post-election Conference, arguing that Clause Four created the false impression that public ownership for Labour was an end in itself rather than a means to an end – that of creating a more equal society. He was also well aware of mounting evidence that nationalisation was a vote-loser for Labour. But the party was not ready to surrender what had become a symbol of its historic struggles and it forced Gaitskell to climb down in March 1960 (Jones 1996: 41–64). The rancour generated by the dispute showed how badly damaged was Labour's collective psyche after three successive defeats, a mood that darkened still further when the leadership refused to accept a vote in favour of unilateral nuclear disarmament in October 1960: Gaitskell mobilised right-wing and trade union support and overturned the unilateralist vote at the following year's Conference.

From the depths of crisis, however, the recovery began. During the same 1960 Conference at which Gaitskell pledged to 'fight and fight and fight again' to save his party from unilateralism, *Labour in the Sixties* was presented as an interim policy statement which foreshadowed the 'modernising Britain' theme that helped Labour into power in 1964. At the centre of its analysis was a distinctive socialist approach to the 'scientific revolution'. Endorsing the statement on behalf of Labour's National Executive, Harold Wilson used rhetoric that was to become familiar in the following years: 'The world into which we are moving . . .

is a world characterised by scientific revolution . . . That is why we say today that socialism must be harnessed to science and science to social-ism' (Labour Party Annual Conference Report, 1960: 151). This was to be the way of neutralising public ownership as a divisive issue: traditional-ists took heart from the plans for greater state involvement in industries that were at the forefront of the scientific revolution, revisionists were comforted by the reassurance that there would be no 'shopping list' of whole industries to be collectivised. The approach was spelled out at greater length in June 1961 in *Signposts for the Sixties*, Labour's final general domestic policy statement before the 1964 election manifesto. Peter Shore, one of its authors, explained the thinking in the document:

> *[T]he mood from 1961 onwards was very much in favour of expansion of the public sector in general to make up for these great gaps between the development of people's private standard of living and their social and community services. We were in favour of increased public expenditure and indeed said so and had no doubts about it. And we were also – very much with the Harold Wilson input – in favour of using the public sector in the modernisation and rejuvenation of industry. So all the inhibitions about stopping nationalisation ended by saying – well no it's not nationalisation, it's an extension of the public sector generally to take on tasks which the private sector was failing to perform.*
>
> (interview with the author, July 1993)

When Hugh Gaitskell died unexpectedly in January 1963, Wilson defeated George Brown and James Callaghan in the contest to be his suc-cessor. He inherited a party that by now was in good health. The govern-ment's difficulties had helped Labour maintain a Gallup poll lead since August 1961, policy had been settled with *Signposts for the Sixties* and party organisation had been improved – markedly so from the dark days of 1955 when Labour's National Agent concluded that Labour lost in 35 marginal constituencies primarily because of poor organisation.

Local Labour parties contesting marginal seats were now given extra financial assistance and a permanent Organisation Sub-Committee was established to recruit, train and deploy party workers. Planning for the next election had been under way since October 1961 when a campaign committee was set up to oversee pre-election strategy. In June 1962 a 'Festival of Labour' drew a crowd of more than 100,000 to London's

Battersea Park and, in the same year, a team of advertising artists and copywriters was recruited to help with public relations. Moreover, despite the fact that former Gaitskellites personally detested Wilson, the party united around its new leader for the sake of winning an election. It was soon apparent even to his enemies that Wilson was a superb campaigner. The way he combined extraordinary intelligence and drive with strategic press briefings about his 'ordinary' lifestyle and tastes caught the public mood perfectly. He was the British answer to President Kennedy, but without the sex appeal and stardust. Wilson rejected the fashionable metropolitan society adored by Gaitskell and ridiculed the amateurish Edwardian langour of Macmillan and Home. Instead, he told feature writers, he supported Huddersfield Town football club, he watched *Coronation Street* like everyone else, poured HP sauce over his chips and liked to smoke a pipe. The reverse side of this folksy, working-class projection was his professional image as a tough politician who understood the worlds of automation, atomic power and space exploration. Wilson's political vision was a synthesis of these two sides of his persona. He looked towards a scientific revolution that would create jobs and new prosperity, and a social revolution that would open up opportunities for hard-working, talented individuals like himself, regardless of their class background. This was Wilson's 'New Britain', articulated most forcefully during his 'white heat' speech at the 1963 Scarborough Conference. By the time of the 1964 election even the Marxist Perry Anderson writing in the *New Left Review* had been won over to 'Wilsonism':

> *For the first time in its history, the Labour Party is now led by a man who by any standards is a consumately adroit and aggressive politician. The long reign of mediocrity is over, MacDonald, Henderson, Attlee, Gaitskell – whether honourable or contemptible, the leaders of the Labour Party have always had in common political timidity, tactical incapacity and miserable intellectual vacuity . . . The Labour Party has at last after 50 years of failing, produced a dynamic and capable leader.*
>
> (Anderson 1964: 3–27)

Wilson was a symbol of 'meritocratic' social mobility, having risen from a modest background to become a Cabinet minister in 1947 aged just thirty-one. As a comparatively youthful Labour leader (succeeding Gaitskell when he was forty-six), Wilson was ideally placed to capitalise on the ever more orthodox view that a decade of Conservative rule had left Britain in need of urgent modernisation. The early-sixties vogue for self-critical 'state of the nation' books and articles among the intelligentsia had filtered out to the wider culture via current affairs broadcasting and television satire. As we have seen, Michael Shanks's *The Stagnant Society* (1961), Anthony Sampson's *Anatomy of Britain* (1962), Arthur Koestler's *Suicide of a Nation?* (1964), Nicholas Davenport's *The Split Society* (1964) and Rex Malik's *What's Wrong with British Industry?* (1964) may have diagnosed the British disease differently, but they all agreed that the patient was seriously ill. Not surprisingly, Labour sought to make this a central issue in 1964, continually pressing the charge that the dominance of an old public-school and Oxbridge-educated elite was holding Britain back. In the 'New Britain', they promised, the dead wood would be cleared from the country's boardrooms. The nation's financial, commercial and public life would be opened up to the best available talent, not confined to those who had worn the right school tie.

Labour's self-projection as a party of classless professionals against well-heeled Conservative amateurs – technocrats versus aristocrats – had been well rehearsed by the time the election campaign was under way. Their manifesto attacked the Tory complacency which had produced 'thirteen wasted years' and promised the voters an avalanche of modernising plans. Alongside their overarching National Plan were plans for industry, stable prices, tax reform and the regions. The Conservatives countered by stressing Labour's lack of recent experience in government, contrasting their leader's record as a former Foreign Secretary with Labour's irresponsible flirtation with unilateralism. Despite the months of ridicule that had been heaped on Douglas-Home and his party, opinion polls during the campaign showed the two main parties almost level. Both enjoyed slim leads at some stage in the campaign and the outcome was as close as the polls had predicted.

Labour's aggregate vote had fallen slightly from 1959 and their share of the vote had improved by only 0.3 per cent – on a reduced turnout of 77.1 per cent. The difference in 1964 was the collapse of the Conservative vote, which fell by almost 1.75 million, and the increase of almost 1.5 million in the Liberal vote – this third-party support appears to have been drawn fairly evenly from the two main parties (Jefferys 1997: 191). The average swing to Labour was 3.5 per cent, with their best gains made

TABLE 4.1 ◆ *Results of the General Election, 15 October 1964*

	Total Votes	MPs Elected	Candidates	% Share of Total Vote
Conservative	12,001,396	304	630	43.4
Labour	12,205,814	317	628	44.1
Liberal	3,092,878	9	365	11.2
Communist	45,932	–	36	0.2
Plaid Cymru	69,507	–	23	0.3
Scottish National Party	64,044	–	15	0.2
Others	168,422	–	60	0.6
	27,655,374	630	1,757	100.0

Electorate 35,892,572

Turnout 77.1%

Source: Butler, D. and Butler, G. (1994) *British Political Facts, 1900–1994*, London: Macmillan, p. 217.

in Liverpool, the North-West, Clydeside and Greater London. Scottish and Welsh voters also turned out in force to support Labour, showing the resilience of Labour's working class support. Indeed, the party's own analysis of its victory stressed the importance of Labour's policies on traditional subjects such as housing, education and pensions. But the party increased its share of support, too, among younger and more affluent voters, evidence perhaps of Labour's success in repositioning itself as the party of modernisation and opportunity (Fielding 1993: 42–3). In time, the high expectations that Labour had built up in its 'New Britain' campaign would return to haunt the party in office. But the immediate emotion within the party was relief that the campaign had at last ended the sequence of defeats. As Tony Benn recorded in his diary on Friday 16 October, 'We've waited thirteen years for this' (1987: 154).

CHAPTER 5

On screen

Pilkington and after: the irresistible rise of television

Television's rise to become a near universal presence in people's homes was the most important cultural transformation of the sixties. Between 1961 and 1971 the number of households with a set rose from 75 per cent to 91 per cent. As Milton Shulman pointed out, by the early seventies this meant that there were twice as many televisions as cars or refrigerators in the country, and 'more television sets to be stared at than bath-tubs to be washed in' (1973: 7). This omnipresence changed social life and habits in Britain where, as we have seen, people remained fixed in front of the small screen like nowhere else in Europe, averaging almost 20 hours of viewing per week. As the journalist Keith Waterhouse wrote in *Punch* in July 1966, television had by then become an integral part of the nation's cultural life:

> It's a long time since the Evening Standard *was able to run a series of paragraphs called 'People Without TV' which I remember seemed to include practically everyone in the Government; and the ghastly word 'telly', which once conjured up a whitish flickering vision of awful drab families in Dagenham munching Mars bars and neglecting bingo, has entered the mock-cockney vocabulary of Kensington mums who no longer pretend that they have got it for the au-pair girl.*
>
> (cited in Connolly 1995: 116)

The sixties may not necessarily deserve the 'Golden Age of television' label that Colin MacCabe has attached to the period (1988: 37). But it was the era when British television found its feet, adopting technologies, programme formats and production values that continue to influence the medium's output forty years on. As with any period, television schedules in the sixties were a mixture of good, bad and indifferent programmes. What gives these schedules their unique colouring, however, is the sense that here was a medium that was still young enough to invent itself, but which had been around long enough for programme makers to know what worked. Unlike the pioneers of the sixties who were free to enjoy this cultural form as an adventure playground, each successive genera-tion of programme-makers would feel the weight of traditions that were established during modern television's formative years.

Only two channels competed for audience share in 1960. One was the BBC, whose royal charter and licence fee made it the semi-official state broadcaster. Since the time when John Reith was its first Director General in the inter-war years, the Corporation tended to give listeners and viewers what it thought was good for them rather than too much of what they might enjoy. On the other side there was ITV, a commercial network of regional franchises which made money by selling screen time to advertisers. The battle for ratings between these two channels was a mismatch almost from the start. ITV had only begun broadcasting in September 1955, but it soon won viewers from the BBC with peak-time schedules that were filled with entertainment formats: variety, game shows, westerns, old Hollywood films and soap opera. In September 1960 every one of the top ten most-watched programmes was shown on ITV. Although the ITA (Independent Television Authority) regulated the commercial network and reminded broadcasters that they had a duty to educate and inform their audience as well as to entertain them, there was a growing sense by 1960 that ITV companies had sacrificed high-minded 'Reithian' idealism for the sake of audience share and massive profits, seeing their franchises, in the words of Roy Thomson of Scottish TV, as a 'licence to print money'. It was against this background, and with decisions about the renewal of the BBC charter and the award of a third TV channel imminent, that a Royal Commission was set up in July 1960 under Sir Harry Pilkington to consider the future of British broadcasting.

The Pilkington Committee report of 1962 was largely based on two questionable assumptions: first, that older forms of common folk culture were being eroded by the popular appeal of vulgar television shows; second, that television exerted a powerful influence on people's attitudes and behaviour. It was the Committee's essentially paternalistic mindset that led them to vindicate the public service (in their view worthy) BBC and to criticise the commercial (in their view crassly populist) ITV. As Curran and Seaton argue, 'Pilkington seemed perilously close to despising what was popular and entertaining, and approving only that which was rigorous and demanding' (1997: 179). Although some of Pilkington's recommendations were ignored, the report helped to ensure that the competition to broadcast the new third television channel was won by the BBC and that the Corporation's charter was extended until 1976. In a further fillip to the cause of high-minded broadcasting, the ITA was allowed to 'mandate' certain kinds of serious programmes and to dictate when they were shown in the ITV schedules. So, for example, by the late sixties all ITV franchises had to broadcast one weekday and one weekend play, two weekly current affairs programmes and *News at Ten* (Crisell 1997: 113). ITV responded to Pilkington's criticisms with a programming strategy whose balance of entertainment and more serious material increasingly resembled that of the BBC. Further still, when the ITV franchises fell due for renewal in 1967 a new consortium called Harlech defeated Television Wales and the West in part because it convinced the ITA of its plans to promote artistic, cultural and educational activities in the region (Sendall 1983: 356–7). Although Television Wales and the West had a reasonable broadcasting record, a consortium that better understood Pilkington's benchmarks of 'good' television beat them to the franchise. Public-service broadcasting was now firmly in the ascendant. Perhaps if anti-establishment television existed at all in the sixties it was best represented by brash game shows like Hughie Greene's *Double Your Money*, not satirical sketch shows made by bright young things from Oxbridge.

The government's commitment to public-service broadcasting led to the launch of BBC2 as the third television channel in April 1964. The BBC had lobbied successfully for this, arguing that an additional channel would allow the Corporation to make more experimental programmes and to cater for minority interests. Unlike the two established channels which broadcast on VHF with 405 lines, BBC2 was to use a 625-line UHF transmission system. This meant a higher-definition picture, but in the short term the new technology also meant that only viewers in south-east England could watch BBC2, and only then if they bought new TV sets or had their old ones converted. The new channel was most popular among middle- and upper-class viewers, who were attracted by serious programmes like *Horizon*, *Writer's World* and Malcolm Muggeridge's interrogations of the youth of the day on a show called *Let Me Speak*. By far the most prestigious and successful of the infant BBC2's programmes was *The Great War*, a 26-part documentary series coinciding with the fiftieth anniversary of the outbreak of the 1914–18 conflict. Other landmark programmes included the football highlights show *Match of the Day*, which was initially scheduled on Saturday evenings on BBC2, and the adaptation of John Galsworthy's *The Forsyte Saga*, the last major drama series to be made in black-and-white. By July 1967, when BBC2 began making the first regular colour broadcasts in Britain, the new channel was well established with viewers. In 1971 it became the home of Open University broadcasts, helping to bring higher education to millions of students who were otherwise excluded from the more rigid arrangements of British university teaching.

Pilkington's insistence on the scheduling of 'quality' drama produced a climate in which writers such as Dennis Potter, David Mercer and Trevor Griffiths could develop their talents. The result was a corpus of politically progressive, social-realist plays that owed a debt to the Free Cinema movement of the fifties (see below). When people cite the sixties as a high-water mark of politically committed TV drama they probably have in mind *The Wednesday Play* (BBC 1964–70) – more specifically its 'radical' seasons of 1965 and 1967. *The Wednesday Play* became a frequent target for Mary Whitehouse and other 'clean up TV' campaigners in the National Viewers' and Listeners' Association (see chapter 10). As well as monitoring these dramas for sex, profanity and blasphemy, the activists were also appalled at the topicality of the subject matter. Abortion, homelessness, political corruption, nuclear disarmament, class conflict and anti-colonialism were among the issues that were featured in *The Wednesday Play*. As far as the NVLA was concerned, not only were plays such as *Up the Junction*, *Cathy Come Home* and *For The West* left-wing propaganda, worse still they were paid for by the 'moral majority' of licence payers whose world view was nowhere reflected in the BBC's serious drama output. But perhaps we should not overstate the political significance of these broadcasts. An alternative way of reading them was outlined in Herbert Marcuse's 1968 essay 'The affirmative character of culture'. From this perspective the plays could be viewed as aesthetic imaginings of social problems that transformed those problems into 'spectacle', thereby enabling them to be left unresolved: in other words, what they contributed to was ideological containment rather than a genuinely radical politics (Ridgman 1992: 155). More prosaically, despite the attention focused on them in the literature on sixties television, these single-issue dramas were only a small fraction of output at the time.

So which programmes were most popular in the sixties? Arguably the most important programme of all, *Coronation Street*, was launched on ITV in 1960. This northern-based drama tapped into the enduring popular memory of wartime working-class community, creating a much-repeated formula for social-realist soap opera that continues to thrive. *Coronation Street*'s twice-weekly portrayal of life in the fictitious Manchester suburb of Weatherfield regularly attracted an audience of 20 million, hooking in viewers who tended to leave their sets switched on ITV for the rest of the evening (armchair channel-hopping with a remote control lay some time in the future). *Z Cars* (first shown in 1962) was a successful attempt by the BBC to adapt the gritty *Coronation Street* aesthetic for the police series, producing a show with a documentary feel that was a world away from the comforting homilies of George Dixon in *Dixon of Dock Green*, the BBC's popular police series which had been running since 1955. Producers constantly sought serial dramas and soaps in these years that could build ratings. Two of the most successful dramas were *Maigret* (1960–3), adapted from Georges Simenon's French detective novels and the BBC's most ambitious series production to date, and *Dr Finlay's Casebook* (BBC, 1962–71), a medical drama set in Scotland in the late 1920s, based on the A.J. Cronin stories. Popular soaps included *Compact* (BBC, 1962–5), a twice-weekly series set in the offices of a women's magazine, and *Crossroads* (ITV, 1964–88), a Midlands hotel-based drama that initially ran for more than 4,000 episodes and which was recently revived for audiences in the new millennium. Action-adventure and escapism could be found in shows like *Danger Man* (ITV, 1960–1; 1964–7), starring Patrick McGoohan as a NATO secret service agent, *The Avengers* (ITV, 1961–9), a high-velocity, sexy espionage series, *The Saint* (ITV,

1962–9), in which Roger Moore played the freelance adventurer hero Simon Templar, and *Dr Who* (BBC, 1963–89), the long-running sci-fi series that followed the adventures of a time lord.

Comedy hits included the surreal sketches of *It's a Square World* (BBC, 1960–4), the long-running popular sitcom *Sykes* (BBC, 1960–5) and *The Ken Dodd Show* (BBC, 1959–63). *Comedy Playhouse* (1961–74) was the BBC's showcase for comedy writers and a testing ground for pilot episodes of potential series. The satirical *That Was the Week That Was* (BBC, 1962–3) was a short-lived but influential hit, peaking at around 12 million viewers and becoming the emblem of the early-sixties satire boom. It was followed by other sketch and revue programmes like *The Frost Report* (BBC, 1966–7), *Do Not Adjust Your Set* (ITV, 1967–9) and, at the end of the sixties, the most influential of all, *Monty Python's Flying Circus* (BBC, 1969–70; 1972–4). Perhaps the two most important comedies that were developed in the early sixties were *The Morecambe and Wise Show* (ITV, 1961–4; 1966–8) and *Steptoe and Son* (BBC, 1962–5), both of which were critical and ratings successes whose popularity extended well into the seventies and beyond. *The Likely Lads* (BBC, 1964–6) and *Dad's Army* (BBC, 1968–77) were situation comedies that explored the nuances and prejudices of Britain's class system. Meanwhile Alf Garnett, the fictional cockney anti-hero of *Till Death Us Do Part* (BBC, 1966–8; 1972; 1974–5), satirised 'Little England' jingoism in a show whose irony was lost on some viewers, and which became the most popular comedy programme in the BBC's history.

As we have seen, television mined young people's interest in pop music and the weekly charts with *Cool for Cats* (ITV, 1959–61), *Juke Box Jury* (BBC, 1959–67), *Ready, Steady, Go!* (ITV, 1963–6), *The Beat Room* (BBC, 1964–5) and the country's longest-running pop music show of all which was first shown in 1964, *Top of the Pops* (BBC). Much younger viewers could enjoy children's shows like *Watch with Mother* (BBC, formerly known as *For The Children* in the 1950s), *Playschool* (BBC, 1964–88) and the Gordon Murray animated productions *Camberwick Green* (BBC, made in 1966) and *Trumpton* (BBC, made in 1967). Game shows, quizzes and talent competitions were very popular. Hughie Greene was one of the stars of these formats, hosting the quiz *Double Your Money* (ITV, 1955–68) and the talent-spotting *Opportunity Knocks* (ITV, 1956; 1964–7, 1968–78) in which viewers at home voted for the winner and the studio audience registered their preference via a 'clapometer'. *Criss-Cross Quiz* (ITV, 1957–67) gave contestants the chance to compete for cash prizes three times a week, *Take a Letter*, (ITV, 1962–4) tapped into the British love of crosswords, while *University Challenge* (ITV, 1962–87) was a hybrid of game show and the Reithian ethos of intellectual elitism. But variety was the highlight of peak-time programming, with shows like *Sunday Night at the London Palladium* (ITV, 1955–67) and *The Billy Cotton Band Show* (BBC, 1956–65) guaranteed to attract large audiences.

Tonight (BBC, 1957–65), *Roving Report* (ITV, 1957–64) and *World in Action* (ITV, 1963–93) pioneered television's approach to news and current affairs, adopting a more rigorous adversarial approach to questioning politicians and public figures than had been the case in the more deferential climate of the 1950s. *Grandstand* (BBC, 1958–) set new standards in sports coverage and live outside broadcasts, surviving to become the world's longest-running live sports series. In 1966 the BBC took the unprecedented step of clearing three weeks of its prime-time schedule for live coverage of the football World Cup. Because it was so successful they repeated the strategy for the 1968 Mexico Olympics. In fact, in 1968 over one-fifth of BBC1's output was sports coverage, exploiting to the full the Corporation's exclusive long-term contracts with many of the country's leading sporting bodies. ITV tried to rival *Grandstand* with *World of Sport* (1965–85), but they had to rely on less popular sports such as wrestling and motorcycle speedway to fill up their schedule on a Saturday afternoon. One final notable programme in this brief round-up of sixties schedules was *The Black and White Minstrel Show* (BBC, 1958–78). Here white singers in black make-up performed sing-along show tunes – a useful reminder that at a time when Britain's black and South Asian population was increasing, programme makers were catering almost exclusively for *white* British audiences.

Sixties cinema: New Wave and popular genres

The growing cultural power of television – particularly commercial television – had near-disastrous consequences for British cinema. Between 1955 and 1963 over two-thirds of the audience for films and over half the cinemas in the country disappeared as people stayed at home to watch

TV. Even though the state tried to help by abolishing Entertainments Tax on cinema seats in 1960, little could be done to stop film audiences from simply drifting away (Richards 1997: 149). In much the same way that cinema had superseded repertory theatre as an entertainment form in Britain some thirty years earlier, now cinema was forced to defer to the attractions of the small screen. As the commercial environment in which they operated became tougher, British studios struggled to survive. By the end of the decade, genuinely independent British production of mainstream films had almost ceased. Most of the films that were shown nationally were either made in Hollywood, financed by American sources or shot by a British production subsidiary of one of the major Hollywood studios (Murphy 1992: 258; Hewison 1986: 289). According to film producer David Puttnam much of the damage was self-inflicted. In his view, during the sixties '[Britain] made maybe the longest consistent run of lousy movies that's been managed by any country in the last fifty years history of the cinema' (cited in Murphy 1992: 278). Unquestionably the decade went on to produce its share of dud films, but Puttnam's is an overly negative appraisal of sixties British cinema. A more positive overview can be found in Jeffrey Richards' survey of films and British national identity, in which he claims: 'The 1960s witnessed a revitaliza-tion of British cinema and the emergence of a flourishing and diverse film culture after what was widely perceived to be the "doldrums era" of the 1950s' (1997: 147). Here was the paradox of sixties cinema. Audiences as a whole dwindled at the same time as British-based filmmakers produced a body of critically acclaimed and sometimes commercially successful work. Directors including Karel Reisz, Tony Richardson, Richard Lester, John Schlesinger, Ken Russell and Lindsay Anderson made important films in the sixties, and British studios enjoyed occasional triumphs over Hollywood's dominance of the home market, usually with horror, crime or comedy pictures. This pointed towards a fragmentation of Britain's cinema culture, the corollary of which was that it catered for more plural tastes. On one side there was the popular cinema of *Carry On . . .* , James Bond, pop musicals and Hammer horror. On the other was the bourgeois, metropolitan art-house cinema of the Institute of Contemporary Arts film shows, Arts Labs and the New Cinema Club, supported by a specialist literature that included *Sight and Sound* and *Screen*. The founding of the London Film-Makers Co-Op in 1966 also signalled the development of an oppositional avant-garde cinema that presaged the work of directors such as Peter Greenaway and Derek Jarman in the seventies and eighties (Street 1997: 169–73).

The artistic revitalisation of British cinema was heralded by a 'New Wave' of films in the late fifties and early sixties. This New Wave was a marriage between the visual aesthetic of French *nouvelle vague* cinema and the thematic preoccupations of the social-realist novels and drama of contemporary British writers. It was a left-leaning, highbrow, socially-committed cinema whose impetus came from the Free Cinema movement – which had been launched in 1956 by Anderson, Reisz and Richardson – but whose roots can be traced back to the idealised portrayals of working-class communities in pre-war and wartime documentaries (Eves 1969: 51–66). New Wave films typically tackled 'real' social issues, normally from a young, alienated, working-class or lower-middle-class male perspective. Sex, class, youth culture and working-class affluence were the recurring themes. Consciously or otherwise these themes appealed to what was increasingly a more youthful cinema audience. The films were shot in black-and-white on location in urban provincial settings, sometimes using little-known regional actors. By taking on sensitive themes such as sex and class, and setting their stories in a country whose international power was shown to be on the slide, these films broke away from what Lindsay Anderson called the 'stiff upper class lip' of British filmmaking – the type of film in which usually John Mills or Anna Neagle acted out a backward-looking version of stoical, dignified and decent Englishness. Now audiences were confronted with angry young men whose 'don't let the bastards grind you down' working-class philosophy carried undeniable power. These characters drank heavily, swore casually and had promiscuous sex. They chafed against a rigid class system and the restrictive social and sexual conventions which had been carried over from Victorian times. In an echo of Richard Hoggart's analysis of popular culture in *The Uses of Literacy* (1957) they sometimes yearned for a return to a bygone era of communal and authentic working-class culture, a time in which the pub, the music hall and the football stadium were central to a shared working-class experience, before it was corroded by television and home-centred consumerism.

New Wave films can be seen therefore as cinema's contribution to the 'what's wrong with Britain' debate (see chapter 3). They were also, of course, constructed around a romanticised middle-class vision of working-class life. Subsequently New Wave films have been criticised for their failure to outline any political solutions to the alienation they presented, focusing instead on personalised responses and the refuge that the central characters sought through self-centred, instant gratification. Another shortcoming was that they were heavily masculinised films, a trend that was exemplified by films such as *Room at the Top* (the fourth most popular film of 1959), *Saturday Night and Sunday Morning* (one of the top grossing films of 1960), *The Loneliness of the Long Distance Runner* (1962) and *This Sporting Life* (1963), a clutch of titles that helped to make Richard Burton, Albert Finney and Richard Harris emblems of brooding masculinity on screen: the closest that Britain came to rivalling James Dean or Marlon Brando. Women tended to be marginalised in New Wave films and stereotyped either as 'silly tarts' or 'selfish old bags' (Richards 1997: 154). Indeed the only major New Wave film that featured a female lead was *A Taste of Honey* (1961), a commercial hit that was directed by Tony Richardson and adapted for the screen from her own stage play by Shelagh Delaney. Race and gender were also largely absent from the New Wave agenda, despite the presence of occasional black and homosexual minor characters. Homosexual men were usually either portrayed as exotically quirky characters or as people who deserved the audience's pity because their sexuality left them open to blackmail and prosecution – the latter was the theme of Basil Dearden's *Victim* (1961) in which Dirk Bogarde played a married barrister with homosexual leanings. *Victim* was released four years after the Wolfenden Report had recommended the decriminalisation of homosexuality, yet it was the first English language film to use the word 'homosexual'. Their engagement with topical issues meant that there was always something of the Fabian Society about the British New Wave. The suspicion lingered that the directors were more interested in starting mild-mannered social crusades than they were in making great films. Nevertheless, the New Wave helped to energise British cinema. These films were high-minded, but they were also earthy and more sexually graphic than previous mainstream British productions. There was nothing, perhaps, to rival the work of Godard, Truffaut or Fellini, but at least the films were more ambitious than most of what British studios had delivered so far. The New Wave was over by 1964 as audiences grew tired of their grim *mise-en-scène* and as filmmakers searched for new subjects, not least the glitz and artifice of what would become known as 'swinging London' (see chapter 6). But the movement left a legacy of earnest 'kitchen sink' realism in British filmmaking that was to reappear later in the decade in works such as Ken Loach's *Poor Cow* (1967) and Peter Collinson's *Up the Junction* (1968). Also, towards the end of the decade Lindsay Anderson's film *If . . .* (1968) used the setting of life in an English public school to resume the attack on the New Wave targets of class privilege, conformism and sexual repression.

New Wave was the dominant aesthetic in serious British cinema in the early sixties, but it was only a small part of the industry's total output. Comedies had been a consistently successful area of domestic film production since the silent era and they seemed to be in good shape as Britain entered a new decade. In 1959 the top two box office films were comedies: *Carry On Nurse* and *I'm All Right Jack*. In 1962 thirty-six British comedies were released. Time, however, appeared to be running out for the genre and in 1964 only eleven British comedies were released (Murphy 1992: 236, 238). Fortunately, one of the most popular series of all British films kept the peculiarly native comic tradition alive. The *Carry On* series began in 1958 with *Carry On Sergeant* and went on to include almost 30 other titles over a period of 20 years. As Jeffrey Richards has commented, the *Carry On* films drew on the rich comic heritage of music halls, seaside postcards and Max Miller, portraying 'a world of fat ladies and overflowing bosoms, nervous honeymoon couples and randy jack-the-lads, chamber pots and bed pans' (1992: 232). The comedy worked around the stereotype of British repressed sexuality, with the staple jokes consisting of innuendo and *double entendre*. Setting the films in institutions – *Carry On Nurse, Carry On Teacher* (1959), *Carry On Constable* (1960) – or within film genres – *Carry on Cleo* (1964), *Carry On Cowboy* (1966), *Carry On Screaming* (1966) – allowed the filmmakers to play around with recognisable situations and cinematic conventions, milked for all they were worth by the often brilliant comic acting of an ensemble cast. There was an innocent charm to the earlier *Carry On* films that was lost in the more 'permissive' climate of the late sixties. A similarly understated approach worked well in other successful comedies of the period such as *The League of Gentlemen* and *School for Scoundrels*, both of which were released in 1960. But as the country experienced wider social and cultural changes in the later sixties, film comedy lost its way. There were occasional successes, not least *The Italian Job* (1969), a crime-comedy caper that starred Michael Caine, Noel Coward and a trio of Mini Coopers driven through Turin. But as a whole the genre floundered towards the sex comedies and adaptations of television sit-coms such as *On the Buses* in the seventies (Murphy 1992: 255).

Another success story for sixties British cinema was the Hammer studio's horror films. Hammer was helped by a deal which gave them the right to remake Universal's 1930s horror pictures, enabling them to produce a run of features which drew on the dark gothic tradition of Mary Shelley and Bram Stoker. Until 1965 Hammer horror production was centred at Bray in Buckinghamshire, where the studio assembled a talented team that included the director Terence Fisher and the actors Peter Cushing and Christopher Lee. *The Curse of Frankenstein* (1957), *The Brides of Dracula* (1960) and *The Kiss of the Vampire* (1962) failed to impress most critics at the time, but they performed well enough at the box office for Hammer to secure a US distribution deal. Perhaps the films were popular in the late fifties and early sixties because they 'seemed to bring excitement and colour into a dull, conformist society' (Murphy 1992: 171). A more nuanced explanation has been offered by Jeffrey Richards, who argues that Hammer horror films were a 'symbolic and mythological counterpart to the New wave and swinging London' (1997: 165). He continues:

> *Hammer films consistently pointed up the contrast between the ordered, bourgeois normality of Victorian England and the forces of unreason and excess lurking below the surface. In particular, they celebrated their anti-heroes' single-minded gratification of their desires . . . Initially symbols of a ruthless and exploitative upper class, they [Frankenstein and Dracula] soon became transformed into the heroes of an era of sex, style and 'anything goes'.*

> (Richards 1997: 166)

In short, they tapped into a *zeitgeist* that would eventually become more explicitly manifest in the late sixties counter-culture.

Perhaps the ultimate icon of sixties British cinema, however, was James Bond, a secret agent in the Boys' Own tradition of Bulldog Drummond and Dick Barton whose first big screen appearance came in *Dr No* (1962). Commercially the Bond formula turned out to be bullet-proof, with the next two films in the series, *From Russia With Love* (1963) and *Goldfinger* (1964), becoming the top-earning films in Britain in those years. The pictures were adapted from Ian Fleming's best-selling novels by Albert Broccoli, an American co-founder of Warwick Films, and Harry Saltzman, a Canadian producer at Woodfall Films. Despite having some difficulties financing the first Bond picture, Broccoli and Saltzman were convinced that the key to the formula's appeal was lavish production values, typified by the use of exotic locations, spectacular action sequences and high-tech gadgetry. They also liked to give audiences lingering shots of the female form – the obvious examples are the camera gazing on Ursula Andress as she rose from the sea in *Dr No*, and on Shirley Eaton as she lay semi-naked, dead and painted from head to toe in gold in *Goldfinger*. Sean Connery was in many eyes the surprise choice for the lead role, but he made it work. Connery played Bond as a classless sophisticate, a man who could be the final word in highly-controlled professionalism but who always found time to indulge his tastes as an urbane playboy. In a culture that was increasingly preoccupied with materialism and sex, Bond was a practised consumer of elite brand goods who travelled without luggage and rarely failed to satisfy his voracious sexual appetite. (Ironically the only screen star in the country who could eclipse Connery's popularity in the sixties was Julie Andrews, the wholesome star of Britain's most popular imported film of the decade, *The Sound of Music*.) The Bond sequence rolled out across the rest of the decade, with titles such as *Thunderball* (1966) and *You Only Live Twice* (1967) proving that hit films could be made in Britain. Sensing that the spy genre could be taken in other directions, Harry Saltzman spent some of his time away from the Bond films producing a more low-key portrait of a British intelligence agent at work. Michael Caine starred as Harry Palmer in three films, *The Ipcress File* (1965), *Funeral in Berlin* (1967) and *Billion Dollar Brain* (1967), the plots of which became ever less comprehensible. In terms of sustaining the home film industry, the problem with the Bond series was that while the films were largely shot in Britain, using British crews, technicians and actors, the financial backing came from Hollywood's United Artists studio. As a result, most of the profits were taken back to the US and invested in Hollywood features.

This repatriation of earnings to Hollywood underscored the nature of the challenge that faced the British film industry in the sixties. It lacked the kind of state support that de Gaulle committed to the French film industry, and it struggled to compete successfully against Hollywood's commercial might. There was a brief period around 1965–7 when Hollywood executives saw that British films had a youthful charisma that they hoped to capture for their own pictures. The main US studios set up bases in Soho and poured money into making films in Britain. But the bubble soon burst. Earnings from British productions were disappointing, meanwhile big-budget flops like *Star!* (1968) and *Hello Dolly* (1969) back home forced the studios into retrenchment. Also, the success of Peter Fonda's *Easy Rider* (1969), the tale of two drop-outs riding across America on motorcycles, alerted the studios to a new generation of home-grown talent that could make films for younger audiences. By the early seventies Hollywood studios' British subsidiaries had either been scaled down or closed.

CHAPTER 6

. . . .

'Swinging London' and the 'long front of culture'

'Swinging London', changing fashions

Britain's capital city stood as an emblem of national self-confidence and cultural renaissance during the high sixties. 'Swinging London' was a mythical fusion of design, architecture, boutique fashion and pop culture, the seal being set – at least as far as one part of the UK was concerned – by England's World Cup victory at Wembley in July 1966, the focal celebrations for which spilled out westwards from Trafalgar Square to the players' post-match party at the Royal Garden Hotel. London was seen to be at the heart of the wider social and cultural loosenings of the sixties, soaking up influences from the provinces and abroad and morphing them into an exotic motif of hedonism, modernity and affluent liberation. This newly-fashioned identity was then transmitted for wider national and international consumption via a range of media. The *Daily Telegraph* read the signs earlier than most, labelling London 'the most exciting city in the world' in a weekend edition in April 1965. Here, American journalist John Crosby name-checked the capital's main night spots – Annabel's in Berkeley Square, the Ad Lib Club and Ronnie Scott's jazz den in Soho, the Marquee on Wardour Street, the Scene on Great Windmill Street – and performed a roll-call of the fashionable glitterati, dukes and duchesses, designers and media darlings, whose presence had made London 'the gayest, most uninhibited, and – in a wholly new, very modern sense – most wholly elegant city in the world'. A more powerful piece of myth-making came exactly one year later, when the US magazine *Time* carried a front-page feature on 'London: The Swinging City', focusing on how the capital had reinvented itself from being the centre of a once-mighty empire into a city that now set the social and cultural markers for the rest of the world. As one of the female editors who worked on it recalled, the article also gave a licence to indulge 'the fascination among the senior editors for mini-skirts' (Green 1998a: 86). Central to both of these commentaries was the idea of a newly apparent 'classlessness', based on the observation that many of the leading 'swinging London' celebrities came from working-class or lower-middle class backgrounds. Photographers such as David Bailey, Brian Duffy and Terence Donovan were East-End working class – the press was delighted when the 'unstuffy' Bailey wore a light blue sweater and green corduroy trousers for his wedding to actress Catherine Deneuve in August 1965 – while actors such as Michael Caine and Terence Stamp were drawn from a similar social milieu. Now they could afford to drive Rolls-Royces and mix easily with the youthful offspring of Britain's major titled families, whose acquiescence in the development of classless relations was seen as crucial to the 'swinging London' phenomenon. When the Beatles were awarded their MBEs at Buckingham Palace in October 1965 it was taken as proof positive that a new classless age had truly arrived.

Of course 'swinging London' was always a highly selective composite, based predominantly on the fashionable western districts of Soho, Chelsea, Mayfair and South Kensington. It ignored the council housing estates, corner shops and greasy cafés that typified most of the city. It also sat uncomfortably alongside alternative narratives of the 'state of the nation', such as the rediscovery of poverty by social researchers in late 1965 (see chapter 9), or people's absorbtion in the horrific details of the Moors Murderers' trial in April–May 1966. But, as with all mythical constructions, it corresponded to an important imaginative reality, and the myth had a cultural resonance which transcended the tiny cliques who made up London's interconnected 'scenes'. By 1962 London already employed more than one-fifth of the country's working population (Rycroft 2002: 578). As the *Time* article noted, some 30 per cent of its total population was in the 15-to-34-year-old age bracket, and an influx of post-colonial immigrants meant that London had a more cosmopolitan ethnic mix than anywhere else in the country. Between 1965 and 1967 all of these factors helped to make the congested capital city an important gathering point for creative expression across a range of cultural forms, the combination of which produced a new aesthetic that was widely shared throughout the rest of Britain. Fashion was at the leading edge of this phenomenon, pushed forward by design pioneers like Mary Quant and John Stephen, and continued by art-school graduates who had spent their time at college studying fine arts and graphic design as well as fashion. Indeed, as fashion rose to high prominence during the era of 'swinging London', so its status as an academic discipline within the art colleges also gradually improved. A prime force here was Mary Quant, who gained a national profile after she opened Bazaar, her first shop, in the King's Road in 1955, designing and selling 'sexy' clothes such as brightly coloured mini-skirts and skinny-ribbed sweaters to the young Chelsea set. The store was a magnet for those who wanted entry into the fashionable scene. Before he became the Rolling Stones' manager, Andrew Loog Oldham was employed to dress the Bazaar windows – a job he likened to an apprenticeship for designing record covers (Oldham 2000: 94). Quant's ability to conceive and implement new design ideas almost daily ensured that there was a constant turnover of new stock in her store. Ten years later she was being described as 'the major fashion force in the world outside Paris' (cited in Booker 1969: 22). Quant and the art-school-trained 'fashion girls' who followed her lead absorbed Pop Art and pop music references into their design and retail strategies, making *haute couture* and luxury fashion look out-of-date in comparison with their own off-the-peg clothes (McRobbie 1998: 35–6). The mini-skirt was integral to the new look, designed as a symbol of sexual freedom and modelled by the catwalk icons Twiggy and Jean Shrimpton, whose tiny waistlines were an ironic counterpoint to the post-austerity abundance of the sixties. Barbara Hulanicki, whose Biba boutique had a clientele that included *Ready, Steady, Go!* presenter Cathy MacGowan, offered her own explanation for the new style. 'The postwar babies had been deprived of nourishing protein in childhood and grew up into beautiful skinny people. A designer's dream. It didn't take much for them to look outstanding' (1983: 79). The infantile 'dolly bird' look became the dominant style represented in fashion magazines like *Petticoat* and *Nova* which in turn fed the public appetite for the uniform. As Angela Carter commented in a piece for *New Society* in 1967, clothes such as this had a significant social and psychological function as 'disguises' which 'give a relaxation from one's own personality'. More constructively, she suggested: 'Style means the presentation of the self as a three-dimensional art object, to be wondered at and handled. And this involves a new attitude to the self which is thus adorned' (Carter 1967: 866). It was important, therefore, that boutiques selling the latest style spread from the capital to other towns and cities, modelled on stores like Bazaar and Biba which became, as Angela McRobbie observed, focal points for youth culture as well as a place in which to adorn the self.

> The boutiques were as innovative in design as the clothes they stocked. They didn't look like any other shops. The items were not priced beyond the budget of the working-class girls who spent substantial sums each week, while the fast turnover of stock as well as the reputation these shops got from the publicity they attracted in the fashion magazines and the daily press (in particular the Sunday newspaper colour supplements), meant that they came to represent the ultimate consumer fantasy for ordinary girls and young women up and down the country.

(McRobbie 1998: 37)

Those who lived too far away to visit the most fashionable boutiques were not left behind entirely. Since 1963 Quant had mass-produced new fashions and sold them wholesale to the mass market. But it was not only women who gained from this explosion in high-street fashion. Men's clothes similarly benefited from an injection of creative energy at this time. John Stephen was a pioneer who had moved from Glasgow to London in the fifties and established himself as the high priest of 'Mod' fashion with his four Carnaby Street stores: His, Mod Male, Domino Male and Male W.1. By the time of 'swinging London', Carnaby Street was fast becoming a tacky tourist trap, but a new sensibility about men's fashion had become a permanent feature of popular culture. Coloured shirts and boldly patterned ties – if ties were worn at all – replaced the dominant grey-and-white look of the fifties. Denim jeans and T-shirts (which often carried names and slogans) became ubiquitous among the young and not so young, signalling a new informality in dress. Elasticated 'Chelsea' boots and collarless jackets benefited from their association with the Beatles, as did the trend towards longer hair which was accompanied by the increased production of cosmetics and dressings for male hair (Byrde 1979: 171).

Fashion was now big business, and it matched perfectly the other descriptors for Pop Art which the artist Richard Hamilton had set out in 1957: it was popular, transient, expendable, low-cost, mass-produced, young, witty, sexy, gimmicky and glamorous (McRobbie 1998: 36). Fashion retail strategies also had an impact beyond the rag trade, inspiring the designer Terence Conran who opened his first Habitat furnishings shop in the Fulham Road in 1964. Conran, who had designed the Knightsbridge branch of Mary Quant's Bazaar, made Habitat more of a boutique than a traditional furniture store and he later went on to offer a highly stylised catalogue and mail order service. 'Swinging London' was the hippest place in the world to buy a lifestyle. For those who lived beyond its immediate reach, there was always at least the opportunity to absorb some of its influences via the style magazines and weekend colour newspaper supplements.

The cultural power of the capital was further accentuated by television and film producers. *Adam Adamant Lives!* (1966–7), for example, was a BBC fantasy series in which Gerald Harper played an Edwardian gentleman-adventurer who was drugged and frozen alive in 1902, only to thaw out intact and perfectly preserved in mid-sixties London. More importantly, 'swinging London' became the dominant motif of mid-sixties British cinema, displacing the northern industrial towns and black-and-white social realism of the early-sixties 'New Wave'. In line with the more optimistic sensibility that they depicted almost all films were now shot in colour, often with a *mise-en-scène* that emphasised bright primary colours (Silvio Narizano's 1966 film *Georgy Girl* was the last 'swinging London' picture to be shot in black and white). Although directors handled the subject matter in a variety of ways, adopting differing moral approaches to metropolitan permissiveness, all were inspired by London's relatively short-lived reputation as the world's most fashionable city. As well as the thematic interest there was a commercial imperative behind the production of such pictures. At a time when the average age of cinema audiences was falling, these films, with their references to pop, fashion and pre-marital sex, had an obvious youthful appeal. Pop-group movies which married British R&B, youth culture and Pop Art aesthetics were precursors of the genre. *A Hard Day's Night*

(1964) and *Help!* (1965), both of which featured the Beatles, and *Catch Us if You Can* (1965) starring the Dave Clark Five, signposted the direction to take to capture the target demographic and featured some of what became the visual clichés of 'swinging London' films – E-type Jaguars, red buses, mini-skirts. By 1965 the genre was fast becoming established. In this year Dick Lester (who had directed *A Hard Day's Night*) released *The Knack*, a film which examined the differences between physical sexual attraction and more profound emotional love. It showed how a shy schoolteacher named Colin (played by Michael Crawford) could win the love of Nancy (Rita Tushingham), a country girl who had been drawn to London's glitz. In order to do so, Colin had to compete against the attentions of his more sexually experienced and confident rival, Tolen (Ray Brooks). *Darling*, which was also released in 1965, starred Julie Christie as Diana Scott, an amoral but spontaneous girl who wanted to have it all (sex, wealth, celebrity) but who found only emptiness once her dreams came true. Despite its 'swinging' backdrop *Darling* was in essence a traditional morality tale, full of cautionary portrayals of how relationships that were built on fantasy rather than truth led only to pain and failure. A similar moral grounding can be seen in Lewis Gilbert's *Alfie* (1966), one of the most emblematic of all 'swinging London' films in which Michael Caine played a 'working-class Don Juan' (French 1966, cited in Murphy 1992: 143). Alfie's amorous wanderings leave behind a string of hurt females, including the abandoned mother of his child and a married woman who has to resort to an (illegal) abortion in his seedy London flat after a casual sexual liaison. But there is at least a trajectory of developing self-awareness sketched out in the film, at the end of which Alfie shows some genuine remorse and attempts to settle down in a monogamous relationship. As Alfie explains in his final address straight to camera, despite having 'a bob or two, some decent clothes, a car' to his name his life choices have not given him 'peace of mind'. And as he says 'if you ain't got that, you ain't got nothing'. Michelangelo Antonioni's film *Blow Up* (1966), scripted by the playwright Edward Bond and adapted from '*Las babas del diabolo*', a short story by the Argentinian modernist Julio Cortazar, signalled a deeper sense of unease at mid-sixties London permissiveness. David Hemmings plays Thomas, a fashion photographer (in the mould of Bailey and Donovan) who believes he has witnessed a murder as he shoots off film casually in a London park. He pursues the beautiful suspected murderess (Vanessa Redgrave), but all the while seems interested in the murder primarily as the inspiration to make a piece of art. Thus the film meditates on issues of artifice, affluent decadence and moral relativism. Antonioni trains a wearily cynical eye on the fantasy he perceives to be at the centre of 'swinging London', but whether his audience responded to depictions of a pot-smoking party in Chelsea, casual sex in the photographer's studio and a guitar-smashing performance by the Yardbirds in quite the way he intended is another matter. MGM's press release for the film left to one side Antonioni's philosophical ruminations and emphasised instead the youth appeal of the modern London setting, 'where teenage pop singing groups have their records sold in shops owned by people their own age, and photographers who have barely started shaving drive Rolls-Royces with radio telephones' (cited in Lev 1989: 135).

By the time that the genre's final batch of films was released – *Here We Go Round the Mulberry Bush, I'll Never Forget What's 'Is Name, Smashing Time* (all 1967) – signs of exhaustion were all too apparent. More importantly in 1967 'swinging London' was about to surrender its *zeitgeist* status to the counter-culture and the 'summer of love', imaginative constructions which were largely reactions against the excessive materialism of the London scene of the previous two years. As Simon Rycroft observes, however, 'swinging' and 'underground' London were not completely antithetical ideologically. Their cultural politics sprang from similarly abstract notions of the relationships between society, nature and technology (2002: 581). They were both based around counter-hegemonic strategies which allowed people (if only in their heads) to resist more traditional, and still dominant, moral and cultural values. In that sense both also occupied space that was opened up by the 'democratisation' of culture, a long process whose impact was most apparent in the mid-sixties.

Pop Art and the 'long front of culture'

Art was fashionable by the mid-sixties, and fashion was art. It was a productive symbiosis. Clothes designers and poster artists lifted patterns and imagery from fine art works. In the other direction, artists trained in the country's leading academies sought inspiration from the urban pop culture of retail design, brand advertising and new media. The result was an increasingly influential interface between art and commerce, which turned fashionable galleries into thriving businesses and made gallery owners such as John Dunbar and Robert Fraser into 'swinging London' celebrities. Dunbar opened the Indica Gallery in Mason's Yard, London, in 1966, the year after he had married Marianne Faithfull while he was still a student at Cambridge. Fraser's in-crowd credentials were confirmed for a wider public when he was charged alongside Mick Jagger and Keith Richards of the Rolling Stones following a drugs raid on Richards' house in February 1967 (he was sentenced to six months in jail for possessing heroin). The Beatles recruited artists Peter Blake and Richard Hamilton to design their album covers (for *Sergeant Pepper's Lonely Hearts Club Band* and *The Beatles* – more usually known as the *White Album* – respectively). The Rolling Stones were to use Andy Warhol to design the *Sticky Fingers* album cover. And fashion photographers like David Bailey found that their work could be treated and exhibited as fine art. *David Bailey's Box of Pin-ups* (1965) helped elevate him to the position of first iconic photographer of the new age. The box – with accompanying text by journalist Francis Wyndham – contained thirty-six black-and-white studio portraits of the high-sixties 'New Aristocracy', ranging from hairdressers (Vidal Sassoon), interior decorators (David Hicks), models (Jean Shrimpton) and villains (the Kray twins), to artists (David Hockney), actors (Michael Caine) and photographers (Bailey himself, photographed by Mick Jagger). Thus, formerly rigid distinctions between high and popular culture melted to some extent, and a cultural pyramid in which layers were organised according to aesthetic or critical benchmarks gave way to a 'long front of culture' which dispensed with the need for hierarchies of value. This evolution was identified and indeed promoted by art critics like Lawrence Alloway (whose article 'Long Front of Culture' had appeared back in 1959), by the commentators Marshall McLuhan and T.R. Fyvel, and by the artist Richard Hamilton (a key figure in British Pop Art). The Arts Council – the body that had emerged from wartime as the main state agency for promoting the arts – was also sanguine about this levelling effect. In the 1965 White Paper, *A Policy for the Arts*, Britain's first Minister for the Arts, Jennie Lee, acknowledged that the traditional cultural hierarchy was breaking down:

*. . . [D]iffusion of culture is now so much a part of life that there is no
precise point at which it stops. Advertisements, buildings, books, motor
cars, radio and television, magazines, records, all can carry a cultural
aspect and affect our lives for good or ill . . . It is partly a question of
bridging the gap between what have come to be called the 'higher' forms
of entertainment and the traditional sources – the brass band, the
amateur concert party, the entertainer, the music hall and pop group
– and to challenge the fact that a gap exists. In the world of jazz the
process has already happened; highbrow and lowbrow have met.*

(1965: 15–16)

The Arts Council's agenda here mattered, not least because of its
rising profile and status in the sixties – whereas, for example, its budget
had been static in the fifties, between 1960 and 1964 Arts Council funding more than doubled. Labour's return to power in 1964 ushered in a
further period of funding growth, thereby endorsing Anthony Crosland's
view in *The Future of Socialism* that with poverty and unemployment
seemingly under control, legislators should turn their attention to the
'spheres of personal freedom, happiness and cultural endeavour' (1956:
520). The Arts Council's grant rose steadily from £3,205,000 in 1964–5 to
£3,910,000 in 1965–6, £5,700,000 in 1966–7, £7,200,000 in 1967–8 and
£9,300,000 in 1970–1 (Hewison 1986: 58). True, most of this money
was spent on the metropolitan (usually London) centres of elite culture.
The Royal Opera House, Sadler's Wells Opera, the National Theatre, the
Royal Shakespeare Company and the major art galleries all drew heavily
on the Council's coffers. But some of the funding went to artists and writers, smaller theatre companies and orchestras. Regional arts associations
benefited, so too did art forms which had previously been ineligible for
grants – jazz, for example, was supported in 1967 when Graham Collier
was given a small award – and a fraction was spent on encouraging
'experimental' projects. As Robert Hutchison recognised, here was the
real source of the Arts Council's power: its official capacity to conceptualise and identify the arts and the artistic. By giving approval to some
artists and withholding it from others, the Council legitimised some
kinds of creativity and ignored the rest (1982: 13–14). It was therefore
significant that the Council preferred to promote contemporary work in
the visual arts, often produced by graduates from the art colleges that

had proliferated in the wake of the 1944 Education Act and the 1960 Coldstream Report. Whether or not this new generation of contemporary artists produced work of high merit was in some respects less important than the fact that there were wider opportunities for people to study, experience, practise and exhibit art. Art colleges had a cross-class social role:

> *Art schools were a haven for imaginative people otherwise neglected by the educational system. Few would become commercially successful artists, but the relative freedom of the art schools encouraged experiments with style. For working class students they were an escape from the factory, for middle-class students they were the entry to bohemia.*

> (Hewison 1986: 63)

Art school graduates brought their aesthetic sensibilities to bear on a number of cultural forms in the sixties. Nowhere was this more evident than in popular music, where the roll-call of musicians who came from an art school background includes some of the key names in sixties rock: Lennon and McCartney, Eric Clapton, Pete Townsend, Keith Richards, Ray Davies, Jeff Beck, Eric Burdon, David Bowie and all of Pink Floyd. Unlike their fifties counterparts, this generation of musicians demanded extensive artistic control over writing, production, album cover design, marketing and the lighting and staging of live shows. When Pete Townsend smashed his guitar into an amp at the end of a show he was at least aware that he was drawing on a tradition of 'destructive' art. Pop music was one important medium which helped to filter some fine art influences to a wider audience. Another was television, with arts pro- grammes such as the BBC's *Monitor* (1958–65) and *Omnibus* (from 1967) bringing the visual and other arts to a mainstream, if not necessarily a mass, audience. The increased interest in art was reflected in the rising circulation of art journals like *Art and Artists*, *Studio International*, *Art Forum* and *Arts Review*. It was a good time too for contemporary art venues. The Tate, the Whitechapel and the Institute of Contemporary Arts all flourished in London. The Walker Art Gallery in Liverpool suc- cessfully hosted the John Moore's biennial exhibition, and the Whitworth in Manchester put on important shows of younger artists' work (Sillars 1992: 272).

What of the art itself? Above all the mid-sixties art boom was driven forward by Pop Art, a form which originated in the early fifties. Pop Art developed out of a series of meetings of the Independent Group at the ICA, where a group of like-minded friends – Richard Hamilton, Lawrence Alloway, the architects Peter and Alison Smithson, the artist Eduardo Paolozzi and the architectural historian Reyner Banham – gathered to discuss their visions of contemporary art. The Independent Group had a shared preoccupation with modern technology, commercial design and mass-media culture, and so they were naturally predisposed towards art forms that absorbed and recontextualised these influences. Pop Art played around with the distinctions between high art and the iconography of modern popular culture. Its comic book aesthetic unashamedly celebrated post-war affluence and the new consumer culture, particularly the US hard commercial culture of brand advertising, pulp magazines and Hollywood films. Pop Art thus in a sense reversed the normal current of *avant-garde* movements: whereas its predecessors developed in opposition to mainstream culture, Pop Art positively luxuriated in the new materialist 'paradise'. It was Pop Art's greatest strength, producing images that were glamorous, sexy, witty and euphoric, using visual references that were familiar to anyone who watched television, put posters on their walls, read magazines or shopped in the high street. The first well-known British example of this aesthetic is Richard Hamilton's iconic illustration, *Just What Is It That Makes Today's Homes So Different, So Appealing?*, a collage of magazine images which he produced for the 1956 'This is Tomorrow' exhibition. By the early sixties British Pop Art was seeping into a wider public consciousness via the publicity surrounding the annual 'Young Contemporaries' exhibitions held at the Whitechapel Art Gallery. These exhibitions raised the profile of the artists Peter Blake, Joe Tilson, Richard Smith, David Hockney, Patrick Caulfield and R.B. Kitaj, all of whom had studied at the Royal College of Art. Although their work was highly individual and eclectic rather than part of a highly-defined 'school', each of these artists at least absorbed some aspects of Pop Art's sensibility into their painting. They also profited from the media perception that they were part of an artistic movement which, in common with early twentieth century Dadaism, sought to expand the parameters of art by challenging conventional tastes. Thus they benefited from the very commercialism that underpinned much of their work, selling their art in a buoyant market that was crowded for a time with private galleries and dealers. Ironically, however, the form's worship of consumer culture came to be seen as Pop Art's greatest weakness. Critics on the radical left dismissed Pop Art as a decadent irrelevance. To them, it was a form which built on a complacent acceptance of the ideology of affluent consumerism, failing utterly to engage with the realities of the modern world and the forces that reshaped society. Other critics, who were simply bored by it, claimed that Pop Art continually recycled the same idea. To some cynical observers, the wider public interest that Pop Art had helped to generate in the visual arts was superficial. They claimed that it was merely a consequence of weekend newspaper colour supplement hype and a fleeting sense that art galleries were fashionable places for poseurs. Worse still, the growing market for contemporary art was seen to have a corrosive effect on the artist, with the true spirit of the *avant-garde* giving way to a commercialised art boom. Hugh Adams made this complaint about the art world of the sixties:

> The leeches on the artist's back multiplied: in the world of 'You've never had it so good' galleries proliferated, art institutions expanded, and the media presentation of the artist as pop idol rescued him from his lonely attic . . . Roaring young lions of the early sixties became sleek, purring, sedentary ones later, their art consequently soft, and sufficiently accessible for the manipulators and middle-men to be able to package producer and bland product alike.

(Adams 1978: 32)

Although it was an emblematic feature of sixties visual culture, Pop Art was only a fraction of what the art world offered at the time. Among older British artists, Francis Bacon and Frank Auerbach produced some of their best paintings in the sixties. Crowds still flocked to see the old masters in museums and galleries. The highest prices at a Sotheby's art auction in 1967 were paid for a Cézanne and a Picasso (Sillars 1992: 271). Among contemporary styles, Neo-Dada, New Realism, Op, Kinetic, Tachism, Hard-Edge, Colour Field, Minimalist, Conceptual, Event and Earth were all part of a bewildering array of artistic categories referred to in the sixties and early seventies. These styles often overlapped or had a dynamic relationship with each other, significantly blurring distinctions between painting, sculpture and performance art. For example, in sculpture Anthony Caro and his students at St Martin's School of Art – the 'New Generation' – used industrial materials and modern building techniques to produce work that had more in common with architecture than classical sculpture. They bolted and welded steel plates and sheet metal together, laid iron poles on the ground, arranged girders, filled canvas sacks with plaster and put their work on the floor rather than on pedestals. Their sculptures were accessible, allowing spectators to engage with the pieces and explore their spaces freely, rather than passively admire them as rarefied works of art. It was part of an increasingly prevalent trend towards an elision of the artistic work and the process of spectatorship, with the intention being that spectators would experience art as a total environment. The sculptures could also be seen as three-dimensional abstract paintings, sharing some of Pop Art's predilection for recycling, recontextualising and demystifying the artistic process. Coming from the opposite direction, the paintings of Allen Jones and Derek Boshier, whose canvases were shaped to match the subject matter they depicted, displayed the sense of spatial awareness found in 'New Generation' sculpture. It was present too in Bridget Riley's Op Art, in which black lines were arranged on a white background in ways that gave the viewer the illusion of movement. Riley's abstract geometric patterns soon inspired fashion designers who printed them on to fabrics and sold them to the fashionable set. The humming wave effect of these Op Art pictures also had something in common with the stroboscopic lighting used by rock bands later in the decade. It was another example of how a long front of culture was established by the high sixties. If there was a unifying theme to an otherwise diverse field of British visual art in this period, it was a desire to make galleries and art works more accessible and enjoyable. Reverence and stuffiness in art were to be avoided at all costs in these self-consciously new times.

CHAPTER 7

◆ ◆ ◆ ◆ ◆ ◆ ◆ ◆ ◆ ◆ ◆ ◆ ◆ ◆ ◆ ◆

Labour's first term and the politics of race

New government for new times: Labour in power, October 1964–March 1966

Labour's election victory in October 1964 itself became a symbol of new times. It meant that for a while at least Labour's image was that of a modern, even fashionable, party. Its reforming plans to create a 'New Britain' re-energised politics after the drifting final years of Conservative rule. Here, it appeared, was a government with constructive answers to the 'what's wrong with Britain?' soul-searching of the early sixties. But the downside of raising public hopes that it would reinvigorate the country after thirteen years of Tory rule was unrealistic expectations of Labour's possible achievements in office. It made the eventual sense of anti-climax even harder to bear. The virulence of the criticism that the government was to endure from 1966 onwards was inversely proportional to the heady optimism it had encouraged two years earlier. No doubt many of the difficulties it later faced were of its own making, and Wilson can be held responsible for the over-ambitious rhetoric used in the election campaign. But from the beginning Labour was also unfortunate to be confronted with such powerful external constraints and problems.

The first of these was the parliamentary arithmetic. Labour did not sweep the Conservatives from office in October 1964, it squeezed them out in the tightest of contests. Harold Wilson had to wait until the Friday afternoon following polling day for confirmation that his party had finally gained a parliamentary majority. By the time the final result was declared, Labour's lead over all the other parties was just four seats. After thirteen years in opposition, victory by any margin was welcome, but Wilson knew that he needed a larger majority to have any chance of pursuing a radical agenda. That day would come, but for now Wilson had to concentrate on survival and governing, as he told one interviewer, 'by the seat of my pants'. When he went to Buckingham Palace to tell the Queen that he could form a government, Wilson chose to wear a short black coat rather than a more formal morning coat as was the custom. It was a minor but telling detail, symbolic of Labour's determination to align itself with new times and break away from the past. Opportunities to exploit such symbolism had to be taken, partly because the size of Labour's majority would make it difficult for them to push through headline-grabbing reforms, but also because the personnel that made up the administration were drawn from the traditional stock of Britain's political elite. Labour had sneered at the Conservatives for being the 'Establishment' party before the election, but new ministers usually came from the same middle-class, public-school-educated intelligentsia as their Tory predecessors. Several members of Wilson's Cabinet had been pupils at Eton, Harrow or Winchester and almost half of the Cabinet had been to Oxford. Another link between this government and its predecessors was the balance between the sexes in its upper ranks, with only Barbara Castle's appointment at Overseas Development preventing a male monopoly of Cabinet posts. Moreover, as Lord Longford noted in 1965, about half of his Cabinet colleagues were committed Christians, making this one of the last traditional Christian family Cabinets of the modern age. It was ironic that it took office just as the sixties was entering the period that came to be seen as the high point of permissiveness and wider cultural change.

Expectations about the new administration's agenda were certainly high among Labour supporters, the business community and even civil servants. But the other binding constraint holding the government back was the economic legacy of Home's Conservatives. Wilson was briefed by officials about the worrying scale of Britain's balance of payments deficit, and the consequent pressure that this would exert on the exchange value of sterling, within minutes of entering Downing Street. Thus it was that

Wilson in his memoirs claimed that the first hundred minutes in government in October 1964 set the pattern for the first hundred days (1974: 24). The projected deficit for 1964 was £800 million, roughly twice what Wilson and his colleagues had been expecting. The news meant that Wilson and his two senior economic ministers, James Callaghan (Chancellor of the Exchequer) and George Brown (Secretary of State at the Department of Economic Affairs), were required to make a decision about whether or not to devalue the currency on their first Saturday morning in office. It was a tough choice to make just days after a gruelling election campaign and less than twenty-four hours after Labour's narrow victory had been confirmed. For a number of reasons – some economic, others political – Labour's troika agreed to defend the exchange rate. There was no certainty that a swift surgical devaluation would have the desired economic effect, and there was at least a chance that planned expansion would eventually earn enough foreign currency to correct the deficit. Politically, Wilson had made his reputation as a Shadow Chancellor, flaying the Tories' inability to deliver faster economic expansion: now was the time for audacity, not retreat. He was also desperate to avoid a repeat of the sterling crises of 1931 and 1949, adamant that *his* government would at last establish Labour's reputation for economic competence.

Almost at once, therefore, many of Labour's plans had to be put on hold. Sizeable increases in public spending, whether for social projects or as investment to promote faster economic growth, would panic the foreign exchange markets and undermine the defence of sterling. So *largesse* was to be distributed within strict limits only and an orthodox defence of sterling was to supersede the goal of a growth rate that would match Britain's main international competitors. The government's barely visible majority in the Commons was soon reduced still further when the attempt to parachute the Foreign Secretary, Patrick Gordon Walker, back into parliament cost Labour its seat at the Leyton by-election in January 1965 (Gordon Walker had surprisingly lost his West Midlands constituency of Smethwick in the general election after local Conservatives highlighted his liberal views on immigration). This setback intensified the belief in the senior reaches of the government that its overriding priority was to survive in office long enough to control the timing of the next election. If the administration could avoid, or at least ride out, serious defeats in the Commons and hold on to its overall majority at further by-elections, Labour could appeal to the country for a stronger mandate whenever the outlook was favourable, probably within eighteen months to two years. In his memoirs Wilson gave credit to Ted Short, the government's Chief Whip, for marshalling Labour MPs in defence of the party's fragile major- ity (1974: 52). But the Prime Minister himself contributed more than anyone to the government's survival by keeping his party united and its morale high. Cabinet appointments were balanced between Wilson's old Bevanite colleagues on the left and the Gaitskellites on the right who had voted against him in 1963. In fact the combined right-wing of the party were given most of the spoils, largely because of their previous strength in contests for shadow Cabinet posts. Arthur Bottomley, Herbert Bowden, Tom Fraser, Ray Gunter, Denis Healey, Douglas Houghton, Douglas Jay and Frank Soskice were all appointed to Cabinet. The left's standard bearers were Barbara Castle, Richard Crossman and Anthony Greenwood, together with the leader of the transport workers, Frank Cousins, brought in to keep the trade unions settled. Wilson's Westminster colleagues and supporters in the country also took heart from the way he constantly outshone his opponents and critics, not least Alec Douglas-Home who was regularly knocked around at Prime Minister's Questions until he was jettisoned by the Tories in July 1965. His replacement, Edward Heath, soon trailed Wilson by a distance in the opinion polls (Butler and Butler 1994: 252).

The tightness of the parliamentary arithmetic did not entirely absolve Labour from answering the question: what was this government *for*? The first answers were provided in the Queen's Speech on 3 November 1964, which promised among other measures the renationalisation of iron and steel, the repeal of the 1957 Rent Act and the restoration of rent control, a new law to protect trade unions from legal action resulting from strikes, a law to compel companies to disclose political donations, and a free vote on the abolition of the death penalty. After years of frustration in opposi- tion this was heady stuff for the left. They were cheered even more a week later by Callaghan's first budget, which increased pensions, widows' benefits and other social security payments by £345 million per year. The Chancellor also announced that prescription charges – a totem of Labour's socialist credentials – would be abolished from February 1965. Such enlightened social payments were made in the face of opposition from the financial markets, whose response to Labour's first budget since Gaitskell's had split the party in April 1951 was to sell sterling. This set the tone for the following months: on one side a new government anxious to prove it was making a difference, on the other currency dealers dumping sterling because they doubted the government's seriousness about tackling Britain's deficit.

The centrepiece of Labour's first term was the National Plan (the first and only such plan in British history), published by George Brown in September 1965 as the work of the newly created Department of Economic Affairs. It was inspired in part by the French model of indicative planning and set a series of five-year targets, together with a check list of thirty-nine actions by which the Plan's aims were to be achieved. Both the Confederation of British Industry (CBI) and the Trades Union Congress (TUC) gave their support, even if they harboured doubts about the optimistic forecasts the document contained. The problem was that the conception of the Plan owed as much to political calculations as it did to economics. After despairing at 'thirteen wasted years' of Conservative rule and promising a new 'white-hot' age of science-led growth, Labour had to set itself eye-catching targets to match its campaign rhetoric. Thus the Plan envisaged a 25 per cent increase in output by 1970, setting accompanying targets in areas such as labour productivity and export performance, and promising supply-side improvements in education and training, research in high-tech industries and action against monopolies. All of this was to be achieved within a ceiling on public expenditure growth, met in part by reductions in overseas spending. As a declaration of faith in the government's ability to micro-manage the economy, free from the restraining influence of the all-powerful Treasury, the Plan was a presentational triumph. But what choked it from the start was the Chancellor's need to damp down consumer demand and reduce public spending to defend the exchange rate. In April 1965 Callaghan had increased direct and indirect taxation. The following July he held back £350 million of public investment in schools, hospitals and local authority projects. Further cuts would follow as the government retreated against the currency speculators. In essence, Labour's modernisation strategy and the National Plan were one and the same: within a year both were left in ruins.

The Labour left complained throughout the first term that the government had lost sight of its socialist principles, taking only scant comfort from Wilson's reassurance that the defence of sterling was merely phase one of a more radical project, to be followed by phase two in which more 'positive policies' would be pursued (Crossman 1979: 138). The diaries of Wilson's former Bevanite colleagues – Benn, Castle and Crossman – show them constantly manoeuvring for influence within the 'court of King Harold', sometimes chiding him for snubbing the left, other times wanting to believe that Wilson truly was the Bolshevik surrounded by Tsarists he had claimed to be on becoming leader in 1963. But the longer they waited for Wilson to reveal his radical intent, the more angered and embarrassed they became at the course their government was taking. Spending cuts were one grievance, another was the wage restraint pushed by the Prices and Incomes Board after it was established in February 1965. The success of the Labour right-wing rebels Woodrow Wyatt and Desmond Donnelly in blocking plans to renationalise steel in May 1965 was seen by Barbara Castle as 'the worst blow yet for the Government' (Castle 1990: 17). More galling still was the refusal of Labour's 'Big Three' to allow the Cabinet to debate the merits of defending sterling rather than devaluing. At a special weekend Cabinet meeting at Chequers in September 1965, Castle brought up two further issues. The first was immigration policy. Here Labour faced the charge of disowning its internationalist heritage by tightening up entry controls into Britain (see below). The second was the Vietnam war, an issue which eventually became the left's main indictment against a government which they increasingly felt had betrayed them. Anger at the war was what pulled together otherwise diverse oppositional forces in Britain and beyond at this time. It was the 'left litmus paper' in the sixties (Walker 1987: 201). In the left's view unless you opposed the war you must be for it. And it was the Wilson government's consistent diplomatic support for American policy in Vietnam, even though Britain committed no troops to the conflict, that enraged them. They were right to suspect that this support was part of the price to be paid for the US Federal Reserve's help in defending sterling. Frank Cousins had asked Wilson in May 1965 why he had not taken a firmer stand against American policy in Vietnam. 'Because we can't kick our creditors in the balls', came the reply (Goodman 1979: 492–3). But in any case Wilson was neither the first nor the last British Prime Minister to protect the Atlantic alliance by all means necessary, cultivating his personal relations with President Johnson with some success. Johnson welcomed Wilson's effort to use the Commonwealth as a mediator in the search for a diplomatic solution to the Vietnam conflict in June 1965. The initiative also bought him some time with the Labour left, at least until the Americans extended the war by bombing oil installations in the North Vietnamese cities of Hanoi and Haiphong in June 1966.

The Labour government's policy on Vietnam found stronger support among Conservatives than it did within its own ranks. A broadly bipartisan approach was also apparent over the Rhodesian situation, a diplomatic problem which Labour inherited from Douglas-Home's government. In November 1965 this problem escalated into a crisis when Ian Smith's white supremacist regime in Rhodesia declared independence on the basis of an apartheid-style constitution that guaranteed white minority rule. Despite urgings from some quarters that British troops be used to force the Smith government to climb down, economic sanctions were the favoured tool. Sanctions against Rhodesia combined principle and pragmatism, avoiding a potentially messy armed confrontation at a time when the government was expecting to seek early re-election. A bonus for Labour was the embarrassment that sanctions against Rhodesia caused for Edward Heath, whose Conservative Party split three ways on the issue. Right-wing Tories opposed any action against their white 'kith and kin' in Africa, some on the Conservative left supported the Wilson line, and Heath tried to steer the rest of the party along a middle course which backed limited but not 'punitive' sanctions. Tony Benn was delighted at how the Tories were:

> splitting up and splintering before our eyes. Heath is a pathetic figure, kicked this way and that, and is incapable of giving firm leadership. Home and Selwyn Lloyd are really running the Tory party now and are much firmer on Rhodesia than Heath. Our massive lead of 18.5 per cent in the Gallup polls reflects a failure by Heath and the fact that Harold is emerging as a father figure for the whole nation.
>
> (Benn 1987: 354)

With this lead in the polls, and following a morale-boosting hold at the Hull North by-election in January, during which Labour increased its majority, Wilson called an election for March 1966. Labour appealed for a mandate to complete the tasks it had begun eighteen months earlier and

TABLE 7.1 ◆ *Results of the General Election, 31 March 1966*

	Total Votes	MPs Elected	Candidates	% Share of Total Vote
Conservative	11,418,433	253	629	41.9
Labour	13,064,951	363	621	47.9
Liberal	2,327,533	12	311	8.5
Communist	62,112	−	57	0.2
Plaid Cymru	61,071	−	20	0.2
Scottish National Party	128,474	−	20	0.2
Others	201,302	2	49	0.6
	27,263,606	630	1,707	100.0

Electorate 35,964,684

Turnout 75.8%

Source: Butler, D. and Butler, G. (1994) *British Political Facts, 1900–1994*, London: Macmillan, p. 217.

was rewarded with a 97-seat majority. It was a 'doctor's mandate' to continue working, this time with greater authority. As Ben Pimlott argued: 'The election was the culmination of a fifteen-year journey by the Labour Party and its Leader. Wilson and his party had promised a social revolution: now was the time' (1992: 400).

The politics of race and immigration

Race and immigration were two of the most high-profile issues facing the Wilson government. Indeed the development of parts of the country into more multi-ethnic and multi-cultural places was one of the most profound social and cultural changes to transform sixties Britain. The influx of migrants from the New Commonwealth – India, Pakistan, the West Indies and newly independent African territories – was predominantly an English phenomenon, and even then its impact tended to be confined to the major conurbations of Greater London, the West Midlands, the North West and the North East. But despite this geographical specificity, race and immigration policy remained at the top of the political agenda throughout the decade, occasionally erupting into public debate and dominating the front pages and airwaves. In February 1965 Richard Crossman, the Minister for Housing and Local Government, judged immigration policy to be the 'hottest potato in politics' (1979: 73). Three years later, tens of thousands of London dockers and meat porters marched through Westminster in support of Enoch Powell's call for a halt to further large-scale immigration into Britain. The issue was not one of over-population: on balance the country was a net exporter of population throughout the sixties (as had long been the case), with the flow of migrants who left the UK usually exceeding new arrivals by some 20,000 to 60,000 annually. Rather, what was at stake was the widespread perception that the flow of immigrants from the New Commonwealth into the UK (running at about 70,000 a year during the 'bulge' period of 1965–74) was eroding long-held conceptions of white British national identity. A former colonial power which had internalised notions of racial superiority at all levels of society, and which had successfully fought two major wars in the last fifty years, in some senses assumed that it had earned itself the right to permanently fix notions of (white) Britishness. Adjusting to the realities of post-war and post-colonial migration was for many the most unwelcome feature of changing times.

At the level of high politics, race and immigration policy was focused on two principal areas: controlling the numbers and tackling a culture of racial discrimination. The former was always easier to achieve than the latter. In 1962, following the previous year's strong demonstration of support for immigration controls at their party conference, Macmillan's Conservative government passed the Commonwealth Immigrants Act. Its primary purpose was to limit the influx of non-white immigrants from the New Commonwealth, restricting entry into Britain to those citizens who had been granted vouchers by the Ministry of Labour. These vouchers were the key to the gate, with priority given to those migrants who had employment already arranged in Britain (category A) or who possessed skills or qualifications which were in short supply (category B). All other intending migrants (category C) went on to a waiting list, with ex-servicemen given a front place in the queue. There was never any question that Britain sought to limit migration from the predominantly white Dominions of Australia, Canada, and New Zealand, nor from white South Africa; neither did the Act apply to the Irish Republic, which had reciprocal citizenship arrangements with the UK. The main significance of the legislation lay in the way it conceptualised non-white immigration as a problem that had to be checked by entry restrictions. Thus began the 'numbers game' approach to immigration, the logical outcome of which

PLATE 1 ◆ *British Prime Minister Harold Wilson and President Johnson take time out from talks on Vietnam to pose for pictures in Johnson's office at the White House, February 8, 1968.*

© Bettman/Corbis.

PLATE 2 ◆ *23 April 1968: Demonstrating dock workers, holding banners in support of Conservative politician Enoch Powell, march past Monument in the City of London, on their way to the House of Commons.*

PLATE 3 ◆ *Anti-Vietnamese War Demonstration, London, 1968.*

PLATE 4 ◆ *British soldiers patrol the streets of Belfast during the period of civil unrest in July 1970.*

© Hulton-Deutsch Collection/CORBIS.

PLATE 5 ◆ *Carnaby Street, the 'Mod' Scene.*

PLATE 6 ◆ *29 August 1970: Isle of Wight Pop Festival. From the hillside, camping pop fans look down on the jammed area behind the fence.*

© Bettman/Corbis.

PLATE 7 ◆ *The Beatles, 'All you need is love'. L–R: George Harrison, Paul McCartney (front), Ringo Starr, John Lennon, 1967.*

© Hulton-Deutsch Collection/CORBIS.

PLATE 8 ◆ *Barclaycard advertisement.*

The Advertising Archive, Ltd.

PLATE 9 ◆ *General Charles de Gaulle, French statesman and President of the Fifth French Republic, speaks in Paris in 1967 about the United Kingdom's entry into the European Economic Community.*

PLATE 10 ◆ *31st October 1969: The Queen's Buildings housing estate in Southwark, London.*

Photo by Evening Standard/Getty Images.

PLATE 11 ◆ *Family hugging outside home, 1960s.*

© Hulton-Deutsch Collection/CORBIS.

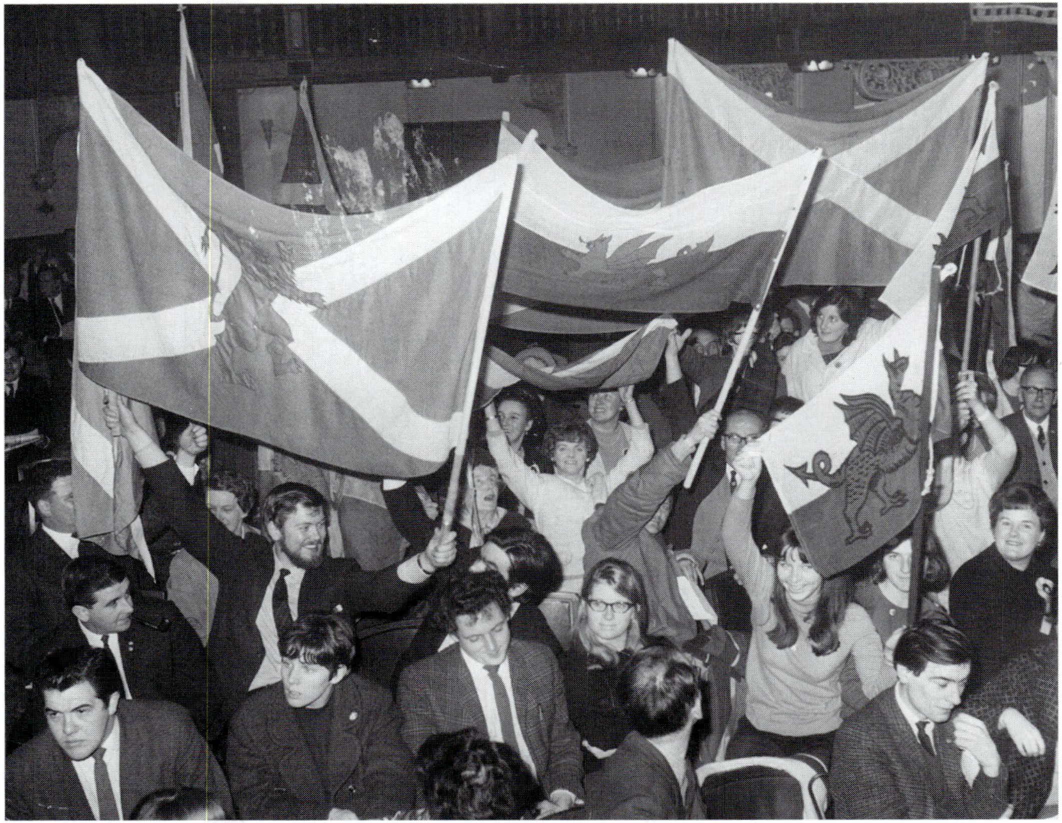

PLATE 12 ◆ *16 November 1967: Members of the Scottish National Party and Plaid Cymru (the Welsh National Party) during a joint conference at Caxton Hall in London, celebrating Scottish Nationalist Winifred Ewing MP taking her seat at the House of Commons.*

Photo by Wesley/Keystone/Getty Images.

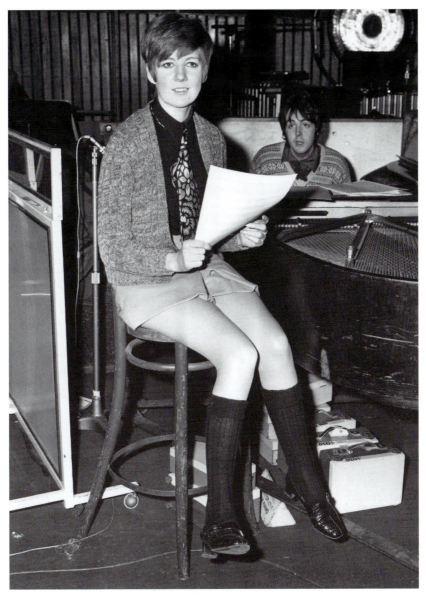

PLATE 13 ◆ *Cilla Black at Chappell Studios, London, recording 'Step Inside Love,' composed for her by Paul McCartney (background).*

© Hulton-Deutsch Collection/CORBIS.

PLATE 14 ◆ *The Kray twins at home after having been questioned by police about the murder of George Cornell in 1966.*

© Hulton-Deutsch Collection/CORBIS.

PLATE 15 ◆ *Richard Hamilton, My Marilyn, 1965. Screenprint on paper. Tate Gallery, London.*

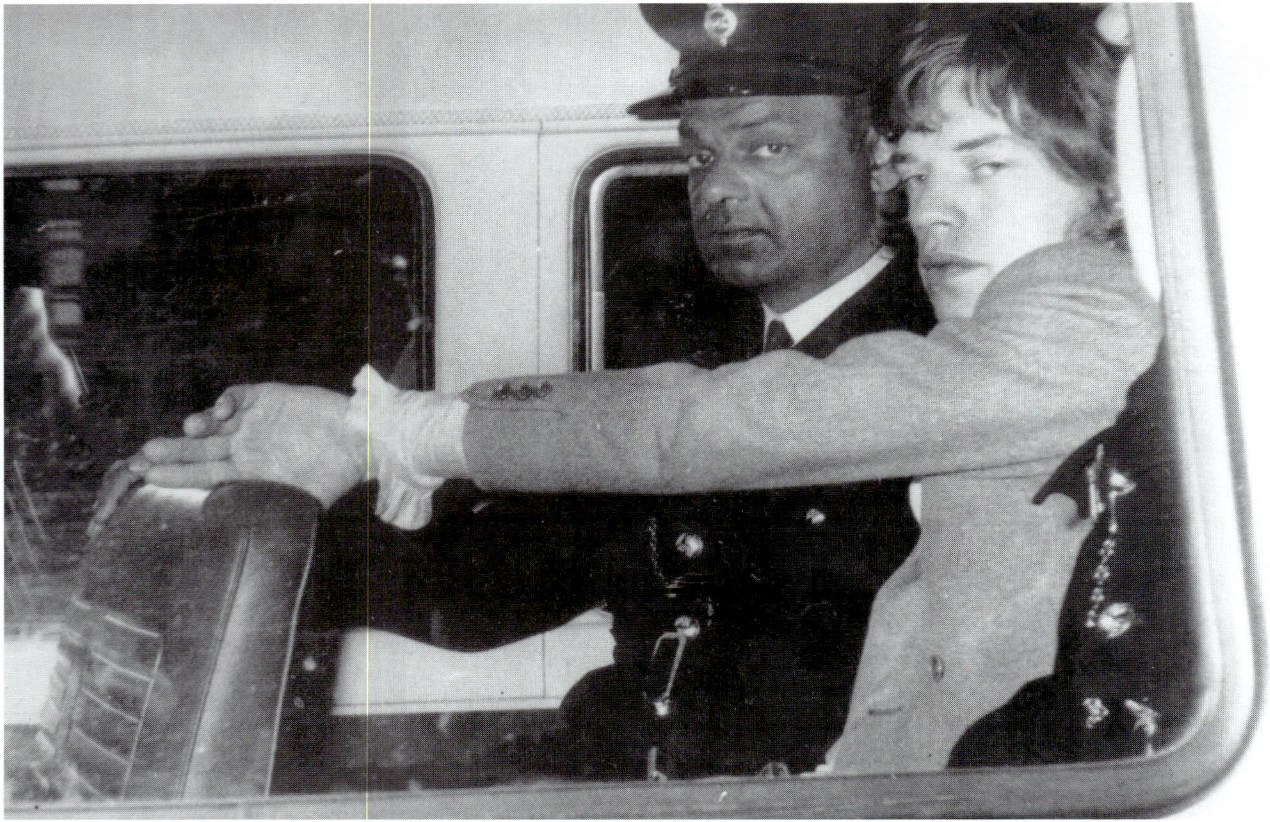

PLATE 16 ◆ *Mick Jagger, singer of British pop group The Rolling Stones, is driven to Brixton prison to begin a three-month sentence for drug offences. He was released pending an appeal the next day.*

Photo by Keystone/Getty Images.

– at a time when opinion polls showed some 70 per cent public support for controls – was a progressive tightening of restrictions. Ironically the Act led to a rush of immigrants from the Caribbean, scrambling to arrive before the new restrictions came into force. Another unforeseen consequence was that, whereas migration had previously occurred back and forth between Britain and the New Commonwealth depending on the fluctuations of the trade cycle, the new legislation encouraged a trend towards permanent migration (Holmes 1988: 263).

Labour had strongly opposed the 1962 Act, led by Gaitskell's moral objections to what he regarded as a racist measure which would damage Commonwealth relations. The political problem for Labour, however, was that the liberal views of the leadership were not widely shared among the party's core working-class support. The view of the West Ham Constituency Labour Party, for example, was fairly typical, calling in 1961 for all immigrants to undergo medical examinations and for entry to be restricted only to those who had arranged housing and employment in advance (Donnelly 1994: 225). The possible electoral damage of a perception that Labour was 'soft' on immigration became apparent in the West Midlands' constituency of Smethwick in the 1964 election. Patrick Gordon Walker (Shadow Foreign Secretary) was defeated by the Conservative candidate, Peter Griffiths, who fought an essentially single-issue campaign which pledged his support for tougher entry controls and highlighted Gordon Walker's liberal contributions to the debate on the 1962 Act. 'If you want a nigger neighbour, vote Liberal or Labour' was the slogan coined by Griffiths' campaign supporters, who engineered a victory that defied the national swing towards Labour. Wilson took a seemingly tough stance when the Commons reassembled and controversially declared that Griffiths would be treated as a 'parliamentary leper'. But the new Prime Minister was pragmatic enough to read the wider signals. For the first time, racism had been injected into national politics and it had damaged Labour electorally (Hiro 1991: 44). Within months of taking office, Labour dropped its objections to the 1962 Act and renewed the legislation, even tightening up on ways in which the restrictions were being evaded. In August 1965 it went a stage further and issued a White Paper, 'Immigration from the Commonwealth', which cut back the number of entry vouchers issued annually from 20,800 to 8,500 and abolished category C. As Barbara Castle, who fought the White Paper in

Cabinet, noted in her diary, this meant 'picking all the skilled workers for ourselves. This "one-way technical assistance" was nauseating', she added (1990: 24). Crossman mused that the White Paper would 'probably have a deeper undermining effect on the moral strength of Harold Wilson's leadership than any other thing that we have done' (1979: 132). But he saw no easy way of avoiding the electoral imperative of taking a 'tough' stand on entry controls, writing in his diary on the day the White Paper was published:

> *This has been one of the most difficult and unpleasant jobs the*
> *Government has had to do. We have become illiberal and lowered the*
> *quotas at a time when we have an acute shortage of labour. No wonder*
> *all the weekend liberal papers have been bitterly attacking us.*
> *Nevertheless, I am convinced that if we hadn't done all this we would*
> *have been faced with certain electoral defeat in the Midlands and the*
> *South-East. Politically, fear of immigration is the most powerful*
> *undertow today.*
>
> (Crossman 1979: 132)

Unease at Labour policy was assuaged slightly by the adoption of a 'twin-track' strategy in which the government combined tighter entry controls with measures designed to ease racial integration and outlaw racial discrimination. The need for such measures was becoming ever more difficult to ignore as the daily routine of Britain's still small immigrant population came to include casual discrimination, ingrained racist attitudes within institutions such as the police and local authorities, and in some cases violent racial abuse. Pressure groups such as the Birmingham Immigration Control Association and the Southall Residents' Association made life worse by presenting Britain's majority white urban population as the true victims of population movement, claiming that essential public services in their locality were being overrun by the pressure of new arrivals. Labour, at least, had some credentials in attacking such prejudices, with party members prominent both in the Movement for Colonial Freedom and the anti-apartheid campaign. During the long years in opposition, backbench Labour MPs such as Fenner Brockway had tried to use Private Members' Bills to outlaw racial discrimination but had been frustrated by the Conservatives. Now in office they had a chance to make some headway. In March 1965 Maurice

Foley was appointed to the new post of Ministerial Co-ordinator of Policy on Integration, with the main tasks of liaising with voluntary sector race relations agencies and reviewing the role local authorities could play in promoting racial integration. More importantly, Frank Soskice, the Home Secretary, drew up what became the first Race Relations Act. Soskice enlisted Conservative frontbenchers to help draft the legislation, the advantage being that cross-party cooperation defused a potentially explosive issue, forging a bi-partisan consensus around a set of injunctions which could be sold to a doubtful public. The disadvantage of the tactic was that Soskice was unable to prevent the Conservatives from drawing most of the teeth from the Act. Although the legislation aimed to outlaw racial discrimination in public places, discrimination was not made a criminal offence in 1965. Instead, complaints were to be referred to a new Race Relations Board which would then attempt to conciliate between the two sides. The Board's powers, however, were so limited that it could not even compel witnesses to attend hearings. From the moment it was created, the Board, chaired initially by Mark Lennox Boyd, called for an extension of its powers. Another crucial omission was that housing and employment were not covered by the Act, leaving landlords and employers free to discriminate on racial grounds. Not surprisingly, therefore, the immediate impact of the Race Relations Act was minimal. But, if nothing else, it at least set down a marker of acceptable behaviour and provided a starting point for more ambitious extensions (Saggar 1992: 80). The Race Relations Board was also able to sponsor research which eventually helped to convince policy-makers that racial discrimination was occurring on a large enough scale to justify further and tougher legislation later in the decade.

· · · · · · · · · · · · · · ·

CHAPTER 8

Permissiveness and counter-culture

The permissive era?

The 'liberal hour' arrived in the sixties, heralding what Marwick described as the 'end of Victorianism' (1990: 141–53). Advertising and the media became more graphically sexualised, symbolised at the decade's close, on 18 November 1969, by the first appearance of (model Uschi Obermeier's) bare nipples in a centre-page spread in Rupert Murdoch's newly-acquired *Sun* newspaper – the topless 'page three girl' would arrive a year later. There were major reforms of the laws relating to capital punishment, abortion, divorce and homosexuality. The wider availability (and use) of contraceptives – including the Pill from early 1961 – made for greater sexual freedom and a reduced risk of unwanted pregnancy. The sheer joylessness of Sundays was no longer so rigidly imposed. Restrictions on gambling were relaxed and censorship of books, plays and films was liberalised, if not abandoned entirely. Of course there were limits. A permissive state is not the same as a permissive society. People may have had more freedom to do all kinds of things in the sixties (and indeed they may have welcomed it) but they did not necessarily exercise that freedom. Individuals often expressed liberal attitudes on issues of personal morality but behaved in ways that were little different from their more morally buttoned-up predecessors. Also, surveys consistently highlighted the continued power of moral conservatism across age ranges and class divisions throughout the decade. Commenting on a survey in *New Society* in November 1969 illustrating deep popular unease about liberal law reforms, strong support for the death penalty and even higher levels of support for the notion that 'too much publicity was given to sex', the editor Paul Barker asked: 'Shouldn't one talk about the Cautious Sixties rather than the Swinging Sixties?' (1969: 850).

The permissive reputation of the sixties, however, has stuck. In large part this is because the legislative framework regulating sexual behaviour and public morality in Britain since Victorian times was overhauled during the period. Permissiveness in this sense was handed down from above rather than taken from below. As Christie Davies argued in *Permissive Britain*, the period saw a shift in moral attitudes among lawmakers from 'moralism' to 'causalism': in essence, rather than judge a given activity against a fixed set of Christian ethics, the question for legislators was whether the social consequences of permitting such an activity were predominantly beneficial or harmful (Davies 1975: 3). The first breakthrough in this new moral paradigm came when Penguin Books re-issued D.H. Lawrence's *Lady Chatterley's Lover*, a novel exploring the sexual relationship between the lady of a great house and her husband's gamekeeper. The book in its uncut form had been banned since the 1920s because of its (for the time) graphic sexual content and 'Anglo-Saxon' vocabulary. The decision to re-issue came in the wake of the 1959 Obscene Publications Act, which stated that a work could be defended against an obscenity charge provided it had sufficient literary merit. It also followed a successful test case brought by Groves Press in the United States, where publication of Lawrence's novel was now allowed on the grounds of its 'redeeming social importance'. When Penguin Books were prosecuted for issuing *Lady Chatterley* they were able to call in their defence a formidable collection of writers, intellectuals, churchmen and the 'great and the good' to testify to the book's literary qualities. Against them was the prosecution counsel, Mervyn Griffiths-Jones, the high-cheek-boned and poker-backed veteran of Eton, Trinity Hall (Cambridge), the Coldstream Guards and many previous obscenity cases (in Kenneth Tynan's description) whose patronising manner alienated rather than impressed the jury (Connolly 1995: 10–12). The five-day trial became a symbolic contest between an old public-school patrician elite and a post-Butler-Act grammar school generation. It was resolved in favour of those who no longer wanted to be told what they could read. Penguin's victory and the publicity generated by the court case helped them to sell two million copies of *Lady Chatterley* within the year, and it encouraged other publishers to take a more adventurous approach to their catalogue. As the decade wore on, the police and prosecuting authorities became increasingly reluctant to take action against publishers. However, they did not give up intervention completely. John Cleland's *Fanny Hill* (1963), Alex Trocchi's account of drug addiction in *Cain's Book* (1964), William Burroughs's *The Naked Lunch* (1964) and Hubert Selby Junior's descriptions of sex, excess and gang rape in *Last Exit to Brooklyn* (1966) all led to court cases (all were eventually permitted publication). Moreover, the Obscene Publications Act was not the only weapon the authorities could employ. In January 1970 three directors of the counter-cultural paper *International Times* were charged and convicted of conspiracy to corrupt public morals and outrage public decency – because the paper's personal columns contained gay contact adverts. They were each fined and sentenced to twenty months' imprisonment. The following August, another underground publication *Oz* was charged with obscenity because of its 'School Kids' Issue' of April 1970; following the trial in June–July 1971 its three editors were initially given custodial sentences of between nine and fifteen months, but these were overturned on appeal (Green 1998b: 350–377). The state, in other words, was prepared to allow publishers much greater latitude, but it reserved the right to issue reminders that some boundaries remained.

Roy Jenkins had played a role in shaping the Obscene Publications Act and had been one of the defence witnesses in the *Lady Chatterley's Lover* trial. His 1959 book *The Labour Case*, written for the election of that year, contained a chapter called 'Is Britain Civilised?'. Here he reiterated Tony Crosland's argument in *The Future of Socialism*, where he had written that in the blood of a socialist there should always run 'a trace of the anarchist and the libertarian, and not too much of the prig and the prude' (1956: 355). The state, Jenkins agreed with Crosland, should not impinge excessively on people's private lives and personal morality, nor should it exceed its powers to punish those who transgressed the law. Both of them calculated that in an affluent society in which the manual working class was apparently shrinking, the old 'holy trinity' of Labourism – full employment, welfare and nationalisation – was not enough to win elections. Labour needed new modern projects, and a programme to increase personal freedoms would at least attract support from bourgeois liberals. When Jenkins was appointed Home Secretary in December 1965 he found himself with the power to act on his own advice. The subsequent burst of reforms were not government policy as such – the key pieces of legislation involved matters of conscience and were carried via Private Members' Bills and free votes. But it was the new Home Secretary who sought out backbench sponsors for the Bills and who ensured that sufficient parliamentary time was made available for them to complete their journey into law.

The Sexual Offences Bill was the first such measure, eventually passing through the House of Commons between 10.00 p.m. and 6.00 a.m. on 3–4 July 1967. This reform finally reversed the 'Labouchere amendment' of 1885 which had covered all homosexual acts with a blanket of illegality. It represented victory at last for the Homosexual Law Reform Society, which had been pressing since 1958 for implementation of the Wolfenden Committee report's main recommendations on homosexuality, published in 1957. The Labour backbencher Leo Abse, whose previous attempts at reform in this area had failed, led the Bill through the lower House, deploying arguments in favour of reform which he later described as 'absolute crap – and I knew it', but which were designed to position the debate on the least hazardous moral ground. During the Bill's passage sceptics were reassured that there was never any question of homosexuality being endorsed as a valid sexual orientation. Instead, it was argued, homosexuals should be seen as unfortunates who suffered from a psychological malfunction, deserving pity and treatment rather than imprisonment. Moreover, the law as it stood amounted to a 'blackmailer's charter', leaving vulnerable men open to the kind of extortion that had been shown in the film *Victim* (1961), in which a criminal threatened to expose a barrister's hesitant connections with a homosexual 'underworld'. The Sexual Offences Act was carefully limited in its scope. It was in tune with Wolfenden's view in 1957 that the intention of reform was not to give 'a general licence to adult homosexuals to behave as they please'. The new law decriminalised homosexual acts in private between two adult men (defined as aged 21 and over, five years above the age of consent for heterosexual sex), except in the merchant navy and the armed forces which were excluded from the Act entirely. Northern Ireland also remained exempt from this law until 1981, when decriminalisation was effectively imposed on the whole of Ireland by the EEC. Reform essentially arose from the utilitarian philosophical position which held that the criminal law should be used to serve the public good rather than to impose a particular pattern of moral behaviour on individuals. The Act never challenged the assumption that homosexuality was 'abnormal', and it insisted that individual freedoms in this area could be exercised only behind closed doors. Definitions of 'public decency' meant that activities such as importuning in public lavatories and cruising grounds remained offences. The police were keen to enforce this distinction between private and public behaviour: between 1967 and 1976 the number of prosecutions of males for indecency trebled and the number of convictions quadrupled (Weeks 1989: 275). Thus the Gay Liberation Front, which was founded in October 1970, was less than satisfied with the 1967 Act, insisting that further change had to recognise the absolute validity of homosexuality as a sexual orientation. The next advances, they argued, had to be won by the gay community themselves rather than be handed down from on high by an elite (Weeks 1989: 285–6). The most difficult challenge they faced was to defuse popular hostility towards homosexuality. Geoffrey Gorer's 1969 survey of attitudes among under-45s in England found that there was much work to do. Only 12 per cent of his sample displayed even a 'tolerant' attitude towards homosexuality, meanwhile 24 per cent expressed 'revulsion' and a further 22 per cent 'pity' (1973: 255).

In the same year the Sexual Offences Act was passed, the Liberal backbencher David Steel's Bill to legalise abortion also became law. It was a controversial measure that was opposed by a national campaign led by the Catholic Church, and it was almost frustrated by a cross-party alliance of MPs (which included Leo Abse and other supporters of homosexual law reform) who hoped to see it fall through shortage of parliamentary time. Again the reformers were grateful to Roy Jenkins for helping to ensure that the Commons sat throughout the night on 13–14 July, and for threatening to keep it sitting through Friday and Saturday night if necessary, so that the Bill could complete its third reading. The new law permitted an abortion within the first 28 weeks of pregnancy provided that two doctors confirmed it was necessary either on medical or psychological grounds. Thus, for the first time, an abortion could be allowed on 'social' grounds, rather than exclusively on the narrow justification that a termination was required to safeguard the mother's health. In effect the responsibility for policing abortion passed from the police themselves and the courts to (usually male) doctors. There was no question, however, that abortion was now being defined in terms of a woman's 'right to choose'. As Steel himself stated, the reformers were not aiming to leave an open door for abortions on request. Their main object-ive was to stamp out the trade in back-street abortions, destroying the market for the kind of dangerous and degrading operations that had been brought to wider public attention in the iconic 'swinging London' film *Alfie* (1966). The argument for reforming the abortion laws, therefore, was won on utilitarian rather than narrowly moral grounds: legalised abortion was a lesser evil than unregulated abortion. Reformers also hoped that by improving the provision of sex education and counselling, there would be fewer unwanted pregnancies and terminations. In reality the number of abortions climbed sharply, rising from 35,000 per annum in 1968 to 141,000 in 1975; or, put another way, increasing from a rate of 4 per 100 live births in 1968 to 17.6 in 1975 (Weeks 1989: 275). The fact that women clearly were using abortion as an adjunct to other forms of birth control led campaigners such as the Society for the Protection of the Unborn Child to seek to reverse, or at least amend, the 1967 Act. This in turn produced a rearguard defence of the legislation marshalled by groups that included the National Abortion Campaign. They argued that abortion had to be defended as part of a wider principle: women's rights to control their own bodies.

A Bill to liberalise the divorce laws was also introduced during the 1967 parliamentary session but failed through lack of time. It later resur-faced and became the Divorce Reform Act of 1969. Before this change in the law a married person was required to prove that their partner had committed a matrimonial offence (usually adultery) for a divorce to be granted by the courts. The 1969 Act introduced the 'no fault' divorce, based on the concept of an 'irretrievable breakdown' in marriage. A couple who had lived apart for two years could obtain a divorce if both partners gave their consent; if separation lasted for five years a divorce could be granted with the consent of one partner only. Court proceedings now became a more civilised inquest into whether a marriage had finally broken down beyond repair, not a tribunal at which moral blame had to be assigned to one of the parties – a process which had frequently relied on surveillance evidence collected by private detectives. The task of the divorce courts was to end 'empty shell' marriages with as much fairness and as little distress as possible to the concerned parties. Ultimately, it was hoped that the new law would help to *support* marriages that had a chance of survival, because whereas before the proof of a single adulterous act alone was sufficient grounds for divorce, now the petitioner had to show that the marriage was no longer sustainable. Once again, however, the law of unintended consequences took effect and reform was followed by an acceleration in a divorce rate that had been rising steadily anyway since the 1910s. In the mid-fifties the divorce rate stood at around 7 per cent, by the early 1970s the figure was 10 per cent and climbing. Between 1970 and 1979 the divorce rate among the under-25s trebled, and doubled for those over 25. By the end of the seventies, one in three marriages ended in divorce (though most divorcees remarried), leading to fears that the concept of a 'marriage for life' had been fatally undermined, with all that implied for family and wider social life in Britain (Weeks 1989: 274).

The significance of the opening-up of personal freedoms allowed by the law in the sixties should not be under-estimated. But nor should the reforms be misread as evidence in the wider debate about permissiveness. Although there were specific factors that helped to explain the timing of reforms in the 1960s, efforts to change the laws as they related to censorship, homosexuality, abortion and divorce had been gathering pace since at least the 1950s and in some cases much earlier. Reforms, in other words, were not purely products of a changed moral climate in the sixties, but were the end points of a more gradual process of liberalisation (Fisher 1993: 163–4). In addition, a range of data from opinion polls and social surveys act as a cautionary brake against easy assumptions about sixties permissiveness. The term itself is most commonly associated with the changes in sexual behaviour and attitudes that were believed to have occurred at the time. But, paradoxically, this is one area where the data for measuring change are limited and fragmentary – there was no British equivalent, for example, of the Kinsey report, a US study of sexual behaviour (Davies 1975: 61–2). The two issues in this sensitive field which did seem to preoccupy researchers in Britain were levels of promiscuity and the incidence of pre-marital sexual intercourse. Michael Schofield's 1969 fieldwork for *The Sexual Behaviour of Young Adults* found that only 17 per cent of his sample of 25-year-olds had had more than one sexual partner in the past year (1973: 179). Geoffrey Gorer's survey for the *Sunday Times* in the late 1960s found that a quarter of men and nearly two-thirds of women said they were virgins when they married (Weeks 1989: 254). When the *Sun* asked the same question about pre-marital virginity of its working-class readership in 1971, it found a similar response among men, but 90 per cent of its female respondents stated that they had been virgins on their wedding day (Chippindale and Horrie 1990: 28). Investigating the allied issue of the use of contraception, Gorer's survey *Sex and Marriage in England Today* (1971) found that only 18 per cent of married couples under 45 used the birth control pill, with its use lower still among single women who often found the Pill difficult to obtain. Although the Pill was marketed in Britain from 1963 onwards, it was not made available to single women until 1967. Indeed, the Family Planning Association had only officially begun to give advice about contraception to unmarried women in 1966. Essentially, the Pill was most commonly used by middle-class married women and students. Some women in any case declined to use oral contraception because they feared possible damaging side-effects; it also seems that some men were reluctant to surrender their control over contraception.

Marriage as an institution remained as popular as ever in the sixties, with marriage rates climbing to a peak in 1972 as the post-war 'baby boomers' reached their mid-20s. Gillian Tindall's *New Society* article in May 1968, 'Housewives-To-Be' also found that adolescent girls were as likely as their fifties predecessors to envision their future primarily as housewives and mothers (794–5). Most schools, moreover, were reluctant to provide sex education for their pupils. The more permissive climate of the sixties, therefore, took some time to feed through into behaviour and attitudes. But if we accept that permissiveness was about more than simply personal and sexual morality, that it included such things as autonomy and individualism – 'doing your own thing' – then perhaps its more immediate impact was felt in what was known as the counter-culture.

Counter-culture

The counter-culture (sometimes called the underground) was imported from west-coast America to Britain in the middle of the sixties, functioning primarily as a kind of short-lived, utopian parallel universe for the disaffected young middle class. It was never a homogenous movement with a clearly identifiable membership or manifesto. It was more ephemeral and unstable than that, ranging widely across fields and activities, drawing in an assortment of drop-outs, hippies, students and weekend bohemians with varying levels of commitment, held together in the main by opposition to the Vietnam war and a shared interest in exploring the limits of self-expression and personal freedom. In its most overtly political form, as the embryonic cultural base of New Left politics, the counter-culture drew some inspiration from Mao's cultural revolution in China and looked outwards to the creation of a new society, free from the dominance of bourgeois values, the protestant work ethic and authoritarian controls on freedom. As well as promoting the cause via the underground press and discussion forums, the counter-culture's politically committed followers, split into an array of left-wing groups, such as the International Marxist Group, the International Socialist League and the Socialist Labour League, went head to head with the state's forces with student demonstrations, civil rights marches and anti-war protests across the country. But this was for a minority. For most, the counter-culture was what Charles Shaar Murray called 'a gorgeous, playful and decadent exercise in life-style' (1989: 20). The psychedelic, flower-power imagery provided the dominant aesthetic of the later sixties, and in 'make love not war' the counter-culture coined one of the sharpest advertising slogans of the post-war period. Cynics could dismiss the counter-culture as a self-indulgent, drug-fuelled interlude for a privileged, work-shy minority who would settle down to steady careers once the taste for an alternative lifestyle was out of their system. But such cynicism ignores the heightened sense of idealism that ran through the bloodstream of the counter-culture: idealism about self-fulfilment, free expression, communal values, racial and sexual politics, a clean environment, the nature of work and the opening-up of cultural spaces. The promotion of these ideals was to have consequences throughout the seventies and beyond.

Despite its apparent novelty, the counter-culture drew on a long tradition of resistance to social norms and cultural orthodoxies. Romantic writers of the eighteenth and nineteenth centuries, for example, bequeathed a legacy to the sixties alternative spirit, using opium to escape the constraints of rationalism and producing a radical literature that challenged both received wisdoms and the authority of organised religion. Mick Jagger summoned this Romantic spirit at the Rolling Stones' Hyde Park concert in July 1969, when he read Shelley's poem 'Adonaïs' in memory of Brian Jones, the band's recently dead guitarist (Green 1998b: 116–7). The European *avant-garde* of the early twentieth century was another source of inspiration, feeding into the counter-culture's rejection of formal constraints and artistic conventions in favour of spontaneous 'happenings' and experimentation in Arts Labs around the country. More immediately, the American beat writers of the fifties provided the role models for the alternative lifestyle. Finding nothing to hold their attention in post-war, affluent, consumerist America, the beats went 'on the road', travelling, drinking, taking drugs (marijuana, benzedrine, morphine), listening to jazz and mythologising their experiences in verse or prose form. Neal Cassady, famed for his punishing stints at the wheel of a 1949 Hudson sedan, best embodied the beat spirit. But the key beat texts were written by others within the clique: Jack Kerouac's *On The Road* (begun in 1948 but eventually published in 1957), John Clellon Holmes's *Go* (1952), William Burroughs's *Junkie* (1953) and *Naked Lunch* (1959), and Allen Ginsberg's poem *Howl* (1955). Ginsberg in particular was an important bridge between the American and British alternative scenes, providing the inspiration for the massive poetry reading of June 1965 which drew an audience of seven thousand to the Royal Albert Hall and marked, perhaps, the arrival of the British counter-culture. At one level the Albert Hall poetry reading was a glorious if chaotic summer party, bedecked in flowers and painted in psychedelic swirls. At another level it was an early gathering of the counter-cultural tribe, as the crowd listened to poets (ranging from the internationally renowned to the almost anonymous), looked around at each other and recognised kindred souls. It was a form of union that prefigured the gatherings at rock concerts and festivals later in the decade.

The Albert Hall poetry readings caught the 'do your own thing' ethos of the counter-culture. Within this ethos, of course, there were counter-cultural entrepreneurs, not least the drug dealers who responded to the rising demand for illicit substances. Counter-cultural clubs such as UFO and Middle Earth provided funds for the underground, so too did one-off events like the Fourteen-Hour Technicolor Dream at Alexandra Palace in the 1967 'summer of love'. It was equally true that mainstream commercial interests lost very little time in seeking profits from the underground – EMI records, for example, who set up their own Harvest label as a thinly-disguised counter-cultural subsidiary in June 1969, releasing records by the Edgar Broughton Band, Deep Purple and Pink Floyd. But, in the main, those at the centre of the counter-culture sought to move away from the passive consumption of commercially-packaged mainstream culture. Their alternative was to open up spaces for cultural participation, creating room for people to remake culture from below. The idea was to give a voice to at least some of those who were excluded from the metropolitan inner circle of cultural production. So, for example, with mainstream poetry publishing dominated by the strong voices of Ted Hughes, Sylvia Plath and Philip Larkin, the 'alternative' response was for aspiring poets to duplicate small print-runs of their own work and distribute these via informal networks at bookshops and readings across the country. Small magazines proliferated, ranging from the innumerable poetry and literary magazines with tiny circulations to the radical politics of Tariq Ali's *Black Dwarf*, or Tony Elliott's London listings magazine *Time Out*. *IT* (*International Times*) was a key underground publication, launched at the Round House in Camden in October 1966 with a party featuring sets from Pink Floyd and Soft Machine. The other was *Oz*, started by Richard Neville in February 1967 as the British version of its satirical forerunner in Australia, and positioned as a more graphic, sexual and loosely psychedelic rival to *IT*. Jim Haynes's Arts Lab, set up in Covent Garden in 1967, was the closest the counter-culture came to having an institutional base. The Lab was a spartan, multi-media venue, open through the night, offering films, theatre, rehearsal space, concerts and dance. It was a place for people to meet, eat and drink, until it collapsed through lack of funds in autumn 1969. Haynes' aim had been to recreate the participatory art-and-life-style ethos of his Paperback Book Shop and Traverse Theatre in Edinburgh. The attempt was short-lived, but it inspired some fifty similar ventures in places like Manchester, Birmingham, Brighton, as well as Paris and Amsterdam, some of which remain as permanent centres for the arts. Fringe theatre groups multiplied from the mid sixties in a milieu in which, as Robert Hewison noted, 'there were sound reasons for the theatre to become the principal form through which the politics of the counter-culture found their most lasting expression' (1986: 188–9). Taking their lead from Joan Littlewood's post-war Theatre Workshop and the writers' theatre at the Royal Court,

the new theatre groups aimed to integrate aesthetic and political radicalism. Above all, perhaps, they wished to attract a new audience to the
theatre, experimenting with lunchtime shows, street theatre, community
theatre, improvisations and synergies with poetry, music and dance.
Among the many groups which formed at this time were agit-prop
companies offering politically-committed street theatre. The Cartoon
Archetypal Slogan Theatre was one example, formed by Claire and
Roland Muldoon in 1965 with a preference for 'the shock tactics of the
avant-garde while being defiantly not "arty"' (Rowbotham 2000: 181).
Another was the People Show, which specialised in a 'non-theatrical
theatre' that was best understood as performance art – such as their 'happening' in the bookstore, Better Books, when they wrapped themselves
up in fabric to become living sculptures.

For anyone interested in the ideology of the counter-culture, one
notable shortcoming of the British underground was its failure to produce a major native theorist. European and American gurus were left to
fill the void, with their theories interpreted for a wider British audience
by journals such as *New Left Review* or in more slogan-friendly form
by the underground press. The main social theories they favoured were
engaged in one form or other in a dialogue with Marxism. Herbert
Marcuse, a German intellectual who fled to the United States after helping to reinterpret Marxism for modern times as a member of the Frankfurt
School of critical theory between the wars, told readers of *One
Dimensional Man* (1964) that freedom in modern industrial society was
illusory. Individuals thought they were free, he argued, but in reality
their spiritual and intellectual lives were stunted, leaving them to accept
their place in capitalist society and settle for the materialism and consumerism fed to them by the mass media. The only possible saviours
he saw were those on the radical fringes: students, 'third world' and
black revolutionaries and hippies. In the post-war French academy
structuralists such as Claude Lévi-Strauss, Jacques Lacan and Louis
Althusser held sway, showing, among other things, how bourgeois ideology located individuals in a system of relationships that was necessary
for the maintenance of existing class relations – hence the frequent references to the malign effects of 'the system' in the sixties. Also in France,
post-structuralists like Roland Barthes, Jacques Derrida and Michel
Foucault provided sixties revolutionaries with the intellectual tools to

understand why a cultural revolution targeting bourgeois values, norms and power had to precede any worthwhile political revolution. Political and social structures, they argued, were neither natural nor absolute realities: instead they were imposed by dominant (bourgeois) ways of thinking which made out that the status quo was pre-ordained. Thus political revolution first had to involve an assault on the very *language* itself that transmitted bourgeois values and which served to underpin bourgeois ideological hegemony. Across the Atlantic, Timothy Leary, a Harvard psychologist until his experiments with LSD brought his dismissal in 1963, approached liberation from a different perspective. After taking his first 'magic mushrooms' in August 1960, Leary became the guru of the psychedelic age, founding both the *Psychedelic Review* and the International Federation for Internal Freedom. Here he preached the gospel of mind-expanding drugs as a route to heightened self-knowledge and personal freedom from the multi-layered constraints on the individual imposed by society. Long months of transcendental meditation were one way of tapping into the unconscious material of the mind. A much quicker way was to use drugs to short-circuit the body's central nervous system. This was the philosophy that led Allen Ginsberg in 1966 to urge all healthy Americans over the age of 14 to take at least one acid 'trip', so that they could see 'the New Wilderness of machine America' as it really was (MacDonald 1995: 13–14). Leary famously summed up this particular road to enlightenment with the mantra: 'turn on, tune in, drop out'. Perhaps the closest British equivalent to Leary was R.D. Laing, a Glaswegian psychiatrist who used LSD himself, as well as in the treatment of his patients. Laing was central to the British 'anti-psychiatry' movement which questioned conventional definitions of mental illness as an objective condition. Drawing on Michel Foucault's groundbreaking analysis in *Madness and Civilisation* (originally published as *Folie et déraison* in 1961) the anti-psychiatrists argued that madness was a socially-determined state, defined for the wider society by the medical and political authorities. Moreover, anti-psychiatrists believed that people often exhibited what were defined as the 'normal' symptoms of mental illness because of pressures exerted on them within socially-constructed institutions such as the family. Laing's writings, including *The Politics of Experience* (1967), reached a wide international audience, having an obvious appeal to those who sought confirmation that societal norms were artificial constructs (and therefore easier to reject) rather than objectively-defined 'true' states. Together with like-minded colleagues, he also pioneered new methods of treating schizophrenia at Kingsley Hall, east London, between 1965 and 1970, replacing the factory-like structures of traditional institutions with a communal approach to treatment that stressed the value of natural healing.

The other significant contribution made by Laing and the anti-psychiatrists to the counter-culture came when they convened the 'Congress for the Dialectics of Liberation' conference at the Round House in Camden in July 1967. It was here that the different factions involved in the long front of the liberation struggle met, bringing together theorists such as Laing and Marcuse with the physical force advocates of the revolutionary left, notably the American black power activist Stokeley Carmichael. Perhaps the conference picked up rather than initiated a changing sensibility, but there appeared to be a definite hardening of mood among participants. Far from 'demystifying violence', as it had originally intended, the conference suggested there was a growing appetite for direct action. Parts of the underground seemed intent on moving from what Gramsci had termed 'passive revolution' or a 'war of position' to a new phase of active revolution (1971: 106, 243). Counter-cultural politics was gaining primacy over counter-cultural art, and the politics of choice was confrontational. Some kind of clash with the repressive machinery of the state, it seemed, could no longer be delayed: the scene was set for the street politics and student unrest of 1968.

The counter-culture's political ambitions were never realised, but its values and aesthetics were a rich source of material for those who wished to remake their own identities, or who wanted at least to believe that they could fashion a greater sense of autonomy for themselves. It was always the case that, outside a core 'in-crowd' who defined the British scene – documented in Jonathon Green's oral history *Days in the Life: Voices from the English Underground* (1998a) – most of those who were inter-ested in the counter-culture experienced it in mediated ways. They read the magazines, wore the freaky clothes, tuned in to John Peel's late-night show on Radio One, listened to the Beatles' albums from *Revolver* (1966) and *Sergeant Pepper's Lonely Hearts Club Band* (1967) onwards, or to rock groups like the Doors, Jefferson Airplane and the Grateful Dead, and perhaps went to the Isle of Wight festivals of 1968, 1969 and 1970.

So despite the counter-culture's essentially anti-capitalist stance, most people who engaged with it did so via simple acts of consumption. The underground for them was a set of commodities. But, as cultural studies has taught us, self-reflexivity – the cultivation of the self, physically as well as psychologically – is intricately bound up with the process of consumption (Mort 1996: 6). One of the important points about the counter-culture was that it provided a new liberationist fantasy with which people could connect. Of course it also had its downside. As Sheila Rowbotham, whose connection with the underground was more active than most, recalled:

> I could see the tribe-like underground possessed its own snobberies and conceits like any other social world. In rejecting the ways of 'straight' culture, hippies surreptitiously introduced implicit conventions of their own. Exclusivity and hierarchy appeared and were policed with the sneering snobbery of 'cool'. The hippie subcultures which formed, renouncing these hip aristocracies, were, in their turn, rapidly to be soured by that curse of those who would purify – sanctimony and pride.
>
> (Rowbotham 2000: 133–4)

Feminists also saw that the narrative of the counter-culture was male-dominated and that its ideal of 'sexual liberation' was typically defined on men's terms. There was a heightened sense among some women that if they rebuffed a sexual advance it would be interpreted as a sign of their 'bourgeois repression'. According to artist Nicola Lane:

> It was paradise for men in their late twenties, all these willing girls. But the trouble with the willing girls was that a lot of the time they were willing not because they particularly fancied the people concerned but because they felt they ought to. There was a huge pressure to conform to non-conformity. . . . What it meant was that men fucked around. You'd cry a lot, and you would scream sometimes, and the man would say, 'Don't bring me down, don't lay your bummers on me . . . don't hassle me, don't crowd my space'.
>
> (Green 1998a: 418–19)

As we will see it was partly in response to these pressures exerted within the counter-culture that the Women's Liberation Movement emerged at the end of the decade.

CHAPTER 9

Poverty and devaluation

The rediscovery of poverty

As the press and culture industries focused on the boutiques and galleries of 'swinging London', it was easy for them to miss the evidence of a disturbing underside to the gaudy materialism and credit-fuelled affluence of the high sixties. On 22 December 1965 two LSE academics, Brian Abel-Smith and Peter Townsend, attempted to counter this ignorance by publishing *The Poor and the Poorest*. It was a sharp reminder that there was an underclass in Britain which the post-war economic boom had simply bypassed. Worse still, Britain's poorest were surrounded on all sides by material abundance and comforts which for them lay constantly just out of reach, perpetual reminders of the widening gap between the 'haves' and the 'have-nots'. *The Poor and the Poorest* was a detailed survey of poverty amid prosperity which showed that the post-war welfare state had not been as effective as some had supposed at lifting people above the poverty line. Across Britain there were millions of individuals and families who frequently faced a day-to-day struggle to make ends meet. Abel-Smith and Townsend, who timed the release of their findings to capture the pre-Christmas headlines and maximise the survey's emotional impact, based their research around a detailed analysis of both the Ministry of Labour's Household Expenditure Surveys and the government's National Assistance Scales. At the press conference on 23 December to launch the survey's findings, the authors ensured that their dry statistics were accompanied with real human stories of poverty:

One mother had £1 a week for each child after rent and fuel had been
paid for. Even small things like soap could not be provided. The children
were verminous, their clothing far from adequate. They had never
possessed anything they could call their own and the younger ones did
not even know what a pencil was. They often had to share a bed with the
parents because of a shortage of blankets. The father had a regular job.

(*The Times*, 24 December 1965, cited in Banting 1979: 72)

The real story, however, was provided by the dry statistics. According
to the researchers' reading of the data, the proportion of the population
living in poverty had climbed from 7.8 per cent in 1953–4 to 14.2 per
cent in 1960. This meant that the number of Britons living on low or very
low incomes had risen from 4 million to almost 7.5 million over the same
period (1965: 57–8). The authors were particularly concerned by their
findings that over 2 million children lived in low-income households.
If the figures were correct, their research pointed to the existence of a
profound social problem, the scale of which had been underestimated
for years. In terms of their headline figure of the numbers living in poverty, Abel-Smith and Townsend were confident about their calculations
– especially the total for 1960. However, they did concede that their
methodology could be challenged on two grounds. First, whereas they
had used *expenditure* as the basis for quantifying poverty in 1953–4,
they used *income* to calculate the number of people who they believed
lived in poverty in 1960 (based on a sample size of 5,000, of whom 3,450
responded). Second, because poverty was a relative concept, their
definition of where the poverty line should be drawn might not be universally accepted.

The starting point for Abel-Smith and Townsend's definition of poverty was the state's national assistance rate, the purpose of which was to
provide a minimum weekly income for every citizen. In fact, they
showed, some 2 million people in 1960 lived below even this official
threshold of an acceptable minimum income. But Abel-Smith and Townsend believed that a more authoritative and sensitive calculation of a minimum weekly budget should take account of cultural norms, rather than
simply calculating how much money a person required each week to live
on without suffering malnutrition. Thus they defined poverty as living
on less than 140 per cent of the state's basic national assistance scale plus

rent and/or other housing costs (a formula dismissed by administrators in Whitehall who believed that it overstated the researchers' case). This gave them a formula for calculating the numbers who lived 'within the margins of poverty', based on a sum which took account of special needs payments and the small amounts of additional income a claimant could receive before their benefit was cut (Timmins 1995: 256). Although references to the 'margins of poverty' were regarded by some as blurring the definition of poverty beyond acceptability, as Audrey Harvey later pointed out, families who lived near the poverty line often moved backwards and forwards across the threshold depending on circumstances. A man might be able to earn a 'fair wage' only so long as he could tolerate working night shifts or overtime; alternatively, a part-time working mother might be forced to drop her job whenever one of her children was ill, thus making a crucial negative difference to the family income (Harvey 1968: 62). To use another example, otherwise reasonable wages might prove insufficient to support a family being charged an exorbitantly high rent. True, in 1965 Labour went on to put in place a Rent Act that guaranteed 'fair rents', but this was rarely used by the poorest tenants (often New Commonwealth migrants) who could not afford expert representation before the tribunals and who feared notices to quit from vengeful landlords. In other words, any attempt to precisely quantify the reach of poverty was always open to challenge. Thus Abel-Smith and Townsend's formula – which gave them their total of 7,438,000 living in poverty in 1960 – led critics to insist that poverty had been redefined rather than rediscovered in the sixties. George Schwartz put the question in the *Sunday Times* Business Section later in the decade: 'What significance and value attach to the definition and measurement of poverty in the Western world and other advanced communities? Before long it will mean non-possession of a colour television set' (18 August 1968, cited in Coates and Silburn 1973: 33). Perhaps anticipating such criticisms, *The Poor and the Poorest* concluded by claiming that if the figure of almost 7.5 million living in poverty in 1960 was wrong, it was probably an underestimation rather than an exaggeration. The reasoning here was that the sample on which the calculation was based under-represented the number of old-aged and sick people in Britain's population (1965: 66).

Even allowing for questions about their methodology, Abel-Smith and Townsend's findings surprised many politicians and commentators. The common wisdom was that the Attlee government's post-war reforms had made Labour's historic mission to eradicate poverty redundant. The National Insurance Act (1946) was believed to have taken care of those whose earnings were interrupted or ended, the National Health Service Act (1946) provided for the sick, the National Assistance Act (1948) established a safety-net of means-tested benefits as a guarantor of minimum income, and family allowances helped to cover the cost of raising children. Furthermore, post-war economic growth and full employment meant that the new welfare state could be adequately funded. As early as 1951, Seebohm Rowntree's third report on conditions in York, *Poverty and the Welfare State*, calculated that only 1.6 per cent of the city's population now lived in poverty – compared with a figure of 18 per cent in 1936. *The Times* was moved to report that Rowntree's findings constituted 'a remarkable improvement – no less than the virtual abolition of the sheerest want'. For those who cared to look, however, there was no shortage of evidence to contradict this complacent optimism. In 1952 Peter Townsend had first challenged assumptions about the post-war reduction of poverty. His analysis was shared throughout the fifties and sixties by the left-wing weekly newspaper *Tribune*, whose writers regularly drew attention to problems such as slum housing, low pay and social neglect in an otherwise affluent society. 'The tightrope of poverty in the Affluent Society' and 'Poverty Amid Plenty Is Back in Britain', for example, were both used to headline stories in 1962. In the same year Paul Foot wrote a major piece on rising unemployment in Scotland which ended with a call for a 'crash programme to turn the hovels of Scotland into decent homes'. A series of books, pamphlets and articles appeared at the time which echoed this theme, written by authors such as Audrey Harvey, Harriett Wilson, Richard Titmuss and Dorothy Cole. Perhaps most powerful of all was the survey of St Ann's in Nottingham, supervised by Ken Coates and Richard Silburn. *Poverty: The Forgotten Englishmen* was published as a Penguin Special in 1970. Several findings emerged from the literature. Not only did the poor (of course) have the lowest incomes, they were also in every sense under-privileged. The effect was of a vicious cycle of poverty. The poor inhabited the worst housing, they were treated in the most dilapidated hospitals and their children went to the most run-down and under-staffed schools – from which there was very little chance of progressing to university and thus to a graduate job. Overwhelmingly, it seemed, rather than promote greater equality, the welfare state operated in favour of the affluent and articulate middle classes. Too often, those most in need failed to claim the benefits to which they were entitled – whether these were rate rebates, free milk for the under-fives, or the free school meals that were claimed by only a quarter of those children who were eligible. And as the *British Hospital Journal* pointed out at the time, 'a right cannot be called a right if people do not know it exists' (cited in Titmuss and Zander 1968: 4).

Another recurring feature of the 'rediscovery of poverty literature' was the agreement about which social groups were primarily affected. Old-age pensioners, the long-term unemployed, late-middle-aged men who were chronically sick, widows, and children who lived in low-income (usually larger) families were all most likely to feel the effects of poverty. Few, if any, of them could do much in the short term to pull themselves clear of the poverty line. Instead they had to stretch their meagre incomes far enough to cover the cost of living, sometimes far enough to buy the affluent society's cast-offs at places like Sneinton Market in St Ann's, Nottingham, the area studied by Coates and Silburn in 1966–8.

> *Either at Sneinton, or in the dingy little stores which announce 'houses cleared', you can often save heavily if you value your pennies more than your pride, or sometimes more than your comfort. A new pair of shoes? For two bob you can find a nice pair of second-hand ones, with only very small holes, which nearly fit. You can get the kiddies' breeches at the same shop. If the old man needs a suit, a rummage through the barrows can find him a lovely one for thirty bob, if you know where to look, and he doesn't mind a bit of slack at the back. To an outsider, the meanness, the sad shabbiness of poverty, comes alive in these little shops, with their tired fat ladies scratching a living from the clothes of the recently dead.*
>
> (Coates and Silburn 1973: 74)

Pensioners and children in low-income families were a cause of particular concern to poverty campaigners. As they pointed out, it was clear that the basic pension was simply too low to meet many retired people's needs, yet perhaps as many as 3 million elderly people never claimed the extra means-tested payments to which they were entitled, either because the complexities of the welfare system left them confused about their full entitlements, or because they were too proud to ask for additional support. This, remember, was a generation born in the age of late-Victorian self sufficiency which had then gone on to imbibe the discourse of wartime stoicism and the ethic of scarcity twice in fifty years. At the other end of the age spectrum, the 2.25 million children whom Abel-Smith and Townsend identified as living in poverty could hardly be held responsible for their hardship. Nor was it necessarily the parents who were at fault. Half a million of these children were in households where a male breadwinner was employed, but on such low wages that the family would theoretically have been better-off on state benefits. The trap here, however, was that if a wage-earner in this position gave up their job and claimed benefits, it would trigger a policy known as the 'wage-stop'. This meant that any subsequent state payments would be held at the level of the person's previous wages when they stopped work. Until the wage-stop was abolished in 1976 it was a cardinal principle of Britain's benefit system that no-one should be able to become better off by giving up work.

The accumulating evidence pointed to the fact that millions of children who lived in low-income families needed immediate state support if they were to escape an endless cycle of poverty. In pursuit of this aim, the Quaker social affairs committee helped to set up the Child Poverty Action Group (CPAG) in March 1965. This collection of enlightened campaigners naively believed that once they set out the facts of family poverty to Wilson's government there would be swift remedial action: namely an increase in the value of family allowances. Memorandums were sent to government ministers setting out the facts of family poverty and journalists were briefed so that the campaign was kept in the public eye. So confident were the CPAG that they would achieve their objective within a few months and thereafter disband, they never even opened a bank account until almost a year after their formation. Yet far from provoking an immediate policy change, the government delayed increasing family allowances until October 1967; and far from being a short-lived organisation the CPAG remains a campaigning force some forty years on. The CPAG's initial optimism was soon replaced by a recognition that a long hard campaign lay ahead. In his January 1967 Fabian Tract, *Poverty, Socialism and Labour in Power*, Peter Townsend announced that he was 'extremely critical' of the government's social policies in its first two years. In his view, much more had to be done by an administration that proudly proclaimed, at least in certain contexts, its socialist credentials. Most urgent, he argued, was the increase in family allowances that was eventually granted later that July. A list of other proposals followed. There should be an all-round improvement in state benefits for the long-term sick, the disabled and fatherless families. The wage-stop had to be abandoned. A more comprehensive plan for wage-related social security was a priority. 'Threadbare sections' of social services – areas short of doctors, under-developed community-care services, poor schools, under-staffed hospitals – had to be strengthened. Finally, there should be a genuine redistribution of income and wealth via taxation and incomes policies: as the data confirmed, most poor families did not exist on state benefits, but included a male wage-earner on very low wages (27–9). Without these measures, Townsend concluded, Labour would fail to achieve its two aims of national prosperity and social justice.

> *Good deeds have been done. But they are no more than hot compresses on an ailing body politic . . . The Labour Government is compromising too readily with entrenched interests, is avoiding the need to confront racial and social prejudice with moral authority, is failing to introduce institutional change and is forgetting that in this growingly more complicated world it must, like Alice, run even faster to stay in the same place and to preserve, still less extend, existing human rights.*
>
> (Townsend 1967: 31–2)

One successful feature of the CPAG was that it provided a model for subsequent single-issue pressure groups – such as the Low Pay Unit and the homeless charity Shelter – that came later in the sixties. Also, partly thanks to their campaigning efforts, social exclusion remained a current (if not pressing) public issue. Television films such as *Cathy Come Home*, which told the story of a homeless young couple whose children were taken into care, at least presented a 'state of the nation' narrative, focused on those who were usually marginalised in the culture (BBC 1966). The partial collapse of the Ronan Point system-built tower block in May 1968 also drew attention to the crumbling state of Britain's high-rise housing stock, home to some of the country's poorest tenants. Ultimately, however, the problem the campaigners faced was that while Labour ministers paid lip-service to the concept of greater equality, the government's domestic agenda was constantly shaped by other priorities. Most pressing of all were the twin issues of sterling's exchange rate and levels of public spending. In the battle to defend sterling, measures to tackle poverty were regarded in the Treasury as simply too expensive: the constructive ideas of the CPAG and others were to be lost in a blizzard of public spending cuts.

Devaluation: Labour in power, March 1966–January 1968

Despite being re-elected with a secure majority for the first time in its history, Labour's post-election glow did not last long. Within weeks of its triumph in March 1966 the government was forced on to the defensive, never fully recovering its confidence for the remainder of its time in office – perhaps, as Kenneth Morgan has argued, never looking like being a dominant party of government again until Tony Blair became party leader in 1994 (1997: 240). The central problem was the state of the economy. In May, the National Union of Seamen began a two-month strike which seized up the docks, hit Britain's already fragile balance of payments and tested the government's resolve to hold the line on its incomes policy. On 23 May, with over 500 ships immobilised, a State of Emergency was declared. A month later the Prime Minister drew on MI5 briefings and unhelpfully blamed the seamen's dispute on communist elements within the union – what he referred to as a 'tightly knit group of politically motivated men' – who were holding the state to ransom at a time of acute economic strain (Wilson 1974: 307). 'Completely bonkers' was Peter Shore's verdict on a remark that only heightened sympathy for the seamen, who were now seen to be fighting against a Labour government which aligned itself with employers and the security services rather than the unions (Benn 1987: 436). By June, the Treasury was once again supplying the Prime Minister with almost hourly reports of the worsening exchange position. By July, an atmosphere of crisis threatened to overwhelm the upper reaches of government. Brown, a convert to devaluation, was constantly on the verge of resignation. Callaghan, who periodically conceded the case for devaluation before reverting to his former position, was forced to issue ever more gloomy economic papers to the Cabinet, showing how Britain's trade deficit was now exceeding the Treasury's worst fears. Wilson, who had ordered the burning of an earlier

Treasury paper which recommended devaluation, had a paranoid fear that former Gaitskellites were plotting to make either Brown or Callaghan Prime Minister while he was away in Moscow on a diplomatic mission. On top of all this, Frank Cousins resigned as Minister of Technology (in protest at a Prices and Incomes Bill which he denounced as 'fundamentally wrong in its conception and approach') and the Carmarthen by-election was lost to the Welsh nationalists *Plaid Cymru*.

This was the background of political turmoil and personal enmity against which the Cabinet was finally allowed to formally discuss devaluation on 19 July. Wilson, Callaghan and Healey led the Cabinet majority of seventeen against the measure; a temporary alliance of three pro-Europeans, Brown, Crosland and Jenkins, and three left-wingers, Castle, Crossman and Benn (who had replaced Cousins in the Cabinet) were the minority in favour of devaluation. There were sound enough reasons why the Cabinet decided to continue the fight for sterling. Devaluation was seen as a short-term 'soft' option, an expedient that would allow Britain to avoid facing up to the fundamental weaknesses undermining its export performance. Moreover, a British devaluation might trigger a chain reaction in other countries, cancelling out the initial competitive advantage of lowering sterling's exchange value. There was a moral dimension to the issue that complicated matters still further. As it was a leading international currency, Britain had obligations to countries holding sterling balances to do what it could to maintain its exchange value. More selfishly, there was within Whitehall an 'overseas lobby' which cautioned that devaluation would weaken Britain's negotiating influence at the 'top table' of global diplomacy. Finally there was the psychological aspect to consider: currencies are regarded as a kind of national totem – 'a strong pound means a strong Britain' – and this was a factor when the political merits of devaluation were weighed. Despite the force of these arguments, however, the decision to defend sterling in July 1966 should be seen as a missed opportunity for the government. This was a time when it could have devalued while it still had a full term in office ahead, years that would have been a valuable breathing space in which to recover from the resulting political damage. As it was they embarked on eighteen months of deflation, lost valuable political support from workers and trade unions in the process, and ensured that when devaluation did take place in November 1967, it was seen as a much more serious defeat than would have been the case if it had happened during a summer when much of the country was distracted by the football World Cup. Even with all their difficulties, an NOP survey showed Labour sixteen points ahead of the Tories in mid-July, three times the lead they had enjoyed at the time of the election (Castle 1990: 73).

The immediate price of the decision to defend sterling was the 'July measures', a major deflationary package which cut public spending by £500 million, increased taxes and set down a six-month freeze on wages, salaries and dividends. This was to be followed by a further six months of 'severe restraint' on pay. It spelled the end of 'purposive expansion' and the lofty ambitions of the National Plan. At home the cuts eventually meant unpopular measures such as more expensive school meals and a reduction in welfare milk. Abroad, it meant a scaling-down of defence commitments east of Suez. Politically, the crisis also marked a permanent downturn in Wilson's reputation; from this point on, as Pimlott noted, the Prime Minister 'acquired the character, which he never lost, of a leader under siege' (1992: 404). Of course he remained in charge, re-shuffling his Cabinet in August and moving Brown from the DEA to the Foreign Office in a straight swap with Michael Stewart. But he never again reached the heights of the previous three years. Nor did the painful treatment of July produce a permanent cure. The immediate signs were encouraging: the balance of payments improved sufficiently for Britain to be able to register a surplus for the whole of 1966, unemployment was low and output was high. The widespread belief that sterling was over-valued remained, however, and it was only a matter of time before there was fresh pressure on the exchange rate. Ironically, George Brown, who had lost the argument for devaluation in the Cabinet, was given the task as Foreign Secretary of preparing Britain's entry into the EEC, a project which entailed massive exchange costs and thus brought devaluation several steps closer. There was never any certainty that the diplomatic tour of European capitals by Brown and Wilson in early 1967 would persuade de Gaulle to allow British membership. But what was agreed almost unanimously was that Britain would have to devalue before it joined the EEC. The application was made in May 1967, shortly after a bad set of trade figures had been announced for the previous month. On 16 May, de Gaulle warned that there were 'formidable obstacles' to Britain's entry, which, although it was a diplomatic setback, fortunately shook neither sterling nor the wider British economy. More immediate trouble came in June when the Israeli victory over the Arabs in the Six-Day War resulted in Iraq and Kuwait imposing an oil embargo against Britain – who, they believed, had assisted Israel. Britain's oil supplies were disrupted for months, putting pressure both on the balance of payments and the currency. Once again, however, it was Labour's strained relations with the unions over pay restraint that precipitated a crisis. Unofficial strikes by dockers in Liverpool, Manchester, Hull, and eventually London through September and October had the same disruptive effect on exports as the seamen's strike of the previous year. As sterling was sold in massive quantities on the foreign exchanges, the Cabinet was faced with a re-run of the July crisis. The government's waning public popularity was illustrated by three by-election defeats, the first two at Cambridge and Walthamstow West in late September, the third at Hamilton in early November. Shortly after the Hamilton defeat a key Cabinet economic committee met and discussed for the first time the practicalities of devaluation – it was no longer a question of whether, but when. Successive rises in the bank rate had little effect on the market. Only a rescue package from the United States could delay immediate devaluation, but the Americans knew that Britain would never agree to give them the one thing that they wanted in return: stronger support for the war in Vietnam. The political costs of such a deal would simply have been too high. With no other weapons left to defend the currency, the unavoidable decision was taken on 13 November after the Lord Mayor's banquet at the Guildhall (Morgan 1997: 271). Late on Saturday 18 November 1967 it was finally announced that the exchange rate for sterling had been lowered by 14 per cent from $2.80 to $2.40.

For Callaghan as Chancellor, devaluation was a 'political catastrophe'. Wilson ensured that it would be a presentational disaster too for the government, with an ill-judged, upbeat broadcast to the nation in which he said: 'Devaluation does *not* mean that the value of the pound in the hands of the British consumer, the British housewife at her shopping, is cut correspondingly. It does not mean that the pound in the pocket is worth 14 per cent less to us now than it was' (Wilson 1974: 587–9). Wilson did acknowledge in the broadcast that imports would be dearer. But it looked as if the Prime Minister was trying to deny the seriousness of what had happened, and that he was ignoring the hardships suffered in the last two years to defend the pound. Now there would be further sacrifices, as devaluation was accompanied by yet more spending cuts and tax increases. By the time the final details were announced, Callaghan had resigned as Chancellor, swapping jobs with Roy Jenkins at the Home Office. In January 1968 Jenkins outlined the severity of the deflationary package, cutting government spending by £716 million. British forces were to be withdrawn from east of Suez by 1971 and plans to purchase the F-111 strike aircraft were cancelled. At home the housing and roads programmes were cut. More controversially, prescription charges for the NHS were re-introduced – ironically the issue on which Wilson had resigned from Attlee's government in 1951 – and the aim of raising the school leaving age to 16 was deferred. In the vote on the measures on 18 January, 26 Labour MPs abstained because of their opposition to cuts in the social programme. The optimistic forecasts of 1964 now seemed a world away.

CHAPTER 10

1968, cultural crisis and women's liberation

1968

It was the most symbolic year of the sixties. If proof was required of how far events had moved from the conformism of the fifties, it came in 1968. In countries across the world (both capitalist and communist) street protests became the favoured form of political engagement. University campuses, factories and, to a lesser extent, secondary schools provided most of the marchers. Some of those who took to the streets were focused on their own local grievances. Others were galvanised by opposition to the Vietnam War, a conflict that escalated after the Vietcong's Tet offensive in January 1968. Disillusionment with conventional politics was another factor, as were the assassinations of Martin Luther King and Bobby Kennedy, combined with the uninspiring pragmatism of Wilson's Labour government, leading some in Britain and the United States to question the value of the democratic process as a route to change. The consensus of people and state in advanced industrial societies that had held since the end of the war appeared to be in danger. In Paris over a million students and workers fought running battles with riot police on the streets in May. Police brutality against students there led to a short-lived general strike and a counter-attack led by President de Gaulle. As the barricades went up once again in Paris, university towns throughout France lent their weight to a struggle that brought the country to the verge of a political revolution. This insurrection against the French Fifth

Republic had the highest profile of all the events of 'sixty-eight. Perhaps the most poignant was the crushing of the Czech 'Prague Spring' by Soviet tanks in late August. But what made 1968 unique was that from west to east, across the United States, parts of Latin America, West Germany, Spain, Italy and Japan, a wave of strikes, occupations and marches set down a challenge to ruling authorities. Student leaders such as Rudi Dutschke and Daniel Cohn-Bendit became radical icons to place alongside Che Guevara, while Mick Jagger (ever alert to shifts in the cultural mood) sang that the time was now right for 'fightin' in the streets' (the BBC banned the song).

There was always a slightly diluted taste to the British version of 1968. Neither the number of people involved nor the aggressive purity of the confrontations with the (unarmed) British police matched the benchmarks set at the Sorbonne and Nanterre in France or Berkeley and Columbia in the United States. The fact that most of its activists were privileged middle-class students also meant that the upheavals of 1968 were essentially seen as a crisis within the dominant culture rather than a revolt against it. As Stuart Hall has argued, late capitalism in Britain at the end of the sixties suffered a crisis of cultural hegemony – that is, in the ways that capital persuades all groups in society to accept its cultural and moral values as universal, thus masking the coercive nature of the political control it exercises (Hall *et al.* 1978: 240–7). Because the crisis was one of culture rather than politics it was experienced most directly at those sites that transmitted cultural values to the next generation: universities, polytechnics and art colleges (Hewison 1986: 153). But several factors prevented British campus radicalism from making the same impact as its French or American equivalents. First, despite the expansion of higher education in Britain and the slight broadening of the class base of its intake, the size of the British university population was too small for it to be seen as anything other than an elite. Second, almost everyone outside the campuses regarded the issues that caused British students to occupy university buildings as internal institutional matters of minor interest. Unlike in Paris, where the public came to the support of students after they saw French police fire tear gas at young demonstrators and beat them with batons, there was little popular sympathy for rebellious students in Britain. In fact the reverse was more typically the case. Student radicals were seen as work-shy, self-indulgent, rich youngsters who got a kick out of making trouble. In a *New Society* survey published in November 1969, 23 per cent of the controlled sample questioned chose 'student unrest' as the thing they most objected to in the sixties (Barker 1969: 847). Third, the fact that only a minority of the student body were actively engaged in protests meant that the authorities and the press could blame disturbances either on a handful of 'foreign' agitators (Tariq Ali being the target-in-chief), or on tiny fringe political groups such as the International Marxist Group, Socialist Labour League and International Socialism (whose combined membership was probably no more than a few hundred). While surveys suggested that a majority of students were sympathetic to the activities of their more militant peers, most preferred to confine themselves to offering only moral support. A Gallup survey in May 1968 found that in the preceding twelve months only 21 per cent of Cambridge University students had taken part in a protest. At Sussex the figure was 40 per cent (high by historical standards, but a minority all the same). Student apathy, which had been a problem for the National Union of Students (NUS) since its foundation in the 1920s, was still significant in the sixties, despite popular recollection of the period as a golden age of student rebellion (Thomas 2002: 282).

So what were the issues that motivated some students to protest in 1968? The foundation for all other grievances was a simmering disillusionment with the Wilson government. By 1968 there were simply too many areas where the government had let down the hopes it had raised in 1963–4 for a new progressive politics: the most frequently cited were support for the US in Vietnam, racist immigration controls (together with an increase in the fees charged to overseas students), the refusal to use force against the illegal Smith regime in Rhodesia and tough stands taken by the state against striking workers. On top of this were a set of concerns that were specific to colleges and universities. One of the main issues was the right for students to be represented on academic committees and governing bodies. Two of the first such campaigns were at the Regent Street Polytechnic and the Holborn College of Law and Commerce in December 1967. At Hornsey Art School there were disputes over both curriculum content and the granting of sabbatical leave to the student union president, resulting in a six-week long occupation (supported by some staff) that fuelled copycat occupations at art colleges in Croydon and Guildford (Students and Staff of Hornsey College of Art 1969: 29–57, 139–189).

Birmingham Art School and the universities of Aston, Bradford, Hull, Keele, Leeds and Leicester all saw minor disturbances, so too did Essex which earned itself a reputation as the national centre of student radicalism (Marwick 1998: 635–9). Confrontations tended to be sharpest when students intervened to prevent an unpopular speaker from airing their views. Enoch Powell attracted demonstrators at every university he spoke at following his controversial 'rivers of blood' remarks in April 1968 (see chapter 11). In July the Home Secretary, James Callaghan, ignored the authorities' advice to leave Nuffield College by the back door and had a 'fierce confrontation' with Oxford students at which there was 'some suggestion of physical violence' (Morgan 1997: 311). At Essex, three students were expelled after they helped to prevent a scientist from Porton Down, the Ministry of Defence's germ warfare establishment, from delivering a lecture. A sit-in supported by university staff followed and the three were later reinstated. The London School of Economics (LSE) had already seen disturbances in 1966 and 1967, sparked by the appointment as School Director of Dr Walter Adams, then Principal of University College, Rhodesia. Adams, it was claimed, had links with Ian Smith's minority white government. The student campaign to block his appointment involved occupations, marches and suspensions for the ringleaders, but Adams took up his post in September 1967 all the same and the university entered a brief period of calm (Blackstone, Coles, Hadley and Lewis 1970: 151–73; Fraser 1988: 112–4). The following summer, however, perhaps envious of the way French students had paralysed France, and energised by the arrival of 'Red Danny' Cohn-Bendit to feed back on the situation in Paris (Callaghan refused to invoke his powers to keep Cohn-Bendit out of Britain), a minority of LSE students renewed their militant activities. In June they helped to launch the Revolutionary Socialist Students' Federation (RSSF), which listed among its aims the use of the universities as 'red bases' for capitalism's overthrow. In October supporters of the Vietnam Solidarity Campaign (VSC) won a vote at the LSE student union to occupy the School as a temporary headquarters for anti-war marchers who were scheduled to protest outside the US Embassy that month. On the weekend of the anti-war demonstration some 800 students took over LSE buildings and turned them into a rest centre and base for political discussions.

In common with the pattern of events in other countries, opposition to the Vietnam War was a major catalyst for the British street politics of 1968. It was also the one strong bridge that connected disaffected students with a wider body of protesters in the country. As Tariq Ali, the former President of the Oxford Union who became a leader of the radical left, later commented, helping the Vietnamese to drive the Americans out of their country became the 'overriding priority for radicals, socialists and democrats in the West' (Ali 1987: 61). Vietnamese resistance to US imperialism was inspirational. Moreover, as Hewison rightly notes, the issue of Vietnam had a much greater urgency than the CND campaigns of the early sixties: 'the issue was a far more bloodily visible one, thanks to television, than the hypothetical horrors of the Bomb. Emblematically, here were romantic guerrillas pinning down the bureaucrats and technologists of the most powerful and affluent nation in the world' (1986: 158). Thus in place of the Quaker-inspired sit-down protests used by the Committee of 100, the anti-war movement favoured the more aggressive stance of the American Students for a Democratic Society (SDS), whose methods were imported into Britain by US graduate students. In July 1967 Tariq Ali helped to organise the VSC and was at the forefront of the 10,000-strong anti-war protest outside the US Embassy at Grosvenor Square the following October. Buoyed by the success of this first demonstration, the VSC organised a follow-up on 17 March 1968 that saw the Embassy besieged by a crowd of perhaps 25,000 protesters. This was the most violent of all the anti-war marches. Unquestionably some of the demonstrators relished the prospect of a violent clash with the police. Equally, the police hardly shrank from cracking a few heads during fighting that went on for two hours. Dave Clark, a student from Manchester University, recalled how he and a fellow demonstrator dragged a police horse to the ground as it was used to charge the crowd:

> We'd worked out in advance how it could be done. There were theories around that lion's dung would scare police horses, and there was even an expedition planned to Manchester zoo to get some. But I and a bloke from Sheffield University planned that as the horse charged, one of us on each side would grab the reins and pull down. In retrospect it was a

*crazy thing to do because the horse was just as likely to trample you to
death. After we'd done it the police went absolutely barmy, and I took a
real beating from their fists, knees and boots. Fortunately for me, a large
group of people behind me saw what was happening and pulled me
back.*

(cited in Fraser 1988: 161–2)

Although the press reported that 117 police and 45 demonstrators
were treated for injuries, these figures failed to include those beaten
marchers who were hauled away by friends to avoid arrest and who
were left to nurse their own wounds as best they could. That evening's
television news programmes were dominated by images of Britain's most
violent civil protest in living memory, pictures that seemed to confirm
that a new phase of militant activity had opened. The hippie culture of
1967 may have seemed freakish to 'straight' society, but at least it was
essentially passive and self-contained. This latest form of resistance was
heavier and more confrontational. Tariq Ali heightened fears that the
anti-war protesters had subversive intent by claiming that the marchers
had intended to invade the US Embassy 'for just as long as the Vietcong
held the American Embassy in Saigon seven weeks ago' (cited in Thomas
2002: 280). Ali's mischievous remarks were widely condemned in the
media and were followed by calls for a ban on any repeat anti-war
protests by the *Daily Mail*, the *Sun* and politicians from both main parties. When the VSC announced its plans to organise another anti-war
demonstration for October 1968, Callaghan at the Home Office rejected
calls to prevent it and persuaded the Cabinet that the freedom to protest
had to be preserved. As the time of the march approached, several commentators and politicians looked nervously across the Channel at the fall
out of the Paris *événements* and voiced their concerns that the spectre of
revolution was shadowing Britain. A new radical paper, *Black Dwarf*,
appeared in June and attempted to carry the revolutionary message further: its first headline read, 'Paris, London, Rome, Berlin. We Will Fight.
We Shall Win'. The security forces responded to the apparent threat by
bugging telephones, intercepting mail and raiding the offices of fringe
political groups whose ranks had been infiltrated by the Special Branch.
The Times played its part in raising the stakes with a front-page story,
perhaps planted as part of MI5's black propaganda effort, claiming that

armed extremists planned to exploit the crowd cover of the October demonstration as part of a plan to seize key buildings and disrupt communications in central London (Green 1998b: 266–7; Thomas 2002: 289). The paper also made a symbolic point by giving its crime reporters the job of covering the VSC. Tory frontbencher Quentin Hogg joined in the scaremongering by demanding the closure of all mainline London railway stations on the day of the protest (Morgan 1997: 315). Perhaps, as Hall argued, press and politicians were following a deliberate strategy of resignifying what was a distinctly *political* issue into a *criminal* one. Most people in Britain probably supported the right to public protest. So the most effective way to legitimise the coercive response of police and security forces against what were after all legitimate demonstrators was to reclassify them as hooligans who needed to be brought into line (1978: 224).

In fact, the 100,000 anti-war marchers on 27 October were overwhelmingly peaceful. Perhaps the media predictions of violent confrontation and general awareness that the television cameras would be watching for any signs of trouble led most demonstrators to exercise restraint. A sizeable group of five thousand or so broke away from the main march, which the VSC had redirected to Hyde Park, and headed once more for the US Embassy. The resulting fights with the police produced some fifty injuries and forty arrests, far fewer than the confrontation in March. Whatever trouble occurred was confined to the margins. Indeed a more resonant image of the massive October demonstration was that of marchers and police joining together for a rendition of 'Auld Lang Syne'. *New Society*'s survey of demonstrators, which it carried out on the day of the march, suggested that the pre-event publicity had misread the protesters' motives. Far from being the kind of violent troublemakers the media preferred to imagine, the crowd was composed mostly of young, privileged, peaceful idealists. Three-quarters of the marchers were under 24 and over 50 per cent had been to public school or state grammars. Students made up a little more than half of all marchers, with 10 per cent still at school, although almost all of the rest had been through some form of higher or further education. The research suggested that the protesters' radicalism was far-reaching: 96 per cent were against US policy on Vietnam, 68 per cent declared that they were against 'capitalism in general', 65 per cent opposed the 'general structure of British society' and a further 23 per cent were against 'all forms of authority'. But while 70 per cent of the sample expected violence to occur, only 10 per cent thought they would be involved in any violence themselves (Barker, Taylor, de Kadt and Hopper 1968: 631–4). Thus the bulk of the crowd stayed away from Grosvenor Square and listened instead to the speeches in Hyde Park. James Callaghan warmly congratulated the police on their handling of the protest, and the Home Secretary in turn won praise from his Cabinet colleagues for an operation that went a long way towards rebuilding his political reputation after his traumatic exit from the Treasury the previous year. After the violence they had predicted failed to materialise, the press gave generous praise to the police for keeping the peace. 'Police Win Battle of Grosvenor Square' and 'The Day The Police Were Wonderful' were the respective headlines in *The Times* and the *Daily Mirror* the day after the demonstration.

The momentum built up by the anti-war protests in 1968 soon ran out of steam. Perhaps if the VSC had sought to go beyond the single issue of Vietnam and make concrete demands of the Labour government, the sense of purpose would have been maintained. Instead, most students went back to their institutions and only a few thousand die-hards turned out for the anti-war marches of 1969. However, the organising impulse stimulated by the events of 1968 did not entirely dissipate. Lessons learned about the need to organise around a grievance were not forgotten. Some excitement was caused in early 1969 when students sledgehammered down the LSE's new steel security gates, provoking the university authorities to respond with a four-week lock-out and dismissing lecturers (Caute 1988: 324–9). Later there were sit-ins at Manchester and Oxford universities and in 1971 the NUS called a day of action as the Conservative government sought to restrict the autonomy of student unions (Fraser 1988: 290; Chun 1993: 108). In 1972 some student unions offered facilities, accommodation and picket-line support to striking miners. There was also a natural affiliation between the student radicals of 1968 and the civil rights movement in Northern Ireland, which had emerged in the same year in the shape of the People's Democracy organisation (see chapter 11). In short, as Hall argued, the social and political polarisation characterising the 1970s began from the events of 1968 (Hall *et al.* 1978: 242).

The backlash against permissiveness

Student demonstrators, militant trade unionists and Black Power activists all contributed to what came to be regarded as a crisis in the social order in the late sixties. Another component was the generalised concern about the ramifications of high-sixties permissiveness: the sexual libertarianism, pornography, drug-taking and *avant-garde* cultural experimentation that had injected itself into the mainstream of popular culture. In some eyes at least, permissiveness was a cancer that was threatening the nation's moral fibre (Hall *et al.* 1978: 247). Old-money establishment figures might have been willing to sell their houses to the new-moneyed pop aristocracy, but for the most part they found a culture inspired by flash rebelliousness, sexual longing and (for some at least) illicit drugs incomprehensible and threatening. They were not alone. By the late sixties society's moral guardians were intent on tightening up at least some of the social and cultural loosenings of the decade, many of which (if not all) were associated with the vibrant popular youth culture of the time. Their efforts were successful enough to prompt Chris Welch of the *Melody Maker* to take a libertarian stand against establishment attacks on the pop music world in October 1967. In a feature headlined, 'Stop Picking on Pop – why does society want to put pop in chains?' Welch complained:

> *In breathalyser Britain where every new problem is answered by a new law, it is not really surprising pop should be caught up in the swing towards 1984. What is surprising is that so much suppression should be taken lying down.*
>
> (Welch 1967)

He cited several examples of this backlash against cultural freedom. Musicians and singers had been 'hounded' by police (armed with new powers to stop and search suspected drug users under the 1967 Dangerous Drugs Act), who operated on the assumption that all pop artists took drugs. Music venues such as the Majo Club in Sheffield had been closed down as police and local councillors used new powers to revoke clubs' licences (police argued that people going to the Majo had been found with pep pills). Windsor Borough Council, meanwhile, had recommended that an annual Jazz and Blues Festival should be banned from its area, principally because it drew in hippies who were seen sleeping rough in Windsor town. In 'Non-Swinging Britain', wrote Welch, 'people were observed enjoying themselves en masse in a public place, and obviously this could not be tolerated for long'. He might have added to his list of grievances the Marine Offences Act which came into effect on midnight 14 August. This legislation was the government's main weapon in its fight to close down the offshore pirate commercial radio stations which commanded a loyal, and mainly young, audience. If these youngsters wanted to listen to continuous pop they could now tune in to the safe and regulated frequencies of the BBC, which launched Radio One as Britain's first nationwide dedicated pop station on Saturday 30 September 1967 (licensed commercial radio did not arrive in Britain until 1973). Radio One plundered formats and signed up presenters straight from pirate stations such as Radio London and Radio Caroline (Chapman 1992: 194–5, 226–35). But one of the differences between the BBC and the pirates appreciated by the authorities was that the Corporation could be relied upon to anchor its pop presentation in a secure moral context. The BBC did not let them down. In September 1968, for example, the BBC withdrew the group Sly and the Family Stone from *Top of the Pops* after Larry Graham Jr. had been charged with cannabis possession. In May 1969 The Kinks were similarly denied the chance to perform on the show because their song *Plastic Man* featured the word 'bum'. At various other points records by Peter Sarstedt, The Beatles, The Rolling Stones, Serge Gainsbourg and Jane Birkin were all denied air-play by the Corporation.

If there was an identifiable starting point for the backlash against permissiveness it came in February 1967. On 5 February Britain's best-selling Sunday tabloid, the *News of the World*, summoned up its full moral indignation, claiming that Rolling Stone Mick Jagger had taken LSD at a wild party in Roehampton – their reporters in fact had spoken to Brian Jones, not Jagger, and the drug that Jones had cheerfully admitted taking was hashish. Jagger threatened to issue a writ for libel against the paper. The following weekend West Sussex police, acting on a tip-off from the *News of the World*, raided Keith Richards's country pile at Redlands. They took away a collection of recreational drugs and later charged Jagger and art dealer Robert Fraser with possessing substances unlawful under the 1964 Dangerous Drugs Act. Richards was charged with knowingly allowing the drugs to be consumed at his house. In March the newly-formed Scotland Yard Drug Squad raided Brian Jones's London flat and charged him with possession of a variety of illicit drugs. These high-profile raids looked very much like a coordinated attempt by the authorities to make an example of the Rolling Stones, who at the time gloried in their anarchic and decadent image. However, when Jagger and Richards received prison sentences (three months and a year respectively) in June there was a widespread view that the presiding judge had pushed the exercise too far. As Jagger was driven off to Brixton jail, and Richards to Wormwood Scrubs, fans in Britain and the United States protested against the severity of the sentences and even some of Fleet Street wondered whether a proper sense of judicial perspective had been lost during the case. The next day the two Stones were granted bail pending an appeal (Fraser, sentenced to six months for possessing heroin, remained in jail). At the end of July, the Appeal Court conceded that the original trial judge had erred both in his summing up for the jury and in his sentencing. Richards's conviction was overturned and Jagger's prison sentence was changed to a one-year conditional discharge. In the most memorable leading article he ever wrote, *Times* editor William Rees-Mogg argued that it was unacceptable for Jagger to be treated more harshly than anyone else in a British court simply because of his public image. But Lord Chief Justice Parker took a rather different view, warning Jagger as he upheld the appeal against his custodial sentence:

> *You are, whether you like it or not, the idol of a large number of the young in this country. Being in that position, you have very grave responsibilities. If you do come to be punished, it is only natural that those responsibilities should carry higher penalties.*

(cited in Norman 1993: 211)

In broader terms, the trial of the two Rolling Stones was symbolic of a wider contest between traditionalism and a new hedonism, the focal point of which was society's attitude towards recreational drugs. On 16 July 1967 a few thousand demonstrators staged a 'Legalise Pot Rally' in Hyde Park. On 24 July the campaign was pushed forward with a page-long appeal in *The Times* for a reform of the cannabis laws. The advertisement, paid for by Paul McCartney, was signed by some seventy individuals including Labour MP Brian Walden, artist David Hockney, journalists David Dimbleby and Jonathan Aitken, theatre director Peter Brook, writer Graham Greene, and scientist Francis Crick who had co-discovered DNA (Green 1998b: 183). In part, the advertisement was aimed at influencing the Wootton Committee, which at the time was examining the issues relating to drug dependency for the Home Office. When the Wootton Report was published in December 1968 it stated that, on all the available evidence, the long-term consumption of cannabis in moderate doses had no harmful effects. According to their (very rough) estimates there were between 30,000 and 300,000 people in Britain who had used marijuana. Over 3,000 people were convicted for possessing the drug in 1968, the vast majority of whom were white and aged under 25, and the upward trend in the conviction rate was accelerating sharply (Young 1971: 12–13). The Wootton Committee stopped well short of recommending the legalisation of the drug, but they argued that the current laws, which failed to distinguish between cannabis and opiates, were inappropriate and indeed obstructive of further research into the effects of cannabis use. The Home Secretary James Callaghan, however, had set his mind against any reform of the drugs laws and told the Commons that the Wootton Committee had been overly influenced by the 'pro-cannabis lobby'. The *Daily Mirror*, who labelled the report a 'Conspiracy of the Drugged' and the *Evening News*, who called it a 'Junkie's Charter', shared Callaghan's reading of Wootton (Hall *et al.* 1978: 250). Rejecting the report's conclusions, the Home Secretary made clear his own view that the time had arrived to 'call a halt to the rising tide of permissiveness' which he labelled 'one of the most unlikeable words that has been invented in recent years' (cited in Morgan 1997: 320). Callaghan's stern response to Wootton was welcomed on both sides of the House. His final dismissal of the Report's thinking came when he introduced the Misuse of Drugs Act to the Commons in March 1970, a measure that increased the maximum sentence for drug pushers to four-teen years' imprisonment and maintained possession of marijuana as a criminal offence (Young 1971: 202–3). Thus it was, as his biographer remarked, that Callaghan emerged as the 'authentic representative voice' of traditional values at a time of cultural flux, and his tones 'went ringing out over subsequent decades' (Morgan 1997: 320–1). Successive Home Secretaries ensured that cannabis users continued to be arrested and charged, with the drug remaining outlawed for the next thirty years.

Callaghan's call to halt the 'rising tide of permissiveness' was supported by what Stuart Hall called the 'entrepreneurs of moral indignation', who perceived in the late sixties a growing sense of social crisis (Hall *et al.* 1978: 234). The rising profile of the counter-culture, the student demonstrations, the anti-Vietnam protests, the continuing post-devaluation economic crisis and growing hostility towards non-white immigration all contributed to a climate in which a new moral authoritarianism emerged (Weeks 1989: 277). The leading figure in what became a campaign for a moral revival was Mary Whitehouse, who had come to prominence in 1964 as head of the Clean Up TV Campaign (later re-titled the National Viewers and Listeners' Association) which protested about sexual explicitness on television. Whitehouse was then a 53-year-old senior teacher (responsible for art and sex education) in a Midlands secondary school. As Jeffrey Weeks remarked, it would be wrong simply to dismiss her as a 'crank'. Instead we should recognise that there was something 'deeply representative' about her views and campaigns. Whitehouse's profound religious beliefs, her desire for a new Christian-based moral order, her fears about the ways in which the explicitness of modern media had invaded the privacy of the home, all commanded wide support across the social classes in the sixties and beyond (Weeks 1989: 277). Her refusal to accept the validity of a secular and pragmatic morality over one which was grounded in Christian ethical principles struck a chord, even in a society where church-going was in steep decline. Thus, as the sixties wore on, Whitehouse and her supporters, confident that the weight of public opinion was behind them, were in fact encouraged to extend the scope of their moral surveillance. In August 1968, Whitehouse was even given half-a-page by the *Melody Maker* to share her thoughts on how pop music influenced Britain's youth. She had no animosity towards pop music as such, she explained, but she was worried about a sinister minority 'with an unhealthy approach to life' within the business 'who are using the questioning attitude of youth to destroy completely the standards on which society has been built'. Rising rates of sexually-transmitted disease and drug use were proof of this ongoing social breakdown, she argued, which, once complete, would leave the way clear for devil worship and black magic (Whitehouse 1968). More importantly, Whitehouse went on to fight for a reversal of the liberal law reforms that were a defining structural feature of the 'permissive society'. She welcomed the successful prosecution of the *Oz* editors for obscenity in July 1971 for their 'School Kids' issue, but was dismayed when the three had their convictions overturned on technical grounds shortly afterwards, describing this reversal as an 'unmitigated disaster for the children of our country' (Tracey and Morrison 1979: 135). Working with the evangelical organisation the Festival of Light (alongside Cliff Richard, Malcolm Muggeridge and Sir Cyril Black MP) she responded to the freeing of the *Oz* three by organising a Nationwide Petition for Public Decency. The petition was an attempt to give a voice to the 'silent moral majority' and listed amongst its demands a call for the 1959 Obscene Publications Act to be made more restrictive: most writers and publishers at the time took the opposite view and wanted what they saw as a restrictive Act scrapped entirely. As part of its campaign against 'cultural pollution', the Festival of Light also put continual pressure on the British Board of Film Censors in the early seventies to take a tougher line on films such as *The Devils*, *Straw Dogs* and *A Clockwork Orange* which contained graphic scenes of sex and violence (Robertson 1993: 138–50). Pressure was similarly maintained on the BBC to adhere to strict moral guidelines, a cause that was helped by the fact that since 1967 the newly-appointed BBC Chairman, the Conservative Lord Hill, had been willing to meet Whitehouse and listen seriously to her arguments. When persuasion was not enough, the moral rearmament campaigners were eventually forced to resort to the law courts. In 1976 Whitehouse used the archaic blasphemy laws to bring a private prosecution against *Gay News* after it published a poem, 'The Love that dares to speak its name', which depicted a homosexual relationship between a Roman centurion and the crucified body of Christ. The success of this prosecution in 1977 showed that, ten years after the Sexual Offences Act, homosexuality remained surrounded by taboos and a marked degree of popular hostility – legal changes, it seemed, had not changed social attitudes. School sex education was another target for Whitehouse and her supporters (one of whom wrote that schools were in danger of becoming 'moral gas chambers'). There was also an ongoing (but this time unsuccessful) campaign to restrict the opportunities for women to procure an abortion.

Thus it became ever clearer throughout the seventies that the permanence of hard-won sixties freedoms could not be taken for granted. Perhaps this vulnerability owed something to popular misgivings about the value of some of those freedoms in the first place. In November 1969 *New Society* published the results of a survey it had commissioned to measure people's views and preoccupations at the end of the decade. Asked to nominate which sixties changes they most welcomed, 51 per cent of the sample opted for 'better pensions', while only 5 per cent chose 'easier laws for homosexuality, divorce, abortion, etc'. When asked which sixties changes they most objected to, the 'easier laws for homo-sexuality, divorce, abortion etc.' emerged as the highest response (its only rivals as the least popular development in the sixties were 'immigration of coloured people' and 'student unrest', both of which polled 23 per cent). Asked whether there was 'too much publicity given to sex' the survey found that 77 per cent of the sample agreed (the figure for the responses of 16–24 year olds in the sample was rather lower at 59 per cent). Meanwhile, 71 per cent clung to a traditional conception of justice and agreed that 'murderers ought to be hanged': as the magazine's editor Paul Barker commented, these people 'clearly didn't find the 1960s, in one sense, swinging enough'. Summing up the results of a survey which seemed to suggest the resilience of illiberal popular attitudes – even when variables such as age, sex and social class were taken into account – Barker continued:

> Shouldn't one talk of the Cautious Sixties rather than the Swinging Sixties? Hardly any of the obsessions of the metropolitan mass media rate favourably; some of them don't even rate strongly. You emerge with the very strong impression that if the 1960s meant anything special to most people in Britain it was because they got, during them, a better chance to lead a not-too-poor, not-too-insecure life . . . Despite the way the 1960s have often been portrayed, this has not become a wildly changed country, people are not that keen on being disturbed.
>
> (Barker 1969: 850)

Women's Liberation Movement

The Women's Liberation Movement (WLM) emerged naturally out of the student politics of 1968. At a time when *all* forms of authority and oppression were being challenged, women perceived that the time had arrived to pursue their own claims to liberation alongside black civil rights marchers and fighters in South-East Asia. The feminist struggle of the late sixties had a long heritage, but it was also distinctly of its time. Although it is common to refer to the WLM as 'second wave' feminism, it perhaps makes more sense to point to at least three distinct phases in the history of the fight for women's rights. Before the 1960s British feminists had usually focused on the pursuit of specific objectives, most of them to do with notions of female and male equality. In the nineteenth century 'first phase' feminists had fought for equal rights in the public spheres of the workplace, higher education and national politics, culminating in the Suffragette campaign and the award of the vote to some women in 1918. In the inter-war years 'second phase' feminists shifted attention to the private sphere of the family, listing among their demands the provision of reliable contraception and state recognition of the value of mothers' unpaid work within the home by payment of family allowances (the latter was accepted in 1945). The 'third phase' feminisms (deliberately plural) that developed in the late sixties shared some of the objectives of earlier feminist campaigns, but ultimately they were more ambitious and profound than their forerunners: what they aimed at was a radical shift in male-female relations.

Although an otherwise diffuse movement found it convenient to co-alesce around a programme of four demands drawn up by the Women's National Co-ordination Committee in 1970 (equal pay, free oral contra-ception and abortion on request, equal educational and job opportunities, free twenty-four-hour childcare) the WLM was primarily concerned with a more fundamental analysis of contemporary femininity. Those who cared to look could see that, despite the social and cultural changes that transformed so much in Britain at the time, the sixties remained male-dominated. Public life and the workplace were primarily male spaces. Icons of popular culture tended to be male. As we have seen, of the twenty top-selling singles artists in the UK music charts of the sixties only three – Cilla Black, Dusty Springfield, The Supremes – were female. Films overwhelmingly dealt with male-centred narratives, viewing women on screen through the 'male gaze' of a camera lens that was almost always directed by men. The liberationist discourses of counter-cultural politics were similarly male-centred: in some hands they became blatantly sexist. As far as the editors of *OZ* and *IT* were concerned, female assertiveness was best represented via the clichéd signifiers of the dominatrix: stiletto heels, whips and chains. In May 1970 *OZ* at least attempted to redress the balance with its 'Female Energy Issue', featuring Germaine Greer's essay 'The Politics of Female Sexuality' (a dry run for her major book of that year *The Female Eunuch*). But the suspicion remained that *OZ*'s interest in feminist issues was tokenistic and certainly of far less importance than its obsession with sexual libertarianism. What was becoming apparent, to some women at least, was that the way they learned to be feminine arose out of a male-dominated culture, with women forced to operate within the narrow spaces allotted to femininity (Rowbotham 2000: 158).

Awareness of this cultural marginalisation of femininity spread in a variety of ways. Some read influential writers such as Juliet Mitchell, whose groundbreaking analysis 'Women: the Longest Revolution' appeared in *New Left Review* in 1966, or Sheila Rowbotham, who as an editor of *Black Dwarf* declared 1969 to be the 'Year of the Militant Woman'. Rowbotham's *New Left Review* essay in 1968, 'Women's Liberation and the New Politics' was followed by another important piece in *Black Dwarf* the following year, 'Women: the Struggle For Freedom'. For the predominantly university-educated women who made up the readership of these publications, Mitchell and Rowbotham provided a vocabulary and intellectual framework for understanding the nature of the struggle for women's liberation. More significantly still, the increased focus on feminist issues from 1968 onwards led to the development of a country-wide network of 'consciousness-raising' groups. These were the forums in which women met and discussed related issues of personal freedom, self-expression and female autonomy, often going on to draw political conclusions from their own personal experiences. The groups were small and informal and typically involved meeting at a group member's home. By late-1969 the network had spread to some seventy such groups. Significantly, although the WLM is often thought of as a campus-based organisation of young, single women, many of those who attended the consciousness-raising groups were married women with children. What soon emerged from these meetings was how many women felt stifled by their experiences of marriage and family life, with unfulfilling sex regarded by some as merely another household 'chore'. Suzanne Gail's account of married life in 'The Housewife', her contribution to Ronald Fraser's collection of testimonies, *Work*, captured the essence of this alienation (1968: 140–155). Gail was a graduate who, like many others before, had shelved her intellectual and career ambitions after the birth of her first child. As with other females of her generation who benefited from the expansion of higher education, she found that there was a chasm between the world of opportunities that she had been led to expect while a student and the reality of early marriage, young mother-hood and mind-numbing housework. Gail's piece suggested that the loss of identity and self-worth among married women in the United States chronicled by Betty Friedan in her best seller *The Feminine Mystique* (1963) was being replicated in Britain (where the average age of marriage for women in the sixties was 22, and where three out of five births were to women under 25). It was in the 'consciousness-raising' groups that women met and found that there were others like them who looked at their married lives and asked themselves: is this all? If the married idyll that had been pushed at them in women's magazines seemed unrecognis-able from their own negative experiences, women in the groups were at least reassured that this was not because of their own personal shortcom-ings. Instead, they realised that it was the structure of gender relations within the family that was the real cause of the problem, because it was this that left wives with the household chores while husbands were the ones with jobs, money and most of the power. Thus women's subordinate position within the family became a focal point for the WLM who regarded it as the platform on which wider sexual discrimination in society was built.

As we have seen in other contexts, much of the inspiration for the WLM came from across the Atlantic. In the United States Betty Friedan helped to set up the National Organisation of Women (NOW) in 1966, a group which pursued (in their words) a 'truly equal partnership between the sexes, as part of the world-wide revolution of human rights' (cited in Marwick 1998: 679–80). Some sections of the media trivialised Amer-ican feminists as bra-burners after protesters dumped their bras in rubbish bins outside the Miss America pageant in 1968. But NOW was a serious organisation that grew out of wider civil rights activities, anti-war marches and the Students for a Democratic Society movement's campaigning work. The first American National Women's Liberation Conference was organised in 1968, followed within two years by the inaugural British WLM conference at Ruskin College, Oxford in February

1970. Not only did the WLM draw on an organisational model from else-where, its analysis of the history of female subordination also had an internationalist flavour. In common with feminist movements across the west, the WLM reacted against the 'cult of domesticity' that enveloped women after the Second World War. Following the mobilisation of millions of females for the war effort, the return of peace saw a cultural backlash which emphasised both women's domestic roles and a parti-cular construction of femininity, perhaps represented best of all by the ultra-feminine lines of Dior's 'new look' fashions. By 1947 the number of women working in Britain had fallen by about 1.75 million from its wartime peak in 1943. As the sexual division of labour reverted to its pre-war norm, femininity became 'fetishised' and the advertising industry positioned women squarely as 'shoppers-in chief' in the new consumer economy (Coote and Campbell 1982: 12). Younger single women might work, but once they married they were expected to become full-time housewives. As Marjorie Ferguson's analysis showed, women's maga-zines of the period relentlessly pushed the idyll of love, marriage and domestic bliss. Publications like *Woman*, *Woman's Own* and *Woman's Weekly* constantly revisited the same themes: 'getting and keeping your man', 'the happy family', 'the working wife is a bad wife', 'self-help: achieving perfection' and 'be more beautiful' (Ferguson 1983: 44). In early-fifties Britain the Queen and her young family further reinforced this domestic ideal. Thus the limited wartime gains made by women, both in terms of the labour market and their status within marriage, had proven to be only temporary, leaving the WLM determined to press for the social and economic gains that their mothers' generation had been denied.

Again in common with the United States, female activists involved in the radical politics of the sixties' New Left believed that they were marginalised in an environment in which men 'led the marches and made the speeches and expected their female comrades to lick envelopes and listen' (Coote and Campbell 1982: 13). As far as most male activists were concerned, 'bourgeois feminism' was a distraction from the central issue of the class struggle: women's liberation would have to wait until 'after the revolution'. In the meantime, women were expected to make a useful contribution to the revolutionary struggle by making the tea during meetings and satisfying the sexual urges of their male comrades afterwards. As Coote and Campbell argue in *Sweet Freedom: The Struggle for Women's Liberation*, the pressures on women to demonstrate that they were sexually 'liberated' could be intense:

> In the era of flower-power and love-ins, of doing your own thing and not being hung up (especially about sex) 'girls' were expected to do it, and impose no conditions. The more they did it, the more 'liberated' they were deemed to be. It is true that the sixties' counter-culture challenged a lot of old ideas and allowed new ones to blossom; thus far, it nourished the roots of emergent feminism. But at the same time it added a new dimension to the oppression of women – setting them up, in their mini-skirts and mascara, alongside the wholefoods and hippy beads and hallucinogens, in a gallery of new toys with which men were now free to play.

(Coote and Campbell 1982: 19–20)

Sexual liberation, in other words, had profoundly different meanings for men and women. It was bad enough that women in general were expected to be sexually willing, both inside and outside marriage. Worse still, the sex itself so often failed to satisfy them. As Anna Koedt had explained in her widely distributed and influential paper, *The Myth of the Vaginal Orgasm* (1968), what was regarded as the 'norm' of penetrative sex was ideal for producing male orgasm, but it was much less likely to lead to female climax. Echoing the work of William H. Masters and Virginia Johnson in *Human Sexual Response* (1966), Koedt pointed out that the clitoris was the centre of female sexual ecstasy rather than the vagina, which in fact was largely devoid of feeling. This simple biological truth had long been suppressed, however, thereby continually locking women into unfulfilling sex lives and denying them a right to pleasure that was as fundamental as the right to vote or work. Seymour Fisher's survey *The Female Orgasm* (1972) produced some data to support this analysis, estimating that only 39 per cent of women had orgasm during intercourse. Frequently women had been led to blame themselves for the apparent 'frigidity' that prevented them from reaching orgasm. Now at least there was a wider recognition that the penetrative sexual act itself was the problem. Sex became politicised. Feminists categorised the 'norm' of penetrative sex as one more example of the wider male oppression which left women to lead half-lives. For sixties feminists, women's bodies and the sexual act both became important sites of struggle: hence their slogan 'the personal is political'. Anna Koedt, who insisted that sexuality had to be redefined so that women's pleasure need not be seen as dependent on men's, made the point cogently in 1968:

> *One of the elements of male chauvinism is the refusal or inability to see women as total, separate human beings. Rather . . . men have chosen to define women only in terms of how they benefit men's lives. Sexually, a woman is not seen as an individual wanting to share equally in the sexual act, any more than she was seen as a person with independent desires when she did anything else in society. Thus, it is easy for men to make up what facts are convenient about women, as society is controlled so that women have not been organised to form even a vocal opposition to the male 'experts'.*

(cited in Coote and Campbell 1982: 219)

Although the WLM undoubtedly drew on a general reconfiguring of female consciousness that crossed national boundaries, there were also more local issues at stake for British feminists. Of particular interest to socialist feminists were the 'hard' campaigns for equality in pay and workplace rights. In 1968 female sewing machinists at the Ford car plants in Dagenham and Halewood came out on strike in an attempt to win equal pay and grading with their male counterparts. The strike was a significant mobilisation of predominantly working-class women that caught the attention of the national press, even if the newspapers tended to patronise the strike leaders by portraying them as plucky 'girls' popping in for tea and talks with Barbara Castle, the Secretary of State for Employment. The eventual settlement represented a (not overwhelming) victory for the strikers, who secured 95 per cent of the men's rate while losing the battle for regrading. More importantly the strike had a galvanising effect on trade unionists and led to the formation of the National Joint Action Campaign for Women's Equal Rights, whose first rally was held in May 1969. Further encouragement for this campaign came with the Equal Pay Act of 1970, which stipulated that males and females should receive the same pay for doing the same job. Its implementation was delayed until 1975 in order to allow employers time to prepare their payroll adjustments. Also, women would have to wait until 1983 before the Act was amended to recognise the principle of equal pay between the sexes for work of comparable value. But the 1970 legislation was a step forward for female workers and it brought Britain into line with the Treaty of Rome in time for its entry into the EEC in 1973. The Equal Pay Act was thus welcomed, but the facts remained that women tended to be ghettoised in the lowest-paid jobs, and that sexual discrimination reached into every corner of national life. A Labour study group report, *Discrimination Against Women* (1972), gathered together some of the evidence. Although a 1965 Ministry of Labour survey found that more than half the female population aged 16–64 were employed, most of these worked in low-skill, low-pay jobs, with only 5 per cent employed as managers. Much of the increase in female participation in the labour force was due to older married women returning to work after they had raised their children. At the other end of the age-range, girls were more likely than boys to leave school at the minimum age (despite the fact that girls performed better than boys in the 11-plus examination) and females made up only 28 per cent of higher education students in 1970. Perhaps they had had enough of a curriculum that corralled them into studying domestic science. Women were massively under-represented in parliament and men dominated the ranks of government ministers. The report's authors were even forced to concede that their own party was failing to match its professed belief in sexual equality with deeds. At the time it was published there were 950 potential parliamentary candidates on Labour's 'A' and 'B' lists: only 69 of these were women. The gains made by feminists by the early seventies, it was clear, were far outweighed by the inequalities and discrimination that remained to be dismantled. What the WLM had provided above all, however, was a language and a conceptual framework for understanding the nature of the challenge that lay ahead.

CHAPTER 11

Powellism and nationalist politics

Powellism

It was in the middle of the confrontations of 1968 that the debate about race and immigration in Britain was redefined. Opponents of black immigration took the opportunity to argue that the country's changing ethnic composition was one part of a more general crisis threatening social stability in the late sixties. The most forceful advocate of this case was the Conservative politician Enoch Powell, whose comments on race in 1968 shattered the carefully-arranged party truce on the issue that had held for the past three years. The background to Powell's reigniting of the race debate was Roy Jenkins' attempt to extend civil rights for all races in Britain before his move from the Home Office to the Treasury. Jenkins had planned to extend the scope of the 1965 Race Relations Act and further his vision of a multi-racial society in which equal opportunity, cultural diversity and mutual tolerance became the norm (Jenkins 1991: 189). But in order not to disturb the bi-partisan approach to race policy, Jenkins delayed introducing a new Race Relations Bill until there was sufficient evidence that discrimination was widespread enough to warrant further legislation. The onus was thus placed on organisations such as the National Committee for Commonwealth Immigrants and the Race Relations Board to produce the data that would convince both politicians and a sceptical public. Their response was jointly to commission Political and Economic Planning Ltd (PEP) to conduct research on racial discrimination in Britain, the fieldwork for which took place in late 1966 and early 1967. According to an opinion poll taken soon after the report's publication in April 1967, the PEP findings convinced 66 per cent of the public that 'a great deal' or 'quite a lot' of racial discrimination occurred in Britain in the key fields of housing and employment (Hiro 1991: 217–8). However, just as the way was clear for an extension of anti-discrimination legislation, the politics of race were complicated by the legacy of Britain's imperial retreat from Kenya.

When Kenya was granted independence in 1963 the then Colonial Secretary, Iain Macleod, sought to protect its minority racial groups (mainly white settlers and Indians) by allowing any resident of the country to apply for British citizenship. When a strongly nationalistic government embarked on a policy of 'Africanisation' in Kenya in 1967, some of those non-nationals who were pushed out of their jobs and businesses chose to follow up the promises made to them by the British government at the time of independence. Understandably, they believed they had a right to settle in Britain. But as thousands of Kenyan Asians arrived in the autumn of 1967 and the early months of 1968, the Conservative MPs Enoch Powell and Duncan Sandys led a campaign to restrict the numbers allowed entry. Party leader Edward Heath took up the cause, warning of 'serious social consequences' if Kenyan Asians came to Britain 'at a rate which could not be satisfactorily absorbed' (Campbell 1993: 242). The debate about race had shifted from its focus on integration and multiculturalism back to the issues of quotas and the numbers of blacks and South Asians in the UK. On 27 February 1968 Home Secretary Callaghan, anxious not to be seen as 'soft' on immigration, introduced an emergency Commonwealth Immigration Bill which was rushed through both Houses of Parliament within a week. Its effect was to restrict unconditional rights of entry into the UK to those who had close ties to the country by birth, naturalisation or descent (Layton-Henry 1992: 52, 79). This qualification presented no problem to former white settlers in Kenya, but those Kenyan Asians who failed to qualify under the new rules had to take their chances with a voucher system that allowed in only 1,500 of them a year. Michael Foot described the Bill as 'shameful' and was one of 35 Labour MPs who voted against the legislation, together with 15 Conservatives and all the Liberal MPs. *The Times* criticised the Bill as racially discriminatory. Auberon Waugh took a similar view in the *Spectator*, arguing that the Act was 'one of the most immoral pieces of legislation to have emerged from any British Parliament' (Layton-Henry 1992: 52–3).

As a positive counter-weight to a measure that caused dismay among the liberal intelligentsia in Labour's ranks, Callaghan published a new Race Relations Bill in April that went beyond the 1965 Act. The atmosphere in which the Bill was to be debated had already been inflamed by the Kenyan Asians crisis. Then, on 20 April, Enoch Powell pushed the temperature even higher with a speech in Birmingham in which he called for a virtual halt to all further non-white immigration and for a system of voluntary repatriation to be introduced to offset the natural increase in the black and South Asian population that was already settled in Britain. Television cameras were there to record sections of the speech. Powell claimed that he was merely articulating the concerns of his constituents, but his language could hardly have been more inflammatory.

> We must be mad, literally mad, as a nation to be permitting the annual inflow of some 50,000 dependants who are for the most part the material of the future growth of the immigrant-descended population. It is like watching a nation busily engaged in heaping up its own funeral pyre.
>
> (cited in Roth 1970: 352)

Discrimination, deprivation and the sense of alarm and resentment, said Powell, were problems not for the immigrant population, but for the urban white population among whom immigrants settled. He told the story of a terrified pensioner in Wolverhampton who was the only white person left in her street (local newspapers and the BBC 'Panorama' team tried to locate this woman but she was never found). 'She is becoming afraid to go out', Powell explained. 'Windows are broken. She finds excreta pushed through her letter box. When she goes to the shops she is followed by children, charming wide-grinning piccaninnies. They cannot speak English, but one word they know. "Racialist" they chant'. Thus, he continued, to extend race relations legislation in the way that Labour now proposed was to 'risk throwing a match on to gun powder' (cited in Roth 1970: 353–4). The most apocalyptic rhetoric was saved for the conclusion.

As I look ahead, I am filled with foreboding. Like the Roman, I seem to see 'the River Tiber foaming with much blood!' That tragic and intractable phenomenon which we watch with horror on the other side of the Atlantic but which there is interwoven with the history and existence of the States itself, is coming upon us here by our own volition and our own neglect.

(cited in Roth 1970: 357)

The 'river of blood' speech was disowned by Edward Heath, who sacked Powell from the Shadow Cabinet the next day. Among much of the wider public, however, Powell was regarded as a champion, the one politician with the courage to speak on behalf of the 'silent' white majority. His supporters regarded his sacking from Heath's front bench as martyrdom, and an early warning of how anti-discrimination laws were a danger to free speech. Letters of support for Powell poured in by the thousand, far outweighing the correspondence that deplored his views. According to Diana Spearman's analysis of a sample of these letters for *New Society*, most of those who supported Powell cited their fears that continued non-white immigration would undermine the country's culture, heritage and traditions (1968: 667–9). Opinion polls found that between 67 and 82 per cent of people approved the speech. Days after his sacking, London dockers (who reportedly sang 'Bye Bye Blackbird' outside parliament) and meat porters staged walkouts in support of Powell. Similar token strikes took place in Southampton, Norwich, Coventry and Gateshead among other places. Sheila Rowbotham recalled how when she went to teach some Port of London Authority messenger boys at college shortly after the speech, the class stood up and gave her the fascist salute as she entered the room (Rowbotham 2000: 173). More seriously, Powell's speech gave some people a licence to bring their prejudices out into the open. Violent attacks on non-whites increased, immigrants' property was damaged and racial taunts became commonplace. As Mike Phillips recalled, Powell's speech was a turning point for Britain's immigrant population. The message went out clearly that they were not wanted, and many felt enormously threatened as a consequence ('Windrush', BBC TV, 1998).

Powell successfully stirred up emotions on race and immigration issues, but the second Race Relations Bill continued its journey through the legislature. The Act that was passed in October 1968 banned racial discrimination in housing, employment, insurance and other services. The 'No Coloureds' and 'Europeans Only' signs used by employers and landlords were also outlawed along with other forms of racially discriminatory advertising. To enforce the Act, the Race Relations Board was reconstituted with wider powers to investigate claims of racism. Meanwhile the Board's old function of promoting good race relations passed to a new Community Relations Commission, chaired initially by Frank Cousins. In summary the Act was a well-intentioned attempt to advance fairness and racial harmony. In practice, however, it was undermined by some important flaws. First, there were several important loopholes. Employers could discriminate against non-white job applicants in order to maintain a 'racial balance' in their workplace. Also, the new law could not be used as grounds to bring a complaint against the police. Second, the Act proved difficult to enforce in the key areas of employment and housing. Whereas the Race Relations Board found it easy to uphold complaints about discriminatory advertising, it upheld only 10 per cent of the 1241 complaints it received about discriminatory employers up to January 1972 (Hiro 1991: 222). On the very infrequent occasions when the Board took court action against discrimination it sought only nominal damages. Perhaps not surprisingly, the number of complaints it received in the late sixties and early seventies remained at the low level of about 1,000 each year (Layton-Henry 1992: 54–5). This was more a reflection of victims' perception that they would be wasting their time if they complained rather than evidence that levels of discrimination were falling. After all, another PEP report researched between 1972 and 1975 confirmed that, despite the 1968 Act, racial discrimination in employment and (to a slightly lesser extent) housing continued to occur on a large scale .

By the late sixties, therefore, the race debate was far from settled. Despite the Home Office's liberal intentions, racial prejudice remained a normal rather than an exceptional feature of British culture. Within this overall context, however, there was at least a minority who celebrated the cultural impact of post-war immigrants, particularly the arrival of those from the West Indies. The young white hippies of the underground romanticised aspects of black urban culture, chiefly the clothes, the music (jazz, ska and blue-beat) and the marijuana. In cafes such as the

Rio in Notting Dale or the Mangrove Restaurant in All Saints Road, Notting Hill, small numbers of white bourgeois kids bought dope from black dealers and stepped into their own fantasy world of hustlers and black urban cool. The fantasy was based on a caricature of black culture, but at least it was essentially benign. The Notting Hill Carnival, which grew rapidly from its small-scale origins in the early sixties, provided another opportunity to affirm the presence of black migrants, at least in London. In the realm of politics the Campaign Against Racial Discrimination had pushed the case for mutual understanding and racial tolerance since its inception in December 1964. Liberal journalists such as Colin MacInnes, Colin Smith and writers for the underground press, meanwhile, gave sympathetic coverage to the British equivalent of America's Black Power movement – the Racial Adjustment Action Society (RAAS) – and its leader Michael Abdul Malik, better known as Michael X.

Notwithstanding this progressive minority, however, Powell's 'river of blood' speech exposed the depth of hostility towards multiculturalism in the sixties. Throughout the rest of the decade and into the seventies, Powell continued his public crusade against immigration, arguing that a 'true' British national identity could only be based on ethnicity and a shared heritage rather than legal definitions drawn up by the Home Office. Black immigrants, he argued, diluted the British 'national character' and were therefore a threat to the country's stability and social cohesion. This was because, Powell reasoned, black immigrants and their descendants would never show allegiance to the dominant cultural norms of white society, while the majority of whites would always see them as alien to their conception of 'Britishness' (Saggar 1992: 176). The immediate beneficiaries of the more openly hostile climate on race that developed through 1968 were the National Front, a party that was formed the previous year from the merger of the League of Empire Loyalists and the British National Party. The Front's membership and support levels steadily increased after April 1968. It only managed to gain 3.5 per cent of the vote in the seats it fought in the 1970 election, but perhaps this owed something to the fact that Heath's Conservatives (despite condemning Powell's views on race) adopted a tougher line on immigration controls in their 1970 manifesto, promising an end to any further 'large-scale permanent immigration'. The resultant 1971 Immigration Act restricted automatic rights of British residency to those who were born in the country, or whose parents or grandparents were British-born (by definition mainly white citizens of the 'Old' Commonwealth). Others would have to apply for a work permit and wait at least five years before they could gain permanent residence. Thus, despite talk of a 'liberal hour' at the Home Office in the sixties, the beginning of the following decade saw an Act that virtually halted black primary immigration into Britain. After Margaret Thatcher captured the Conservative leadership in 1975, attention switched to closing the door on secondary migration – newcomers joining their family who had already settled in Britain. In the late sixties, therefore, popular support for Powellism had pushed Britain towards some of the toughest immigration controls in the world.

A United Kingdom?

Enoch Powell had shown how it was possible to mobilise a particular brand of defensive nationalism in the late sixties, based around the idea that 'white' British national identity was under threat from New Commonwealth migrants. But immigration was not the only dynamic that led some people to fear that the fabric of the United Kingdom was coming apart at the time. Ever since the fifties, the campaign by Scottish and Welsh nationalists (joined by fellow devolutionists in the remoter regions of England) for a reform of the UK constitution had been gathering pace, sparking off a serious debate on this issue for the first time since the 1920 partition of Ireland. In March 1955 the Commons had briefly debated a private member's bill for a Welsh parliament, introduced by S.O. Davies, the Labour MP for Merthyr. The case for Scottish devolution, meanwhile, had been made in the form of a massive petition before the 1950 election, and was regularly articulated by politicians and commentators alike throughout the rest of the decade (Bennie, Brand and Mitchell 1997: 2; Kendle 1997: 158–9). Too often, the reformers argued, the needs of Scotland, Wales and indeed the English regions were ignored at Westminster and Whitehall because ministers and officials were preoccupied with the problems of south-east England. The Conservative and Labour parties, however, were largely unmoved by their arguments, not least because neither *Plaid Cymru* (the Welsh nationalist party) nor the Scottish National Party (SNP) was able to attract enough support – particularly in urban areas – to win parliamentary seats. The breakthrough that shook them out of their complacency came in July 1966, when Gwynfor Evans won *Plaid Cymru*'s first Westminster seat at the Carmarthen by-election (ironically at the expense of a strongly nationalistic Labour candidate, Gwilym Prys Davies). A little over a year later, following the SNP's earlier successes in local elections in the mid-1960s, Winifred Ewing overturned a huge Labour majority and won the Hamilton by-election for the SNP in November 1967. *The Times* read the signs of this victory and called for a commission that would look into the UK's constitutional arrangements and consider the case for setting up local parliaments for Scottish and Welsh affairs. It was now clear that the issue of Celtic nationalism could no longer be pushed into the background: the lesson of Irish nationalism in the previous century was that to delay reform was to invite disaster. In February 1968 Liberal leader Jeremy Thorpe pushed the debate one step further by calling for the establishment of parliaments in Wales, Scotland and Northern Ireland, and for the appointment of a royal commission to examine the feasibility of English regional assemblies. The following April, Thorpe's party published its own blueprint for regionalism, *Power to the Provinces*. The momentum behind the devolutionists' case was irresistible. In April 1969 Harold Wilson bowed to the pressure and set up a Royal Commission on the Constitution, chaired by the economic journalist Geoffrey Crowther.

Such a concession by an English Prime Minister offered Welsh and Scottish nationalists, in theory at least, the prospect of home rule. In Wales this was a testament to the nationalists' success in mobilising popular opinion behind their campaign, in urban areas as well as the Welsh-speaking rural parts of the country. The unifying element in what was at times a diffuse nationalist movement was the desire to preserve the Welsh language, a project whose urgency had been brought into sharper focus by the findings of the 1961 language census, which showed that only 25 per cent of the country spoke Welsh. More alarming still for the future of a separate Welsh identity was the fact that the proportion of native speakers among the young was even lower (Morgan 1981: 359–60, 382). These findings had prompted the veteran nationalist Saunders Lewis to come out of retirement in 1962 to issue a call for the adoption of 'revolutionary methods' to keep alive a language which, he asserted, was the only true basis of nationalist politics or ideology in Wales. The result

was the formation of the Welsh Language Society the same year, supported in large number by university students who employed what were
soon to become the familiar tactics of sit-ins and demonstrations by the
idealistic young in pursuit of a cause. English-language road signs were
defaced, placards were waved and TV studios were invaded by demonstrators who demanded that more programmes in Wales be broadcast in
the Welsh language. Echoing the way that their young counterparts in
other countries were showing a preference for organic culture over the
slick product of major commercial interests, Welsh youth embraced a
burgeoning indigenous pop culture and supported the output of Welsh
folk singers such as Dafydd Iwan (Morgan 1981: 385). A minority chose
to express their nationalism more violently. The 'Free Wales Army', a
fringe group of militants who drew deliberate parallels with the Irish
Republican Army, planted bombs in public buildings and issued death
threats to prominent figures associated with the Westminster government. Their tactics were condemned both by *Plaid Cymru* and the Welsh
Language Society, whose growing authority was boosted in 1967 when
the Welsh Language Act gave Welsh equal validity with English for
official, governmental and legal purposes.

Although the fight to preserve the language was central to nationalist
efforts, there were other issues that contributed to the cause of Welsh
home rule. Certainly *Plaid Cymru* owed much of their spectacular progress in by-elections to the travails of a Labour government being dragged
down by a stagnant economy and recurrent problems with sterling.
Industrial Wales, so long the heart of Labour's electoral support, suffered
more than most regions in the difficult economic climate of the late sixties. Collieries were closed throughout the valleys as part of the government's 'rationalisation' of the coal industry, but the accompanying
programme to replace these lost jobs with factory work made only slow
progress. As a result, unemployment in parts of the country climbed
above 10 per cent. The Welsh Office, set up in 1964 when Labour came to
power, appeared to have neither the budget nor the administrative force
to punch with any real weight in Whitehall and lead a drive for Welsh
economic recovery. As *Plaid Cymru* picked up support from disillusioned
voters who had supported Labour in 1964 and 1966, cynics wondered
whether Wilson's announcement of a royal commission on the constitution was anything more than a delaying device to halt the nationalists'

momentum. If indeed this had been the government's intention, the strategy worked very well. As was the custom with such bodies, the Crowther Commission proceeded slowly, eventually issuing its findings as the Kilbrandon Report in 1973 (Crowther had died in the meantime). In the years in which the commission carried out its work, Welsh nationalist energies were diverted away from promoting the straightforward principle of home rule and towards the minutiae of the proposed *form* of self-government. Matters were not helped by the Welsh Conservatives, who undermined the Commission's legitimacy by refusing to submit any evidence to its proceedings, professing instead their commitment to the sanctity of the union. By the time the Kilbrandon Report was published, the moment of devolution had passed. Perhaps the investiture of the Prince of Wales at Carmarthen Castle in 1969 played a part in promoting emotional support for the Anglo-Welsh union. Perhaps, as Kenneth Morgan has suggested, the success of the Welsh rugby team in beating England with 'embarrassing and monotonous regularity' was satisfaction enough for some nationalists in the late sixties and early seventies (1981: 348). But what was beyond speculation was that by 1970 *Plaid Cymru*'s progress had stalled. In the June 1970 election they failed to win a seat, despite contesting every Welsh constituency. Worse still, they lost Gwynfor Evans' seat at Carmarthen. With the Conservatives back in power, the prospects of Welsh devolution receded into the distance, lying dormant until Labour's narrow election victory in October 1974 left the new government dependent on the support of the nationalist parties and willing to trade Home Rule in return. Few *Plaid Cymru* supporters would have predicted at this time that it would be another twenty-five years before a Welsh Assembly was finally established in Cardiff.

The announcement of the Crowther Commission in 1969 similarly helped to smother the brief surge in support for the SNP which had brought them victory at the Hamilton by-election in 1967 and subsequent success in local council elections. As in Wales, the SNP had benefited from the growing perception that the government's economic policy was driven by the needs of voters in south-east England at the expense of other parts of the UK – even though by the late sixties public spending per head in Scotland was 20 per cent above the British average (Fry 1987: 229). Many Scottish voters saw that Labour's crisis measures to stabilise the exchange value of sterling caused greater difficulties north of the

border than south of it. As the post-war collapse of Scottish industry continued – in coal, steel, shipbuilding and textiles – governments of either
party were criticised for their failure to create sufficient alternative
employment. Between 1955 and 1965 Scotland had the lowest economic
growth rate in Europe. This was despite the fact that the state had spon-
sored several large-scale industrial projects in the post-war years, including the Dounreay nuclear power station at Caithness in the mid-1950s.
The continued retreat from empire also caused particular problems in
Scotland, hitting the old imperial markets for Scottish goods and threatening the continued existence of the popular Argyll and Sutherland
Highlanders regiment (Finlay 1998: 40). The stationing of Polaris nuclear
submarines at Scottish bases, thus making them potential first targets in a
Cold War nuclear strike, was a further grievance. All of these contributed
to the nationalist revival of the sixties, led by remnants of the old
Independent Labour Party (ILP) and CND. When both the Labour and
Conservative parties re-examined their Scottish policies in the wake of
the Hamilton by-election, the message went out across Scotland that
support for the SNP was an effective way of forcing the Westminster
parliament to take notice of Scottish affairs. In 1968 the Conservatives
(temporarily) came out in favour of Scottish devolution. Labour, who
continued to oppose Scottish devolution until the mid-1970s, offered
greater economic assistance for Scotland and bought itself time with the
Crowther Commission. Unfortunately for the SNP, its ability to perform
well in by-elections, when it could concentrate resources and benefit
from a high media profile, was not reproduced in the 1970 general election. As Fry argued, when it came to the serious business of electing
a government for the United Kingdom, Scottish voters – particularly in
urban areas – returned to their old major party allegiances (1987: 219). In
central Scotland this meant working-class voters turning out to support
Labour. Only when recession bit in the early seventies, and the value of
North Sea oil revenues became apparent at about the same time, did the
SNP once more ask serious questions of the main party hegemony. Far
from aiding the Scottish economy, claimed the nationalists, the union
was holding Scottish recovery back because it served to deny Scotland
the full benefit of its oil revenues. However, as the 1973 Kilbrandon
Report surmised, what most Scottish voters seemed to want was a union
that served national needs more effectively and in which Scottish

national identity was properly recognised. This of course fell some way short of a desire for self-government:

> The greatest significance of the Scottish Nationalist movement lies not in its advocacy of separatism but in the means which it has provided for the people of Scotland to register their feelings of national identity and political importance. Nationalist voters, and the obvious sympathy they have attracted from a good many others who would not by themselves be prepared by their votes to endorse a separatist policy, have drawn attention to an intensity of national feeling in Scotland which people outside that country were not generally aware of.
>
> (Kilbrandon Report, cited in Fry 1987: 221)

The failure of the nationalists to secure the required share of the vote in the 1979 devolution referendum seemed to confirm the point. Again in common with *Plaid Cymru*, the SNP would have to wait until the election of New Labour in 1997 to realise their ambition of a devolved parliament, a goal that was a step towards their ultimate aim of an independent Scotland within the European Union.

In Northern Ireland the politics of national identity were more complex and more violently confrontational. The six-county state had been partitioned from the rest of Ireland by the 1920 Government of Ireland Act and the 1921 Anglo-Irish Treaty. For almost fifty years the Westminster parliament had left the running of Northern Ireland to a Protestant and unionist government based at Stormont. In the Republic of Ireland (as it formally became in 1949), and among nationalists in Northern Ireland, the six counties were regarded from the outset as a provisional state. A reunified Irish Republic was their objective, but it remained a distant one as the British Exchequer underwrote the unionist ascendancy at Stormont and turned a blind eye to the sectarian practices used by successive unionist governments against Catholics: after all, the point of partition had been to remove the 'Irish question' from Britain's political agenda. Thus the electoral system, council house allocation and employment procedures were all run in favour of Protestants, supported by the B-Special armed militia, free from any attempt by the government at Westminster to protect the rights of the (sizeable) Catholic minority. By the 1960s the United Kingdom parliament routinely spent less than two hours each year discussing Northern Ireland matters (Coogan 1996: 39).

Within the Home Office, Northern Ireland's affairs were filed away under a 'General' heading (Morgan 1997: 347). Even the warnings of impending crisis provided by the sectarian riots of 1964 and the first deaths in what were to become 'the Troubles' in 1966 failed to persuade the British government to act. Their confidence that Irish nationalism could be contained had been heightened by the failure of the IRA campaign in 1956–62 to force Britain out of the northern state. Only after the Northern Ireland Civil Rights Association (NICRA) was set up in 1967 was Wilson's government forced to consider seriously the position of a nationalist community within a Protestant state.

NICRA was inspired by the black civil rights movement of the United States and later by the student protests of 1968. It developed out of two existing pressure groups, the Northern Wolfe Tone Society and the Campaign for Social Justice in Northern Ireland. Previously, these pressure groups had been encouraged by the fact that about a hundred Labour MPs at Westminster had shown their support for improved civil rights in Northern Ireland via the Campaign for Democracy in Ulster (Buckland 1981: 108, 118). But mounting frustration at their inability to win concessions from Terence O'Neill's Stormont administration, together with pressure for direct action from Catholic areas in the west, led them to adopt street protest as a new and more direct tactic. NICRA's first large-scale march was held in August 1968. It passed off relatively peacefully, but a second march through Derry on 5 October ran into Ian Paisley's Unionist counter-demonstrators and a Protestant police force that apparently relished the chance to beat up some civil rights marchers. As television carried pictures of the violence far beyond the six counties, Wilson urged Unionist leaders to commit themselves to reforms that would meet some of the protesters' demands. By now, however, opinions were hardening on either side of the sectarian divide. On the Catholic side the People's Democracy (PD) was formed by students after the October march, soon emerging as an uncompromising socialist and republican organisation. Leading figures within the PD – which was by no means *exclusively* Catholic – included Michael Farrell and Bernadette Devlin, who became the youngest woman ever elected to Westminster when she stood as an anti-Unionist candidate in the Mid-Ulster by-election in April 1969. Paisley, meanwhile, was the figurehead of a more militant form of Unionism that regarded any concessions by O'Neill towards the Catholic minority as a sell-out. Serious confrontations came during the four-day civil rights march from Belfast to Derry organised by the PD in January 1969 (despite a moratorium on marches called by NICRA in response to O'Neill's plea for them to 'take the heat out of the situation'). The marchers were ambushed when they reached Derry, after which a wave of rioting broke out in which Catholic houses in the Bogside were attacked by a mob which included off-duty policemen.

Violence in the province escalated, including the start of rival bombing campaigns by the Ulster Volunteer Force and the IRA in spring 1969. This was a further blow to O'Neill's position as premier, which had become increasingly untenable since the start of the civil rights campaign. Catholics soon lost faith in O'Neill's promises of civil rights reforms. Within the Unionist community, where there had been a degree of suspicion of O'Neill ever since he had invited Sean Lemass to become the first *Taoiseach* from the Irish Republic to attend a meeting at Stormont Castle in January 1965, O'Neill's credibility as a defender of Unionism had drained away. In April 1969 he resigned and was replaced by James Chichester-Clark. Any faint prospects of establishing some form of peaceful co-existence of the two communities, however, were extinguished during the Protestant marching season of July and August. There were riots throughout the province on 11 and 12 July. When the Orange Order Apprentice Boys marched though Derry on 12 August, Catholics responded with stone-throwing and a two-day siege of the city. On the night of 14–15 August Protestants in Belfast took their revenge on the Catholic community by burning out between 150 and 200 of their homes. In rioting across Belfast, five Catholics and one Protestant were killed (Buckland 1981: 129–31). Faced with the breakdown of local law and order, Callaghan sent in British troops to Derry and Belfast in what he hoped would be a medium-term military response to a crisis. In an effort to find a more permanent political solution to the situation in Northern Ireland, senior British ministers met with their Stormont counterparts on 19 August and issued the Downing Street Declaration. This promised an enquiry into the recent conduct of the Protestant police, a commitment to phase out the hated B-Specials, and pledges to reform local government, voting rights and housing.

The Declaration encouraged hopes of power-sharing and reform via constitutional politics in Northern Ireland. One year later the moderate nationalist Social and Democratic Labour Party (SDLP) was formed, with Gerry Fitt as its first leader. But the Wilson government's decision to prop up Chichester-Clark in the hope that he could carry much-needed reforms, rather than accept that the Stormont parliament had failed and should be replaced by direct rule from Westminster, proved to be a mistake. It was not long before the Catholic communities who had initially welcomed British troops came to regard them as an occupying force. In January 1970 the Provisional IRA emerged in the wake of the previous summer's riots, alarmed at the presence of the British Army on the streets and dismayed by the shift of focus within the nationalist community away from the goal of a united Irish Republic and towards a preoccupation with constitutional politics and civil rights. Throughout the seventies the Provisional IRA fought a campaign against the British presence in Northern Ireland, with bombings and shootings both in the province and across the Irish Sea in England. This contributed to an escalation of violence in which Unionist paramilitaries and the British security services played their parts. In March 1972 a Conservative government at last abolished Stormont and introduced direct rule of the province from Westminster. It was another twenty years before there was a serious prospect of power sharing, following the start of an IRA ceasefire in September 1994.

◆◆◆◆◆◆◆◆◆◆◆◆◆◆◆

Labour crisis and Conservative recovery, 1968–70

Troubles and strife: Labour in power, January 1968–July 1969

Despite the emerging crises demanding ministers' attention at home and abroad, the 'leadership question' overshadowed all government business for months after the November 1967 devaluation. Plotting against the Prime Minister went on almost continuously, coordinated in the main by ex-Gaitskellites who had tolerated Harold Wilson only so long as they saw him as an electoral asset. As Wilson's public approval ratings plunged to depths last seen when Eden was in office, falling as low as 27 per cent in May 1968, they were at last emboldened to move against a man they had long hated. Wilson, they complained, was an isolated leader whose personal insecurities left him over-reliant on a 'kitchen cabinet' of officials, advisers and acolytes led by his political secretary Marcia Williams. Convinced that only a new leader could reconnect the government with the Cabinet, the PLP and the wider party, the dissidents busied themselves preparing the ground for a *putsch*. The plotting lasted for at least eighteen months, until by May 1969 a group was collecting signatures in an effort to force a leadership vote in the parliamentary party. Earlier, the 'Wilson must go' campaign had reached beyond parliament, as Cecil King, chairman of International Publishing Corporation (which owned the *Mirror* newspapers), led a bizarre conspiracy with some of the wilder elements of MI5 to replace Wilson's administration with a National Government. In May 1968 King even tried (unsuccessfully) to persuade Lord Mountbatten to head such a coalition. On 10 May the *Mirror* carried a signed leading article headed 'Enough Is Enough' in which King urged Labour MPs to bring Wilson down (Dudley Edwards 2003: 26–8). The Prime Minister shrugged off King's treachery (King in fact was soon sacked by the IPC Board), but he was much more anxious about his dwindling level of support within the party. Many of his colleagues were now sworn enemies and even his normally loyal friends – Barbara Castle, Richard Crossman, Tony Benn and Anthony Greenwood – feared he was buckling under the pressure of leading a divided and demoralised party. Wilson was forced to devote ever more time and energy to protecting his own position, reshuffling his ministerial team with his mind focused solely on how the changes would shore up his own authority. As the pressure mounted, his ascendancy in the Commons briefly suffered as Edward Heath made ground with the charge that the government had mismanaged the economy. It was a charge that carried some weight, particularly during early 1968, when a second devaluation of sterling seemed a possibility. If that had happened, it is difficult to see how Wilson's premiership could have survived. In such an event, the most likely heirs to the crown were James Callaghan (whose political stock recovered after his departure from the Treasury) and Roy Jenkins. Both were well aware that their supporters inside parliament were working against the Prime Minister, and both at times undermined Wilson by withholding their support on key issues. After these two, Tony Crosland and Denis Healey were mentioned as rising stars and possible alternative leaders. The dilemma that faced each of these challengers, however, was how to bring about Wilson's downfall without delivering the leadership to any of the others. Ultimately, what saved Wilson throughout 1968 and much of 1969 was the lack of agreement about who should replace him.

The background to the leadership crisis was Britain's deteriorating economic position. Far from 'breaking free' after devaluation, the government's popularity nosedived as spending was cut, taxes were raised and home consumption fell. In January 1968 an emergency economic package saw the reintroduction of prescription charges, the postponement of the pledge to raise the school-leaving age to 16 and the withdrawing of free milk in secondary schools. Twenty-six mainly left-wing Labour MPs abstained from supporting these cuts. In part to balance the domestic sacrifices, the timetable for withdrawing British forces from east of Suez was brought forward to March 1971, and the government's planned purchase of American F-111 fighter-bomber aircraft was cancelled. These measures were humiliating for Wilson, whose critics were quick to remind him that he had resigned from Attlee's government in 1951 because it had introduced prescription charges. More serious still, the spending cuts failed to stabilise the economy. In mid March 1968, Wilson and Jenkins were forced into an emergency closure of the London gold market in order to prevent a further run on the pound. This closure required a hastily convened late-night meeting of the Privy Council at Buckingham Palace in order to proclaim a Bank Holiday for the following day. The arrangement took place without the knowledge of George Brown, the Foreign Secretary, who then resigned in protest at Wilson's 'presidential' style of government during an impromptu meeting of half the Cabinet in the early hours of 15 March (Brown 1971: 169–184). Brown had 'resigned' several times before but had been talked round. Despite his genuine anger at Wilson's failure to consult the Cabinet properly before going to the Palace he was prepared to backtrack again on this occasion. But Wilson by now had tired of Brown's volatility and decided that the time had come to cut him adrift. Days later, Roy Jenkins introduced what was then the most deflationary peacetime budget in British history. Taxes were increased by £900 million – mainly on cigarettes, alcohol and petrol – in an attempt to bring about a 1 per cent fall in living standards and reduce the flow of imports into Britain. Jenkins explained to the Commons that he had produced a 'stiff budget' that was to be followed by 'two years' hard slog' to correct the balance of payments. Labour backbenchers cheered the Chancellor's austerity as a giant stride towards economic recovery. The public verdict, however, was less positive. In the aftermath of the Budget, the government lost three seats at by-elections, including George Wigg's Dudley constituency (which Labour had held since 1945) on a swing of 21 per cent. These defeats were part of a dismal by-election record for the Wilson government after March 1966: Labour lost 16 of the 31 seats it defended in this period, more than the party had managed in its entire history since 1900, and a far worse record than any post-war government. Its performance in the May 1968 local elections was equally unimpressive: only 450 Labour councillors were returned. Things were no better for the party in the (rather more limited) local elections of May 1969 (Howell 1980: 275).

With the government lagging behind in the polls, in April 1968 Wilson reshuffled his Cabinet and attempted to re-energise his administration by focusing on two important measures of reform. The first concerned the House of Lords, the second involved trade union law. In 1966 Labour had pledged to take away the Lords' power to delay legislation. But matters became complicated when responsibility for Lords' reform was given to Richard Crossman, then Leader of the Commons. Crossman decided that in place of the relatively straightforward plan to strip the Lords of their delaying powers, a full-scale reform of the Upper House was more desirable. In April 1967 he persuaded Wilson to accept his view. The following September, with Wilson offering strong support, he was able to secure the backing of sceptical Cabinet colleagues. There followed months of intra-party talks which aimed to find a common-ground approach to reducing the Lords' powers and ending the hereditary basis of the Upper House. When the Lords, most of whom not surprisingly opposed reform, fought back by defeating the renewal of sanctions against Rhodesia in June 1968, the cross-party talks were called off. A reluctant Callaghan was delegated to push through parliament a reforming Bill, based on a White Paper that was endlessly redrafted. But as the Bill went to the full House of Commons (as a constitutional measure it could not be taken by a small committee) in February 1969, it ran into severe difficulties. Michael Foot and Enoch Powell, each for different reasons, combined to block its progress. Foot did not want to see a reformed House of Lords given greater legitimacy to challenge elected governments. Powell, meanwhile, objected to any reform of an ancient pillar of the constitution. The two of them marshalled their deep knowledge of constitutional history and parliamentary procedure to prolong the discussion of every line of every clause in the proposed legislation. Faced with the obstructive tactics of two highly-skilled parliamentarians, and with no prospect of introducing reform before the next general election, the Bill was dropped in April 1969. It was a humiliating climb-down, particularly for Crossman and Wilson who had championed the cause since 1967. Despite its large Commons majority, the government had been forced to abandon an important piece of legislation (Ponting 1990: 342–9).

The second major policy initiative at this time, trade union reform, was the centrepiece of Wilson's latest strategy for modernising the economy. Curbing union militancy would also show that his government was prepared to take a tough line against one of the forces seen to be threatening the social order in 1968. The task of delivering reform was given to Barbara Castle, who took over at the new Department of Employment and Productivity because, as Wilson said with unintended irony, she was 'good at getting on with the trade unions' (Castle 1993: 398). Castle shared the Prime Minister's view that the time had come to reform trade union practices. Too often, they agreed, the unions had obstructed the government's economic policies and its plans for restructuring British industry. Pay restraint had proved almost impossible to achieve and militant shop stewards had organised strike action against job losses in the industries the government believed were suffering from surplus capacity. Memories of the 1966 seamen's strike and its damaging effect on sterling were still fresh, and Wilson well knew that there would be wide public support for any action which was seen to curb union power. Unions, for their part, could not see why lower-paid workers should have to accept wage restraint when there were no restrictions on professional earnings and managerial salaries, and no limitations on earnings from capital investment. To the left (both radical and parliamentary) it looked as if the government was intent on disciplining the working classes. Moreover, union members were suffering not only as a result of the government's belt-tightening austerity measures, but also because of its commitment to industrial modernisation. Between 1964 and 1969, for example, a programme of pit closures saw the loss of 45 per cent of mining jobs in the northern region (Howell 1980: 259). As early as 1965, the government had set up a Royal Commission under Lord Donovan to report on the trade unions and generate some momentum for reform. But when the Donovan Report was published in June 1968 it disappointed those who had hoped that it would recommend a tough line against the unions. Rejecting the use of legal sanctions against unofficial strikes as unworkable, Donovan concentrated on measures to reform collective bargaining procedures and to improve the whole sphere of industrial relations. As a series of unofficial strikes in the motor industry ground on through the autumn, and after the TUC decisively rejected a statutory incomes policy at its centenary conference in September, Castle decided that she had to go beyond Donovan and recommend that unofficial strikes could be dealt with only by legislation and penal sanctions. Her proposals were published in the White Paper *In Place of Strife* in January 1969.

Castle argued that *In Place of Strife* was principally about trade union rights, for example the right to belong to a union, and workers' protection from unfair dismissal. Most other observers could see that its real aim was to democratise, delay and if possible defuse strike action (Pimlott 1992: 529). Thus attention focused almost exclusively on the White Paper's view that unions should be obliged not to 'abuse' the strike weapon. To this effect it outlined three penal proposals: there should be a compulsory twenty-eight-day cooling-off period in certain disputes, a pre-strike ballot before some official stoppages, and the Employment Secretary should have the power to impose a solution in intractable inter-union disputes. An Industrial Board was to be set up to impose fines in cases where the new rules were breached – and presumably there was the threat of imprisonment for trade unionists who refused to pay the fines. The proposals split the Cabinet and brought Wilson closer to resignation than at any time in his first period as Prime Minister. Castle defended *In Place of Strife* on the grounds that the government had a democratic duty to restrain the trade unions. Wilson reassured colleagues that a hawkish line on the unions would be a vote winner. In contrast, Callaghan, who led the Cabinet opposition to the White Paper, warned that *In Place of Strife* had no chance of gaining approval either from the TUC or the Labour Party. When the Commons debated Castle's proposals in March, more than 50 Labour MPs voted against the government and about 40 abstained. Later that month *In Place of Strife* was rejected by Labour's NEC, with Callaghan defying collective Cabinet responsibility and voting against the White Paper in his position as party Treasurer. In an attempt to rescue at least some of the proposals and have something to show for their efforts, Wilson and Castle took Roy Jenkins' advice and proposed a short Bill based on the White Paper in April. By now, however, the unions were fully mobilised to resist any attempt at reform. At a special TUC Congress in June, union leaders confirmed their opposition to compulsory legislation and statutory financial penalties. The new Chief Whip, Bob Mellish, warned the Prime Minister on 17 June that Labour rebels would block any attempt to pass a Bill that contained penal sanctions. Following what she described in her diary as '[t]he most traumatic day of my political life', Castle and Wilson were forced into an embarrassing retreat (Castle 1990: 342). In place of legislation they accepted a 'solemn and binding' undertaking from the TUC that member unions would observe the TUC's guidelines on regulating unofficial strikes. The compromise was sufficient to settle what was perhaps the worst party crisis since Ramsay MacDonald had defected to head a new National Government in 1931. Wilson survived, but he never forgot how Cabinet colleagues had deserted him in a moment of crisis. For their part, Cabinet colleagues had seen their faith in Wilson's leadership severely shaken. Tony Benn, whose patience with Wilson had evaporated, captured in his diary on 24 July 1969 the common wisdom in Cabinet that the Prime Minister had been damaged beyond repair by the traumas of the past few months.

> [Wilson] accused Dick Marsh of always leaking, Tony Crosland of always leaking to the journalist Alan Watkins, and complained of Jim Callaghan. He said that he was going to do major restructuring and heads would have to roll. He asked if I would keep an eye out for plots and said that Ministers were meeting in secret and the Campaign for Democratic Socialism was still active . . .
>
> I went out shaken by this, having concluded that the man had gone mad, ought to be removed, that the great case for the parliamentary system was that it did remove people. I just felt contempt for him. Maybe I will get slightly promoted in the reshuffle, if ever it comes in this form in the autumn. But I just feel that Harold is finished.
>
> (Benn 1988: 193)

Conservative recovery and Labour defeat, August 1969–June 1970

Edward Heath's Conservatives were the main political beneficiaries of the overlapping conflicts of the late sixties. As the various themes of protest, permissiveness and rising crime rates coalesced in some people's minds into a generalised threat to civil society, the new authoritarianism of the Conservatives won over sufficient voters to ensure their return to government in June 1970. In the end the victory was a narrow one that caught most commentators (and bookmakers) by surprise. If the polling evidence was correct, it was also one that was achieved largely in spite of Heath's leadership. Despite operating in a political climate that favoured the opposition from at least July 1966 onwards, Heath had failed to build an irresistible momentum behind either his personal or party campaigns. Even the Conservative faithful found Heath's leadership uninspiring, and they were well aware that he usually trailed Wilson in the Gallup poll approval ratings. In fact, the polls showed that many voters would have preferred Enoch Powell as Tory leader. Powell's provocative comments on race had made him a populist hero, not least among those who believed there was more to politics than 'getting the economy right'. Unlike Powell, whose public performances could be magnetic, Heath was a desperately dull speaker and he never escaped the public's perception of him as a dry-as-dust technocrat, even allowing for the favourable press coverage he received after winning the Sidney to Hobart yacht race at the turn of the year in 1969–70. Compounding the party's fears that Heath might take the Conservatives to a third successive defeat, Labour's stand-ing in the polls began to improve after economic recovery became evid-ent in late 1969, reducing the Tories' lead to single figures in the last quarter of that year (Butler and Butler 1994: 252–3). These poll findings were a deep disappointment to the Conservatives who had been working hard in opposition to find a route back to power. In an attempt to restore their electoral fortunes, for example, the party had conducted the largest policy review in their history from 1965 onwards, with MPs, peers and outside experts working on one or more of 23 policy groups, all overseen by Heath. But even these painstaking efforts failed to persuade com-mentators that the Conservatives were fully ready for office because they left important questions about the party's programme unanswered. The circumstances in which a Conservative government should intervene in the economy (in terms of supply-side reforms, wage restrictions or industrial reorganisation) were left unclear. Nor was it apparent whether profitability and industrial modernisation would take priority over the maintenance of full employment as a policy goal under the Conservatives (Johnman 1993: 198). Perhaps most damagingly of all, there was no uni-fying theme apparent in 1969 to tie the various policy strands together in a coherent way – or if there was, Heath was incapable of putting it into words. As far as targeting voters was concerned, the party's research data suggested that women, the skilled working classes and voters aged below 35 were likely to be the 'floaters' who might be detached from supporting

Labour. Heath had also long been convinced that the next election would be won on the centre ground. But with no obvious strategy in place for winning the support of floating voters with centrist policies, a void was left that came to be filled with a more aggressively free-market and socially authoritarian set of policies.

The announcement that the Conservatives had shifted to the right in their search for a way to connect with the electorate came at the end of January 1970. The occasion was a meeting of the Shadow Cabinet to discuss forthcoming election strategy at the Selsdon Park Hotel in Croydon. Perhaps the press briefings that accompanied the meeting exaggerated the ideological coherence of what was decided there. But it was no accident that, at a time of perceived breakdown in the authority of the state, the Conservatives should use Selsdon Park as the departure point for a less consensual and more coercive policy programme. The centrepiece of what emerged at Selsdon was the promise to restore law and order for the 'silent majority', a message that built on an ongoing Conservative campaign that charged the government with failing to tackle both crime and an increasing menace of violent protest. True, the Kray twins had finally been brought to justice in 1969, but their trial allowed the popular press to stoke people's fears about the extent of gangland activity in the capital. Similarly, the demonisation of student and anti-war protesters as criminals and subversives for the past two years had added to the impression that society was stumbling towards lawlessness. The Conservatives declared that the time had arrived for the authorities to fight back. 'Demo Clamp-Down if Tories Get Back' trumpeted the *Sunday Express*. 'The Stainless Steel Tories' was *The Economist*'s cover-story title, neatly summing up the Conservatives' new hard-line image. The *Guardian* took a different view, mildly mocking the way that the law-and-order policies announced at Selsdon were driven by popular fears and stereotypes. The targets of the projected crackdown, wrote the paper, appeared to be: 'student unrest, political demonstrations, the Permissive Society, long hair, short hair and perhaps in time medium-length hair as well' (cited in Hall *et al.* 1978: 274). The authoritarian shift in Conservative thinking reflected popular anxieties (fuelled by politicians, press and 'moral entrepreneurs') that sixties liberalism had been pushed beyond acceptable limits by 1970. It was a signal that the time had arrived for the state to intensify its clamp-down on those who threatened the social order, and for the government to give the police, courts and other state apparatuses the powers to do so. Thus the Tory programme that came out of the Selsdon Park meeting outlined plans to extend the laws of trespass to cover demonstrations, to curb workers' use of the strike weapon and put in place tougher immigration controls. Tax cuts and greater targeting of welfare benefits were also promised as part of a wider agenda for restoring personal responsibility. In the specific context of 1970 it was a widely seductive programme. Harold Wilson labelled the newly-apparent Conservative thinking the brainchild of 'Selsdon Man', claiming that Heath and his colleagues sought to emulate the 'hard-faced' Tories of the 1930s. 'Selsdon Man is not just a lurch to the right', he said on 6 February, 'it is an atavistic desire to reverse the course of 25 years of social revolution. What they are planning is a wanton, calculated and deliberate return to greater inequality . . . The message to the British people would be simple. And brutal. It would say: "You're out on your own"' (Wilson 1974: 954). Wilson's counteroffensive, however, was in some respects counter-productive. His comments portrayed the Conservatives as a party with a strong sense of moral purpose at a time when in crucial respects the details of their programme lacked coherence. It soon became clear, too, that sections of the electorate were more than ready for 'hard' policies on immigration controls and policing. In the aftermath of Selsdon Park the Tories moved into a 10 per cent lead in the polls. Better still for the Conservatives, for many long months the Labour government had been struggling to persuade even some of its usually core supporters that it deserved to remain in office.

There is no doubt that the Labour left believed they had a damning case against Wilson's government by the late sixties. Their list of complaints about what Labour had done in office was recited like a mantra: the government had cut public spending, imposed wage freezes, reintroduced prescription charges, conducted a damaging and over-long defence of sterling, supported America in Vietnam, sold arms to the apartheid regime in South Africa and failed to act decisively against a similarly repugnant government in Rhodesia. Labour, it appeared, had become fixated on economic growth, national efficiency and the securing of popular consent for a new form of corporate capitalism. Indeed, the left complained, the government had been an important agent in the drive to make capitalism operate more effectively in the sixties, using the Industrial Reorganisation Corporation (IRC) from 1966 onwards to sponsor industrial mergers and achieve economies of scale. When Wilson and Castle had proposed to discipline trade unionists with the penal sanctions contained in the White Paper *In Place of Strife*, the 'betrayal' of socialism was seemingly complete. Perhaps, argued the left, Labour's abandonment of its socialist mission explained why individual party membership declined by 12 per cent between 1966 and 1970. Labour's rank and file, it appeared, were increasingly disillusioned and unwilling to remain members of a party that had lost its ideological bearings. In texts such as Raymond Williams' *May Day Manifesto* (1968), or Eric Hobsbawm's piece for *New Society* in January 1970, the left analysed what had gone wrong. Hobsbawm, in a typical example of left critique, was in no doubt about the government's strategic shortcomings:

> *The major fact about the Wilson era so far is that, leaving aside a few stylistic flourishes such as the refusal to create hereditary peers, its achievements seem far more characteristic of centre-right than of centre-left governments . . .*
>
> *The major achievement of the Wilson era so far has been to make big business dramatically bigger and more streamlined . . . It assumes that the problem of baking more national cake is primary, that of sharing it out secondary – or even that it can more or less be left to take care of itself. It reverses the traditional attitudes of the British left and the working class movement. Hence the disorientation of Labour's supporters, which is reflected in the opinion polls and elections of the past two or three years.*
>
> (Hobsbawm 1970: 102)

However, just as Hobsbawm was rehearsing once more the left's indictment of Labour in office, the government was beginning to show signs of recovery. After some two years of continual setbacks, culminating in the double fiasco of *In Place of Strife* and the botched reform of the House of Lords, Wilson's administration finally appeared to have turned a corner in early 1970. The platform on which this was built was renewed economic confidence. With Jenkins' 'two years of hard slog' almost up, the balance of payments moved back into a surplus of £440 million by the end of 1969. In April 1970 Labour enjoyed an opinion poll lead for the first time in three years. As Wilson's Inner Cabinet debated the respective merits of a June or October date for the general election, the local council results of May 1970 provided the decisive push towards a June contest. Labour recaptured several hundred council seats in these local elections, thereby reversing many of the gains made by the Conservatives in 1967 and suggesting that the electoral momentum was once more with the government. Wilson and his senior colleagues took particular heart from the fact that if the voting patterns of May 1970 were replicated in a general election, the result would be a Labour majority of around fifty seats (Ponting 1990: 328). Perhaps, they told themselves, the government was set to reap an electoral reward for its recent prudent stewardship of the economy. Indeed, in contrast to the Tories' irresponsible pre-election budget of 1964, Jenkins had come up with a cautious budget for March 1970. Perhaps, even, the England football team would be on their way to retaining the World Cup in Mexico by the time of the election, thereby lifting the mood of some voters at least (in fact, they lost to West Germany in a quarter-final just before polling day). So when Wilson announced a general election for 18 June he was confident that Labour had done enough to secure a further term in office, albeit with its majority predicted to fall to perhaps twenty seats.

During the election campaign itself, the polls suggested that the outcome would be close. As neither party seemed capable of firing the electorate's enthusiasm the contest was to be won on default. The 1970 election was a referendum to find the least unpopular of the two main parties. Labour fought a relaxed (perhaps in retrospect complacent) campaign and used Wilson once again as the focal point of their appeal. This was a formula that had worked well in 1964 and 1966, and it reflected Wilson's commanding lead over Heath in the personal poll ratings. Labour ministers emphasised their success in steering the economy towards recovery, pointing in particular to the correction of the trade deficit, and offered the electorate 'business as usual'. It was the new breed of hard-faced Conservatives unveiled at Selsdon Park, Labour argued, that threatened to destabilise both the economy and society as a whole. The Conservatives, meanwhile, focused on the rising cost of living under Labour and used a poor set of trade figures for May – showing a deficit of £31 million – to argue that the apparent economic recovery of the past few months was fragile. Wilson's leadership was attacked in the manifesto for producing a 'cheap and trivial style of government'. Tory policies on law and order, immigration, trade unions and tax were presented as the basis for a programme of national renewal after the excesses of the sixties. The party also put into operation its long-planned strategy of concentrating its resources in 70 Labour-held marginal constituencies: 64 of these seats were eventually taken by the Conservatives. As results around the country came through, it became clear that the opinion polls had failed to pick up the scale of the late swing towards the Conservatives. In the most unexpected result since 1945 the Conservatives made a net gain of 66 seats (a post-war record) and came back into government with an overall majority of 30. As Johnman has pointed out, the swing towards the Conservatives across the country was remarkably uniform and the new government appears to have gained support equally across the social classes (1993: 202). The one exception to this was the higher-than-average swing in Wolverhampton, caused by strong local backing for Powell's stance on issues of race and immigration. As well as support for the authoritarian policies already discussed, the Conservatives' own post-election research suggested that their victory owed much to people's fears that difficult economic times lay ahead. Labour was punished for its failures of economic management in 1966–9. The Nuffield survey of the 1970 contest emphasised the degree to which too many voters had simply lost patience with the government to see it re-elected. After years of cuts and recurrent crises under Labour, sufficient voters were willing to turn to the Conservatives to handle the economic problems yet to come.

TABLE 12.1 ◆ *Results of the General Election, 18 June 1970*

	Total Votes	MPs Elected	Candidates	% Share of Total Vote
Conservative	13,145,123	330	628	46.4
Labour	12,179,341	287	624	43.0
Liberal	2,117,035	6	332	7.5
Communist	37,970	–	58	0.1
Plaid Cymru	175,016	–	36	0.6
Scottish National Party	306,802	1	65	1.1
Others	383,511	6	94	1.4
	28,344,798	630	1,837	100.0

Electorate 39,342,013

Turnout 72.0%

Source: Butler, D. and Butler, G. (1994) *British Political Facts, 1900–1994*, London: Macmillan, p. 217

Conclusion

'What's wrong with Britain?' an anxious elite of commentators and opinion formers had asked in the early sixties. Britain, they argued, was a post-imperial nation in decline, led by a complacent and decadent political class whose slow decline into irrelevance was to be symbolised above all by the Profumo affair. Moreover, British society was gripped by an outdated class structure and an unhealthy obsession with US cultural imports. The treatment prescribed by these 'state-of-the-nation' writers, that is, that the country required an invigorating dose of cultural openness and meritocratic social mobility, helped to create the climate in which Labour's 'New Britain' campaigns of 1964 and 1966 had succeeded. Harold Wilson promised to recover the ground that had been lost after 'thirteen wasted years' of Conservatism. The dominant political discourse that Wilson encouraged was a factor that made the mid-sixties optimistic and heady times. His Labour government bristled with energy and purpose, impatient to implement its plans for national renewal that would take the country into a new age of material and technological progress. Politics and culture fed off one another at this time to produce the mythical composite known as 'swinging London' and a cultural renaissance in which R&B bands, Mary Quant fashion and Pop Art aesthetics were at the leading edge. By 1970, however, most of this optimism had dissipated, drained away by the structural weaknesses of the economy and the government's remorseless use of austerity measures to defend sterling from 1965 onwards. Twenty years later, after a decade of Thatcherism had seen unemployment peak at over 3 million and a credit-fuelled boom had turned to bust, the performance of the Wilson governments looked better by comparison. But this perspective on the government was still in the future. In 1970 voters weighed up what they knew about the present and went to the polls with a striking lack of enthusiasm for either of the main parties, their apathy conditioned by the economic uncertainties and continuing post-imperial malaise of late-sixties Britain (Butler and Pinto-Duschinsky 1971: 345–7). Viewed from a wider perspective, therefore, the optimism and cultural vitality of the high sixties was an exceptional interlude in the country's long post-war history. A fleeting coincidence of demographics, youth-driven popular culture, consumerism, technology and political leadership had left a high-water mark of national self-confidence – at least among some influential groups across the country. It also provided the dominant signifiers of what became the media image of the sixties as a whole. But these signifiers – mini skirts, E-type Jaguars, King's Road boutiques – were only marginal features of a country that was increasingly exposed, in important respects, as a third-rate power after 1945. In retrospect, the anxieties and social conflicts of the late sixties and early seventies were more in line with the trajectory of post-war British development, the dominant motif of which was decline.

The Tories' response to a general anxiety about the 'state of things' in the late sixties was a rhetorical blend of social authoritarianism and free-market 'realism'. It brought them back into power in a tight-run contest in 1970, but 'Selsdon Man' policies were soon overwhelmed by the unfolding crises of the early seventies, the combined effect of which continually undermined the Heath government's authority. The release of wage inflation that had built up under Roy Jenkins' 'iron' Chancellorship led to an explosion of strikes in both the public and private sectors, culminating in an electorally-damaging dispute with the National Union of Mineworkers in 1974. The quadrupling of oil prices in 1973 as a result of the Arab–Israeli war heightened the significance of this dispute. The oil crisis put a temporary halt to Britain's supplies of cheap oil and led eventually to the government's announcement of a three-day working week in order to save fuel. Meanwhile, violence continued to escalate on all sides in Northern Ireland, with the moral legitimacy of the British army's presence there compromised as never before after the 'Bloody Sunday' killing of thirteen unarmed civilians in January 1972: a little over a year later the Provisional IRA began its bombing campaign in England. In March 1974 the Heath government fell from power, its one historic achievement being the formal entry of Britain into the EEC at the beginning of 1973.

However, we should be careful not to imply a simple dichotomy between the 'bleak grim reality' of the seventies and the 'golden age' of the sixties, the optimistic promises of which were somehow betrayed (York 1980: 181). Decades are not hermetically-sealed units, they leak into one another: hence Marwick's use of the 'long sixties' of c.1958–c.1974 as an organising concept. Certainly by the mid-seventies it was hard to avoid the view that aspects of British society and culture had been permanently re-ordered after the experience of the 'long sixties'. Most of these changes had their roots in the post-war years, with their implications only becoming more fully apparent in the 1970s. At the centre of it all were the forces of economic change. It was during the sixties that the domestic-consumer-oriented economy reached an advanced stage, ushering in a new era of popular capitalism whose material benefits were more universally enjoyed than ever before. Although the country suffered a declining share of world exports and a semi-permanent crisis in its balance of payments, average living standards in Britain had never been higher. Materialistic individualism triumphed in the sixties, even though on occasions the Wilson government success-fully persuaded workers to tighten their belts and accept wage restraint for the sake of the 'national interest'. The sixties consumer culture brought undoubted benefits, helping people to enjoy new material comforts and self-defining possessions. But it also came at a price. The self-gratification and consumption that were encouraged initially in an economic context helped to create those aspects of sixties culture that were self-absorbed and privatised. In the longer run it also helped to create an order that was, as counter-cultural activist Sheila Rowbotham recognised, '*more* competitive and less equal than the one we had protested against' (2000: xv).

But the economy was not the only factor to make the sixties an age of individual identity and autonomy. The concern with the self was in part a reaction against the rhetoric of 1940s collectivism and the frus-trated individualism of the austerity years. Among the educated classes, the growing interest in psychotherapy and psychology put personal autonomy at the heart of the human experience – the legacy of this 'doing your own thing' ethos can be found in the New Age spiritualism and best-selling self-empowerment books of the late twentieth and early twenty-first centuries. Conversely, the sixties was the period in which campaigners refined the techniques of organising around a grievance, raising consciousness and bringing pressure to bear on governments, often mobilising pre-existing networks from earlier campaigns. The Women's Liberation Movement, the Gay Liberation Front, Friends of the Earth, Shelter and the Child Poverty Action Group all worked throughout the 1970s and beyond to effect changes or defend hard-won victories, not least the liberal law reforms of the sixties, against an authoritarian backlash. This was the enduring legacy of the counter-culture. It was also in the sixties that the British population comprehended for the first time the full implications of immigration from former colonies and were forced to confront what multiculturalism would mean for traditional conceptions of (white) British identity. Equally, this was the time that Britain's black and South Asian population were confronted with the realities of living in a society in which Enoch Powell's views on race had made him a populist hero. True, there were many who celebrated the cultural diversity and dynamism that new patterns of immigration delivered. From these ranks came the civic campaigners and community activists who worked with immigrants to dismantle the apparatuses of racial discrimination. But more than thirty years after Powell's speech the evidence that ingrained prejudice was a continuing feature of British culture remained. Three examples should suffice. The MacPherson Report (1999) in the wake of Stephen Lawrence's murder found that the Metropolitan Police was infected by 'institutional racism'. The Runnymede Trust's suggestion in *The Future of Multi-Ethnic Britain* (2000) that 'Britishness' should be redefined to reflect the country's ethnic diversity was met with incomprehension and hostility in at least some of the national press. Opinion polls in 2004 showed that most people in Britain continued to believe that too many immigrants arrived in the country each year.

In the end the sixties were not 'good' or 'bad', neither 'swinging' nor 'cautious', neither better nor worse than the fifties, seventies or eighties. Thinking in such dialectical terms about an amorphous entity like the sixties will only produce more sterile debates about the 'myth' or 'reality' of the period, and contending readings of 'what it was really like' back then. The sixties can only be imagined now as a series of overlapping contexts, all offering their own narratives and sources, all of which in turn can be connected together in limitless ways. Recent attempts at the 'sixties never mattered that much' revisionism are as contingent and situated as the more affirmative readings of the sixties, or indeed the apocalyptic conclusions of those who hold the sixties to account for the ills of modern society – no less contingent, for that matter, than the account of sixties Britain offered here. A more interesting line of questioning to pursue in the future is to ask how and why contending readings of the sixties gained authority at particular times. This in turn will open up a space to look at how narratives of the sixties have been mobilised and reworked in the (now) thirty years since the 'long sixties' closed.

Bibliography

Primary sources

Official Papers

Cmnd 2154 (1963) *Report of the Committee appointed by the Prime Minister on Higher Education*, London: HMSO

Cmnd 2601 (1965) *A Policy for the Arts: The First Steps*, London: HMSO

Cmnd 2739 (1965) *Immigration from the Commonwealth*, London: HMSO

Cmnd 2764 (1965) *The National Plan*, London: HMSO

Cmnd 2838 (1965) *The Housing Programme*, London: HMSO

Cmnd 3888 (1969) *In Place of Strife: a Policy for Industrial Relations*, London: HMSO

Advisory Committee on Drug Dependence, Sub-Committee Report, 1968, (1969) London: HMSO

Central Statistical Office (1970) *Social Trends*, no. 1, London: HMSO

Memoirs, diaries and contemporary writing

Abel-Smith, B. and Townsend, P. (1965) *The Poor and the Poorest*, London: Routledge

Abrams, M. (1960) 'Party Images', *Socialist Commentary*, May

Aitken, J. (1967) *The Young Meteors*, London: Secker & Warburg

Alderson, S. (1962) *Britain in the Sixties: Housing*, Harmondsworth: Penguin

Ali, T. (1987) *Street Fighting Years: An Autobiography of the Sixties*, London: Collins

Anderson, P. (1964) 'Critique of Wilsonism', *New Left Review*, no. 27, September–December

 (1965) 'Origins of the present crisis', in Anderson, P. and Blackburn, R. (eds.) *Towards Socialism*, London: Fontana

Bailey, D. and Wyndham, F. (1965) *David Bailey's Box of Pin-Ups*, London: Weidenfeld & Nicolson

Bailey, D. and Evans, P. (1970) *Goodbye Baby & Amen: A Saraband for the Sixties*, London: Corgi

Barker, P. (1969) 'Facing Two Ways: Between the 60s and 70s', *New Society*, 27 November, vol. 14, no. 374

Barker, P., Taylor, H., de Kadt, E. and Hopper, E. (1968) 'Portrait of a Protest', *New Society*, 31 October, vol. 12, no. 318

de Beauvoir, S. (1964) *The Second Sex*, New York: Bantam

Benn, T. (1987) *Out of the Wilderness: Diaries, 1963–67*, London: Hutchinson

 (1988) *Office Without Power: Diaries, 1968–72*, London: Hutchinson

Bergonzi, B. (1970) *The Situation of the Novel*, London: Macmillan

Blackstone, T., Coles, K., Hadley, R. and Lewis, W. (1970) *Students in Conflict: LSE in 1967*, London: London School of Economics and Political Science, Weidenfeld & Nicolson

Bogdanor, V. and Skidelsky R. (eds.) (1970) *The Age of Affluence 1951–1964*, London: Macmillan

Booker, C. (1969) *The Neophiliacs: A Study of the Revolution in English Life in the Fifties and Sixties*, London: Collins

Brown, G. (1971) *In My Way: The Political Memoirs of Lord George-Brown*, London: Victor Gollancz

Butler, D. and King, A. (1965) *The British General Election of 1964*, London: Macmillan

 (1966) *The British General Election of 1966*, London: Macmillan

Butler, D. and Pinto-Duschinsky, M. (1971) *The British General Election of 1970*, London: Macmillan

Caine, M. (1992) *What's It All About? An Autobiography*, New York: Ballantine

Carmichael, S. (1968) 'Black Power', in Cooper, D. (ed.) *The Dialectics of Liberation*, Harmondsworth: Penguin

Carter, A. (1967) 'Notes for a theory of sixties style', *New Society*, 14 December, vol. 10, no. 272

Castle, B. (1990) *The Castle Diaries, 1964–1976*, London: Macmillan

(1993) *Fighting All The Way*, London: Macmillan

Chaplin, M. (1967) *I Couldn't Smoke the Grass on my Father's Lawn: Pot, Girls, and Swingers in London's Ultra-Mod Set*, New York: Ballantine

Coates, K. and Silburn, R. (2nd edn 1973) *Poverty: The Forgotten Englishmen*, Harmondsworth: Pelican

Cockburn, A. and Blackburn, R. (eds.) (1969) *Student Power*, Harmondsworth: Penguin

Cohn-Bendit, D. (1969) *Obsolete Communism: A Left-Wing Alternative*, Harmondsworth: Penguin

Connolly, R. (ed.) (1995) *In the Sixties*, London: Pavilion

Critchley, R.A. (1973) *United Kingdom Consumer Shopping Patterns*, London: International Publishing Corporation

Crosland, A. (1956) *The Future of Socialism*, London: Jonathan Cape

Crossman, R. (1979) *The Crossman Diaries*, London: Methuen

Dallas, K. and Fantoni, B. (1967) *Swinging London: A Guide to Where the Action Is*, London: McCarthy's

Einzig, P. (1969) *Decline and Fall? Britain's crisis in the sixties*, London: Macmillan

Eppels, E. and Eppels, E. (1960) *Adolescents and Morality*, London: Routledge & Kegan Paul

Eves, V. (1969) 'Britain's Social Cinema', *Screen*, London

Fisher, S. (1972) *The female orgasm: psychology, physiology, fantasy*, London: Allen Lane

Fletcher, R. (1962) *Britain in the Sixties. The Family and Marriage: an analysis and moral assessment*, Harmondsworth: Penguin

Foot, M. (1968) 'Credo of the Labour Left – Interview', *New Left Review*, no. 49, May–June

Foot, P. (1965) *Immigration and Race in British Politics*, Harmondsworth: Penguin

(1968) *The Politics of Harold Wilson*, Harmondsworth: Penguin

Friedan, B. (1963) *The Feminine Mystique*, London: Gollancz

Frost, D. and Sherrin, N. (1963) *That Was The Week That Was*, London: W.H. Allen

Gail, S. (1968) 'The housewife', in Fraser, R. (ed.) *Work*, Harmondsworth: Penguin

Gorer, G. (1971) *Sex and Marriage in England Today: a study of the views and experiences of the under–45s*, London: Nelson

(1973) *Sex and Marriage in England Today: a study of the views and experiences of the under–45s*, London: Panther

Gosling, R. (1980) *Personal Copy: A Memoir of the Sixties*, London: Faber

Gould, T. (ed.) (1985) *Absolute MacInnes: The Best of Colin MacInnes*, London: Allison & Busby

Gramsci, A. (1971) *Selections from the Prison Notebooks of Antonio Gramsci*, ed. and trans. Q. Hoare and G. Nowell Smith, London: Lawrence & Wishart

Hall, S. and Whannell, P. (1964) *The Popular Arts*, London: Hutchinson Educational

Halsey, A.H. (1972; 2nd edn 1988) *Trends in British Society Since 1900: A Guide to the Changing Social Structure of Britain*, London: Macmillan

Harvey, A. (1968) *Social Services for All? Part Three*, Fabian Tract 384, London: Fabian Society

Healey, D. (2nd edn 1990) *The Time of My Life*, London: Penguin

Hobsbawm, E. (1970) 'What Labour has done', *New Society*, 15 January, vol. 15, no. 381

Hoggart, R. (1957) *The Uses of Literacy*, London: Chatto & Windus

Hulanicki, B. (1983) *From A to Biba*, London: Hutchinson

Jenkins, R. (1991) *A Life at the Centre*, London: Macmillan

Jephcott, P. (1967) *Time of One's Own: Leisure and Young People*, Edinburgh: Oliver & Boyd

Keeler, C. (1989) *Scandal*, New York: St Martin's Press

Koedt, A. (1970) 'The myth of the vaginal orgasm', in Tanner, L.B. (ed.) *Voices from Women's Liberation*, Chicago: Signet

Koestler, A. (1963) *Suicide of a Nation? An Enquiry into the State of Britain Today*, London: Hutchinson

Laing, D. (1969) *The Sound of Our Time*, London: Sheed & Ward

Laing, R.D. (1964) *The Divided Self*, Harmondsworth: Penguin

(1967) *The Politics of Experience*, Harmondsworth: Penguin

Levin, B. (1970) *The Pendulum Years*, London: Jonathan Cape

Macleod, I. (1964) 'The Tory Leadership', *The Spectator*, 17 January

McLuhan, M. (1964) *Understanding Media: The Extensions of Man*, London: Routledge & Kegan Paul

Marcuse, H. (1964) *One Dimensional Man*, London: Routledge

(1968) 'Liberation from the Affluent Society', in Cooper, D. (ed.) *The Dialectics of Liberation*, Harmondsworth: Penguin

Melly, G. (1970) *Revolt into Style: The Pop Arts in Britain*, London: Allen Lane

Miles, B. (2002) *In the Sixties*, London: Jonathan Cape

Mitchell, J. (1966) 'Women: the Longest Revolution', *New Left Review*, no. 40, November–December

(1971) *Women's Estate*, Harmondsworth: Penguin

Neville, R. (1970) *Play Power*, London: Jonathan Cape

(1995) *Hippie Hippie Shake: the Dreams, the Trips, the Trials, the Love-Ins, the Screw-Ups, the Sixties*, London: Bloomsbury

Nuttall, J. (1968) *Bomb Culture*, London: MacGibbon & Kee

Oldham, A. (2000) *Stoned*, London: Secker & Warburg

Palmer, T. (1971) *The trials of Oz*, London: Blond & Briggs

Parkin, F. (1968) *Middle-Class Radicalism: The Social Bases of the British Campaign for Nuclear Disarmament*, Manchester: Manchester University Press

Quant, M. (1966) *Quant by Quant*, London: Cassell

Rhode, E. (1968) 'British Film-Makers', *The Listener*, 26 September

(1969) 'The British Cinema in the Seventies', *The Listener*, 14 August

Roszak, T. (1970) *The Making of a Counter Culture: Reflections on the Technocratic Society and Its Youthful Opposition*, London: Faber & Faber

Rous, H. (ed.) (1998) *The Ossie Clark Diaries*, London: Bloomsbury

Rowbotham, S. (2000) *Promise of a Dream: Remembering the Sixties*, London: Penguin

Sampson, A. (1962) *Anatomy of Britain*, London: Hodder & Stoughton

(1965) *Anatomy of Britain Today*, London: Hodder & Stoughton

(1971) *The New Anatomy of Britain*, London: Hodder & Stoughton

Sassoon, V. (1968) *Sorry I Kept You Waiting, Madam*, New York: Puttnam

Schofield, M. (1965) *The Sexual Behaviour of Young People*, Harmondsworth: Penguin

(1973) *The Sexual Behaviour of Young Adults*, London: Allen Lane

Scholes, R. (1967) *The Fabulators*, Oxford: Oxford University Press

Selvon, S. (1956) *The Lonely Londoners*, London: MacGibbon & Kee

Shanks, M. (1961) *The Stagnant Society: A Warning*, London: Penguin

Sinclair, A. (1994) *In Love and Anger: A View of the Sixties*, London: Sinclair–Stevenson

Spearman, D. (1968) 'Enoch Powell's Postbag', *New Society*, 9 May, vol. 11, no. 293

Students and Staff of Hornsey College of Art (1969) *The Hornsey Affair*, Harmondsworth: Penguin

Taylor, J.R. (1969) 'Backing Britain', *Sight and Sound*, Spring

Tindall, G. (1968) 'Housewives-To-Be', *New Society*, 30 May, vol. 11, no. 296

Titmuss, R.M. (1962) *Income Distribution and Social Change: A Study in Criticism*, London: George Allen & Unwin

Titmuss, R.M. and Zander, M. (1968) *Unequal Rights*, London: Child Poverty Action Group

Townsend, P. (1967) *Poverty, Socialism and Labour in Power*, Fabian Tract 371, London: Fabian Society

Trevelyan, J. (1973) *What The Censor Saw*, London: Michael Joseph

Veness, T. (1962) *School Leavers: Their Expectations and Aspirations*, London: Methuen

Welch, C. (1967) 'Stop Picking on Pop: Why does society want to put pop in chains?', *Melody Maker*, 21 October

Whitehouse, M. (1967) *Cleaning-Up TV: From Protest to Participation*, London: Blandford

(1968) 'Some pop youngsters are being exploited', *Melody Maker*, 31 August

(1972) *Who Does She Think She Is?*, London: New English Library

Williams, R. (1962) *Communications*, Harmondsworth: Penguin

(1968) (ed.) *May Day Manifesto*, Harmondsworth: Penguin

Wilson, B. (1969) *Religion in Secular Society*, Harmondsworth: Penguin

Wilson, H. (1964) *Poverty in Britain Today*, London: Friends Home Service Committee

Wilson, H. (1974) *The Labour Government 1964–70*, Harmondsworth: Penguin

Wright, H. (1968) *Sex and Society*, London: George Allen & Unwin

Young, J. (1971) *The Drugtakers: The social meaning of drug use*, London: Paladin

Zweig, F. (1961) *The Worker in an Affluent Society*, London: Heinemann

Secondary sources

Adams, H. (1978) *Art of the Sixties*, Oxford: Phaidon

Aldgate, A. (1995) *Censorship and the Permissive Society: British Cinema and Theatre, 1955–65*, Oxford: Clarendon Press

Aldgate, A., Chapman, J. and Marwick, A. (eds.) (2000) *Windows on the Sixties: Exploring Key Texts of Media and Culture*, London: I.B. Tauris

Allsop, K. (1985) *The Angry Decade: A Survey of the Cultural Revolt of the Nineteen-Fifties*, Wendover: Goodchild

Baldry, H. (1981) *The Case for the Arts*, London: Secker & Warburg

Banting, K. (1979) *Poverty, Politics and Policy: Britain in the 1960s*, London: Macmillan

Barnes, J. (1987) 'From Eden to Macmillan, 1955–1959', in Hennessy, P. and Seldon, A. (eds.) *Ruling Performance: British Governments from Attlee to Thatcher*, Oxford: Blackwell

Barr, C. (1986) *All Our Yesterdays*, London: British Film Institute

Beckerman, W. and Clark, S. (1982) *Poverty and Social Security in Britain since 1961*, Oxford: Oxford University Press

Bédarida, F. (2nd edn 1991) *A Social History of England, 1851–1990*, trans. A.S. Forster and J. Hodgkinson, London: Routledge

Bennie, L., Brand, J. and Mitchell, J. (1997) *How Scotland Votes: Scottish Parties and Elections*, Manchester: Manchester University Press

Black, L. (2003) *The Political Culture of the Left in Affluent Britain, 1951–64: Old Labour, New Britain?*, London: Palgrave Macmillan

Bradbury, M. (ed.) (1977) *The Novel Today: Contemporary Writers on Modern Fiction*, Manchester: Manchester University Press

Bradbury, M. and Palmer D. (1979) *The Contemporary English Novel*, London: Edward Arnold

Brake, M. (1985) *Comparative Youth Culture: The sociology of youth culture and youth subcultures in America, Britain and Canada*, London: Routledge & Kegan Paul

Brown, C. (1987) *The Social History of Religion in Scotland since 1730*, London: Methuen

(2001) *The Death of Christian Britain: Understanding Secularisation 1800–2000*, London: Routledge

Brown, G. (1997) 'Paradise Found and Lost: The Course of British Realism', in Murphy, R. (ed.) *The British Cinema Book*, London: BFI

Buckland, P. (1981) *A History of Northern Ireland*, Dublin: Gill & Macmillan

Burnett, J. (3rd edn 1989) *Plenty and Want: A social history of food in England from 1815 to the present day*, London: Routledge

Butler, D. and Butler, G. (2nd edn 1994) *British Political Facts 1900–1994*, London: Macmillan

Byrde, P. (1979) *The Male Image: Men's Fashion in Britain 1300–1970*, London: B.T. Batsford

Byrne, P. (1988) *The Campaign for Nuclear Disarmament*, London: Croom Helm

Campbell, C. (1987) *The Romantic Ethic and the Spirit of Modern Consumerism*, London: Basil Blackwell

Campbell, J. (1993) *Edward Heath: A Biography*, London: Jonathan Cape

Carpenter, H. (2000) *That Was Satire That Was: The Satire Boom of the 1960s*, London: Victor Gollancz

Caute, D. (1988) *Sixty-Eight: The Year of the Barricades*, London: Paladin

Cawthorne, N. (1998) *Sixties Source Book: A Visual Guide to the Style of a Decade*, London: Quantum

Chapman, R. (1992) *Selling the Sixties: The Pirates and Pop Music Radio*, London: Routledge

Chibnall, S. and Murphy, R. (eds.) (1999) *British Crime Cinema*, London: Routledge

Chippindale, P. and Horrie, C. (1990) *Stick It Up Your Punter! The rise and fall of the Sun*, London: Heinemann

Chun, L. (1993) *The British New Left*, Edinburgh: Edinburgh University Press

Clarke. P. (1996) *Hope and Glory: Britain 1900–1990*, London: Allen Lane

Clayson, A. (1996) *Beat Merchants: The Origins, History, Impact and Rock Legacy of the 1960s British Pop Groups*, London: Blandford

Coleridge, N. and Quinn, S. (1987) *The Sixties in Queen*, London: Ebury Press

Connell, R.W. (1997) 'Sexual Revolution', in Segal, L. (ed.) *New Sexual Agendas*, London: Macmillan

Cooke, A., Donnachie, I., MacSween, A. and Whatley, C. (eds.) (1998) *Modern Scottish History, 1707 to the Present. Volume 2: The Modernisation of Scotland, 1850 to the Present*, East Lothian: Tuckwell Press

Coogan, I.P. (1996) *The Troubles: Ireland's Ordeal 1966–1996 and the search for Peace*, London: Arrow

Coopey, R. (1993) 'Industrial policy in the white heat of the scientific revolution', in Coopey, R., Fielding, S. and Tiratsoo, N. (eds.) *The Wilson Governments, 1964–1970*, London: Pinter

Coopey, R., Fielding, S. and Tiratsoo, N. (eds.) (1993) *The Wilson Governments, 1964–1970*, London: Pinter

Coote, A. and Campbell, B. (1982) *Sweet Freedom: The Struggle for Women's Liberation*, London: Picador

Crisell, A. (1997) *An Introductory History of British Broadcasting*, London: Routledge

Crosland, S. (1982) *Tony Crosland*, London: Cape

Curran, J. and Seaton, J. (5th edn 1997) *Power Without Responsibility: The Press and Broadcasting in Britain*, London: Routledge

Davie, G. (1994) *Religion in Britain since 1945: Believing Without Belonging*, Oxford: Blackwell

Davies, A. and Saunders, P. (1983) 'Literature, politics and society', in Sinfield, A. (ed.) *Society and Literature 1945–1970*, London: Methuen

Davies, C. (1975) *Permissive Britain: Social Change in the Sixties and Seventies*, London: Pitman

Davis, J. (2001) 'Rents and Race in 1960s London: New Light on Rachmanism', *Twentieth Century British History*, vol. 12, no. 1

Dean, D. (2000) 'The Race Relations Policy of the First Wilson Government', *Twentieth Century British History*, vol. 11, no. 3

Dell, E. (1997) *The Chancellors: A History of the Chancellors of the Exchequer, 1945–90*, London: Harper Collins

Denselow, R. (1989) *When the Music's Over: The Story of Political Pop*, London: Faber & Faber

Donnelly, M. (1994) 'Labour Politics and the Affluent Society, 1951–1964', unpublished Ph.D. thesis, University of Surrey

Dorey, P. (1995) *British Politics Since 1945*, Oxford: Blackwell

Driver, C. (1983) *The British At Table, 1940–1980*, London: Chatto & Windus

Dyer, R. (ed.) (1981) *Coronation Street*, London: British Film Institute

Edwards, R.D. (2003) 'The P.M., the Press Baron and the Plot', *BBC History*, vol. 4, no. 8, August

Eribon, D. (1992) *Michel Foucault*, trans. Betsy Wing, London: Faber & Faber

Ermarth, E.D. (1998) 'Postmodernism', in E. Craig (ed.) *Routledge Encyclopedia of Philosophy*, London: Routledge, (http://www.rep.routledge.com)

Farrell, J.J. (2nd edn 1997) *The Spirit of the Sixties: The Making of Postwar Radicalism*, London: Routledge

Farrell, M. (1980) *Northern Ireland: the Orange State*, London: Pluto Press

Favretto, I. (2000) ' "Wilsonism" Reconsidered: Labour Party Revisionism 1952–64', *Contemporary British History*, vol. 14, no. 4

Ferguson, M. (1983) *Forever Feminine: Women's Magazines and the Cult of Femininity*, London: Heinemann

Field, C. (2001) ' "The Secularised Sabbath" Revisited: Opinion Polls as Sources for Sunday Observance in Contemporary Britain', *Contemporary British History*, vol. 15, no. 1

Fielding, S. (1993) ' "White heat" and white collars: the evolution of "Wilsonism" ' in Coopey, R., Fielding, S. and Tiratsoo, N. (eds.) *The Wilson Governments, 1964–1970*, London: Pinter

(2003) *The Labour Governments 1964–70, vol. 1, Labour and Cultural Change*, Manchester: Manchester University Press

Findley, R. (2001) 'The Conservative Party and Defeat: the Significance of Resale Price Maintenance for the General Election of 1964', *Twentieth Century British History*, vol. 12, no. 3

Finlay, R.J. (1998) 'National Identity: From British Empire to European Union', in Cooke, A., Donnachie, I., MacSween, A. and Whatley, C. (eds.) *Modern Scottish History, 1707 to the Present. Volume 2: The Modernisation of Scotland, 1850 to the Present*, East Lothian: Tuckwell Press

Fisher, T. (1993) 'Permissiveness and the Politics of Morality', *Contemporary Record*, vol. 7, no. 1

Fountain, N. (1988) *Underground: The London Alternative Press 1966–1974*, London: Routledge

Fox, W. (1944) *The Superpowers: The United States, Britain and the Soviet Union – Their Responsibility for Peace*, New York: Harcourt, Brace & Co.

Fraser, R. (1988) *1968: A Student Generation in Revolt*, London: Chatto & Windus

Frayn, M. (1986) 'Festival', in Sissons, M. and French, P. (eds.) *Age of Austerity*, Oxford: Oxford University Press

Freedman, D. (2001) 'Modernising the BBC: Wilson's Government and Television 1964–66', *Contemporary British History*, vol. 15, no. 1

Fry, M. (1987) *Patronage and Principle: A Political History of Modern Scotland*, Aberdeen: Aberdeen University Press

Fryer, J. (1998) *Soho in the Fifties and Sixties*, London: NPG

Galbraith, J.K. (1958) *The Affluent Society*, London: Penguin

Geraghty, C. (1997) 'Women and Sixties British Cinema: The Development of the "Darling" Girl, in Murphy, R. (ed.) *The British Cinema Book*, London: BFI

Gillett, C. (1971) *The Sound of the City*, London: Sphere

Goodman, G. (1979) *The Awkward Warrior, Frank Cousins: His Life and Times*, London: Davis-Poynter

Graham-Dixon, A. (1996) *A History of British Art*, London: BBC Books

Green, J. (1998a) *Days in the Life: Voices from the English Underground, 1961–1971*, London: Pimlico

(1998b) *All Dressed Up: The Sixties and the Counter-culture*, London: Jonathan Cape

Hall, S. *et al.* (1978) *Policing the Crisis: Mugging, the State and Law and Order*, London: Macmillan

Harker, D. (1980) *One for the Money: Politics and Popular Song*, London: Hutchinson

(1992) 'Still crazy after all these years: what *was* popular music in the 1960s?', in Moore-Gilbert, B. and Seed, J. (eds.) *Cultural Revolution? The Challenge of the Arts in the 1960s*, London: Routledge

Harris, J., Hyde, S. and Smith, G. (1986) *1966 and All That: Design and the Consumer in Britain, 1960–1969*, London: Trefoil

Hebdige, D. (1979) *Subculture: The Meaning of Style*, London: Methuen

Hedling, E. (1997) 'Lindsay Anderson and the Development of British Art Cinema', in Murphy, R. (ed.) *The British Cinema Book*, London: BFI

Hennessy, P. (1996) *Muddling Through: Power, Politics and the Quality of Government in Postwar Britain*, London: Victor Gollancz

(2000) *The Prime Minister: The Office and its Holders since 1945*, London: Allen Lane

Heron, L. (ed.) (1985) *Truth, Dare or Promise: Girls Growing Up in the Fifties*, London: Virago

Hewison, R. (1986) *Too Much: Art and Society in the Sixties, 1960–75*, London: Methuen

(1995) *Culture and Consensus: England, art and politics since 1940*, London: Methuen

Heffer, S. (1998) *Like the Roman: the life of Enoch Powell*, London: Weidenfeld & Nicolson

Hill, J. (1986) *Sex, Class and Realism: British Cinema 1956–1963*, London: British Film Institute

Hiro, D. (2nd edn 1991) *Black British, White British: A History of Race Relations in Britain*, London: Grafton

Hitchens, P. (2nd edn 2000) *The Abolition of Britain: The British Cultural Revolution from Lady Chatterley to Tony Blair*, London: Quartet

Hobsbawm, E. (1994) *Age of Extremes: The Short Twentieth Century, 1914–1991*, London: Michael Joseph

Holmes, C. (1988) *John Bull's Island: Immigration and British Society, 1871–1971*, London: Macmillan

Howard, A. (1990) *Crossman: The Pursuit of Power*, London: Jonathan Cape

Howell, D. (2nd edn 1980) *British Social Democracy: A Study in Development and Decay*, London: Croom Helm

Hutchison, R. (1982) *The Politics of the Arts Council*, London: Sinclair Browne

Hylton, S. (1998) *From Rationing to Rock: The 1950s Revisited*, Stroud: Sutton

(2000) *Magical History Tour: The 1960s Revisited*, Stroud: Sutton

Jackson, L. (1998) *The Sixties: Decade of Design Revolution*, London: Phaidon

Jefferys, K. (1993) *The Labour Party Since 1945*, London: Macmillan

(1997) *Retreat from New Jerusalem: British Politics, 1951–64*, London: Macmillan

(1999) *Anthony Crosland: A New Biography*, London: Richard Cohen

Johnman, L. (1993) 'The Conservative Party in Opposition, 1964–70', in Coopey, R., Fielding, S. and Tiratsoo, N. (eds.) *The Wilson Governments, 1964–1970*, London: Pinter

Jones, M. (1994) *Michael Foot*, London: Victor Gollancz

Jones, T. (1996) *Remaking the Labour Party: from Gaitskell to Blair*, London: Routledge

Kearney, R. (2nd edn 1994) *Modern Movements in European Philosophy: Phenomenology, Critical Theory, Structuralism*, Manchester: Manchester University Press

Kendle, J. (1997) *Federal Britain: a history*, London: Routledge

Kincaid, J.C. (2nd edn 1975) *Poverty and Equality in Britain: A Study of Social Security and Taxation*, Harmondsworth: Penguin

Klee, H. (1998) 'The love of speed: An analysis of the enduring attraction of amphetamine sulphate for British youth', *Journal of Drug Issues*, vol. 28, no. 1

Laing, S. (1983a) 'The production of literature', in Sinfield, A. (ed.) *Society and Literature 1945–1970*, London: Methuen

(1983b) 'Novels and the Novel' in Sinfield, A. (ed.) *Society and Literature 1945–1970*, London: Methuen

Larkin, C. (ed.) (3rd edn 1998) *The Encyclopedia of Popular Music*, London: Macmillan

Layton-Henry, Z. (1992) *The Politics of Immigration: Immigration, 'Race' and 'Race' Relations in Post-war Britain*, Oxford: Blackwell

Lechte, J. (1994) *Fifty Key Contemporary Thinkers: From structuralism to postmodernity*, London: Routledge

Leech, K. (1973) *Youthquake: The growth of a counter-culture through two decades*, London: Sheldon Press

Lev, P. (1989), 'Blow-Up, Swinging London and the Film Generation', *Literature Film Quarterly*, vol. 17, no. 2

Levy, S. (2002) *Ready, Steady, Go! Swinging London and the Invention of Cool*, London: Fourth Estate

Lewis, J. (1992a) *Women in Britain since 1945: Women, Family, Work and the State in the Post-War Years*, Oxford: Blackwell

(1992b) 'From equality to liberation: contextualizing the emergence of the Women's Liberation Movement', in Moore-Gilbert, B. and Seed, J. (eds.) *Cultural Revolution? The Challenge of the Arts in the 1960s*, London: Routledge

Lewis, J. and Wallis, P. (2000) 'Fault, Breakdown, and the Church of England's Involvement in the 1969 Divorce Reform', *Twentieth Century British History*, vol. 11, no. 3

Lewis, P. (1978) *The Fifties*, London: William Heinemann

McAleer, D. (1994) *The Warner Guide to UK & US Hit Singles*, London: Carlton / Little, Brown

MacCabe, C. (1988) 'Death of a nation: television in the early sixties', *Critical Quarterly*, vol. 30, no. 2

MacDonald, I. (2nd edn 1995) *Revolution in the Head: The Beatles' Records and the Sixties*, London: Pimlico

McHale, B. (1987) *Postmodernist Fiction*, London: Methuen

McKibbin, R. (1991) 'Homage to Wilson and Callaghan', *London Review of Books*, 24 October

McRobbie, A. (1990) *Feminism and Youth Culture*, Basingstoke: Macmillan

  (1998) *British Fashion Design: Rag Trade or Image Industry?*, London: Routledge

Maitland, S. (ed.) (1988) *Very Heaven: Looking Back at the 1960s*, London: Virago

Marwick, A. (2nd edn 1990) *British Society Since 1945*, London: Penguin

  (1991) *Culture in Britain Since 1945*, Oxford: Blackwell

  (1998) *The Sixties: Cultural Revolution in Britain, France, Italy and the United States, c.1958–c.1974*, Oxford: Oxford University Press

Masters, B. (1985) *The Swinging Sixties*, London: Constable

Mellor, D.A. (1993) *The Sixties Art Scene in London*, Oxford: Phaidon

Melly, G. (1989) *Revolt into Style: The Pop Arts in the 50s and 60s*, Oxford: Oxford University Press

Meyer, J. (2000) 'Live in Your Head: Concept and Experiment in Britain, 1965–75', *Artforum International*, vol. 38, no. 10

Middlemas, K. (1986) *Power, Competition and the State*, volume 1, *Britain in Search of Balance, 1940–61*, London: Macmillan

  (1990), *Power, Competition and the State*, volume 2, *Threats to the Postwar Settlement: Britain 1961–74*, London: Macmillan

Moore-Gilbert, B. and Seed, J. (eds.) (1992) *Cultural Revolution? The Challenge of the Arts in the 1960s*, London: Routledge

Morgan, K.O. (1981) *Rebirth of a Nation: Wales 1880–1980*, Oxford: Oxford University Press

(1990) *The People's Peace: British History 1945–1989*, Oxford: Oxford University Press

(1997) *Callaghan: A Life*, Oxford: Oxford University Press

Mort, F. (1996) *Cultures of Consumption*, London: Sherlock

Muncie, J. (1984) *'The Trouble with Kids Today': Youth and crime in post-war Britain*, London: Hutchinson

Murphy, R. (1992) *Sixties British Cinema*, London: British Film Institute

Murray, C.S. (1989) *Crosstown Traffic: Jimi Hendrix and Post-War Pop*, London: Faber & Faber

National Deviancy Conference (1980) *Permissiveness and Control: The Fate of the Sixties Legislation*, London: Macmillan

Norman, D. (1989) 'Sociology and the spirit of sixty-eight', *British Journal of Sociology* vol. 40, no. 3

Norman, P. (1993) *The Stones*, London: Penguin

Osgerby, B. (1997) *Youth in Britain Since 1945*, Oxford: Blackwell

Pearce, S. and Piper, D. (eds.) (1989) *Literature of Europe and America in the 1960s*, Manchester: Manchester University Press

Phillips, M. and Phillips, T. (1998) *Windrush: The Irresistible Rise of Multi-Racial Britain*, London: Harper Collins

Pimlott, B. (1992) *Harold Wilson*, London: Harper Collins

Pinto-Duschinsky, M. (1987) 'From Macmillan to Home, 1959–64', in Hennessy, P. and Seldon, A. (eds.) *Ruling Performance: British Governments from Attlee to Thatcher*, Oxford: Blackwell

Ponting, C. (1990) *Breach of Promise: Labour in Power, 1964–1970*, London: Penguin

Porter, D. (1993) 'Downhill all the way: thirteen Tory years 1951–64', in Coopey, R., Fielding, S. and Tiratsoo, N. (eds.) *The Wilson Governments, 1964–1970*, London: Pinter

Rees, H. (1986) *14:24 British Youth Culture*, London: Boilerhouse

Richards, J. (1992) 'New waves and old myths: British cinema in the 1960s', in Moore-Gilbert, B. and Seed, J. (eds.) *Cultural Revolution? The Challenge of the Arts in the 1960s*, London: Routledge

(1997) *Films and British National Identity: from Dickens to Dad's Army*, Manchester: Manchester University Press

Ridgman, J. (1992) 'Inside the liberal heartland: television and the popular imagination in the 1960s', in Moore-Gilbert, B. and Seed, J. (eds.) *Cultural Revolution? The Challenge of the Arts in the 1960s*, London: Routledge

Robertson, J.C. (2nd edn 1993) *The Hidden Cinema: British Film Censorship in Action, 1913–1975*, London: Routledge

Roth, A. (1970) *Enoch Powell: Tory Tribune*, London: Macdonald & Co.

Rowbotham, S. (1989) *The Past is Before Us: Feminism in Action since the 1960s*, London: Pandora

Rule, J. (2001) 'Time, affluence and private leisure: the British working class in the 1950s and 1960s', *Labour History Review*, vol. 66, no. 2

Rycroft, S. (2002) 'The geographies of Swinging London', *Journal of Historical Geography*, vol. 28, no. 4

Saggar, S. (1992) *Race and Politics in Britain*, Hemel Hempstead: Harvester Wheatsheaf

Savage, J. (1993) 'Snapshots of the Sixties', *Sight and Sound*, vol. 3, no. 5

Seldon, A. (1987) 'The Churchill Administration, 1951–1955', in Hennessy, P. and Seldon, A. (eds.) *Ruling Performance: British Governments from Attlee to Thatcher*, Oxford: Blackwell

Sendall, B. (1983) *Independent Television in Britain: vol. 2, Expansion and Change, 1958–68*, London: Macmillan

Shulman, M. (1973) *The Least Worst Television in the World*, London: Barrie & Jenkins

Sillars, S. (1992) '*Caro verbum factus est:* British art in the 1960s?', in Moore-Gilbert, B. and Seed, J. (eds.) *Cultural Revolution? The Challenge of the Arts in the 1960s*, London: Routledge

Sinfield, A. (ed.) (1983) *Society and Literature 1945–1970*, London: Methuen

(1989) *Literature, Politics and Culture in Postwar Britain*, Oxford: Blackwell

Sked, A. and Cook, C. (3rd edn 1990) *Post-war Britain: A Political History*, London: Penguin

Stevenson, R. (1986) *The British Novel Since the Thirties: An Introduction*, London: Batsford

Storey, J. (1993) *An Introductory Guide to Cultural Theory and Popular Culture*, London: Harvester Wheatsheaf

Street, S. (1997) *British National Cinema*, London: Routledge

Swinden, P. (1989) 'Literature at Home', in Pearce, S. and Piper, D. (eds.) *Literature of Europe and America in the 1960s*, Manchester: Manchester University Press

Thomas, N. (2002) 'Challenging Myths of the 1960s: The Case of Student Protest in Britain', in *Twentieth Century British History*, vol. 13, no. 3

Thompson, P. (1993) 'Labour's "Gannex conscience"? Politics and popular attitudes in the "permissive society"', in Coopey, R., Fielding, S. and Tiratsoo, N. (eds.) *The Wilson Governments, 1964–1970*, London: Pinter

Thorpe, K. (2001) 'The "Juggernaut Method": The 1966 State of Emergency and the Wilson Government's Response to the Seamen's Strike', *Twentieth Century British History*, vol. 12, no. 4

Timmins, N. (1995) *The Five Giants: A Biography of the Welfare State*, London: Fontana

Tomlinson, J. (1997) 'Conservative Modernisation, 1960–64: Too Little, Too Late?', *Contemporary British History*, vol. 11, no. 3

(2002) 'The British "Productivity Problem" in the 1960s', *Past and Present*, May, Issue 175

Tracey, M. and Morrison, D. (1979) *Whitehouse*, London: Macmillan

Vahimagi, T. (2nd edn 1996) *British Television: An Illustrated Guide*, Oxford: Oxford University Press

Vansittart, P. (1995) *In The Fifties*, London: John Murray

Vyner, H. (1999) *Groovy Bob: The Life and Times of Robert Fraser*, London: Faber & Faber

Wagg, S. (2002) 'Comedy, politics and permissiveness: the "satire boom" and its inheritance', *Contemporary Politics*, vol. 8, no. 4

Walker, A. (1974) *Hollywood, England: The British Film Industry in the Sixties*, London: Michael Joseph

Walker, D. (1987) 'The First Wilson Governments, 1964–70', in Hennessy, P. and Seldon, A. (eds.) *Ruling Performance: British Governments from Attlee to Thatcher*, Oxford: Blackwell

Weeks, J. (2nd edn 1989) *Sex, Politics and Society: The Regulation of Sexuality since 1800*, London: Longman

(1997) 'Sexual Values Revisited', in Segal, L. (ed.) *New Sexual Agendas*, London: Macmillan

Weiler, P. (2000) 'The Rise and Fall of the Conservatives' "Grand Design for Housing" 1951–64', *Contemporary British History*, vol. 14, no. 1

Wheen, F. (1982) *The Sixties: A Fresh Look at the Decade of Change*, London: Century

Whiteley, N. (1987) 'Interior design in the 1960s: arenas for performance', *Art History*, vol. 10, no. 1

Widgery, D. (1976) *The Left in Britain, 1956–68*, Harmondsworth: Penguin

Williams, B. (1994) *The Best Butter in the World: A History of Sainsbury's*, London: Ebury

Woodward, N. (1993) 'Labour's economic performance, 1964–70' in Coopey, R., Fielding, S. and Tiratsoo, N. (eds.) *The Wilson Governments, 1964–1970*, London: Pinter

York, P. (1980) 'Recycling the Sixties', in *Style Wars*, London: Sidgwick & Jackson

Young, N. (1977) *An Infantile Disorder? The Crisis and Decline of the New Left*, London: Routledge & Kegan Paul

Ziegler, P. (1993) *Wilson: The Authorised Life*, London: Weidenfeld & Nicolson

Index

Abel-Smith, Brian, 131, 132, 133, 136
abortion, 53, 80, 121, 122, 156, 158
    Abortion Act, 120–1
Abrams, Mark, 35
Abse, Leo, 119, 120
Adams, Hugh, 102
Adams, Walter, 146
advertising, 31, 32, 58, 101, 116, 161
affluence, 24, 35, 48, 53, 63, 69, 85, 101,
    131
Affluent Society, The, 25
Africa, 65, 110
Aitken, Jonathan, 154
Aldiss, Brian, 62
Alfie, 96, 121
Ali, Tariq, 12, 126, 145, 147, 148
Alloway, Lawerence, 98, 101
Althusser, Louis, 11, 56, 57, 127
American Students for a Democratic
    Society, 147, 160
Amis, Kingsley, 25, 62
Anderson, Lindsay, 84, 85, 86
Anderson, Perry, 56, 74
Andress, Ursula, 89
Andrews, Julie, 45, 89
'Angry Young Men', 25, 26, 60
anti-apartheid campaign, 114
'anti-psychiatry' movement, 128–9
Antonioni, Michelangelo, 96, 97
Arden John, 50
art colleges, 99–100
Arts Council, 61, 98, 99
Attlee, Clement, 17, 18, 74
Attlee government, 20, 71, 134, 142,
    182
Auerbach, Frank, 102
austerity, 18, 20, 23, 195

Austin Powers, 3
Australia, 112

baby boomers, 1, 26, 27, 35
Bacon, Francis, 102
Baez, Joan, 46
Bailey, David, 92, 96, 98
    David Bailey's Box of Pin-ups, 98
balance of payments, 17, 49, 64, 67,
    105–6, 138, 140, 141, 195
    in surplus, 190
Ball, Kenny, 44
Ballard, J.G., 62
Banham, Reyner, 101
Bank of England, 17
Barber, Chris, 44
Barker, Paul, 117, 157
Barthes, Roland, 11, 57, 60, 127
Bassey, Shirley, 44
Batley Variety Club, 30
'Battle of Britain Sunday', 40
Bazaar, 93, 94, 95
BBC, 4, 19, 26, 50, 78, 79, 152, 156
    BBC2, 4, 79–80
Beach Boys The, 46
beat bohemians, 40–1
beat poets, 42
Beat Room The, 42
beat writers, 26, 40, 125
Beatlemania, 28
Beatles The, 3, 30, 38, 42, 44, 45, 46, 94,
    152
    awarded MBEs, 92
    Hard Day's Night, A, 46, 95
    Help, 96
    Magical Mystery Tour, 45
    Revolver, 46, 129

Beatles The (*continued*)
   Rubber Soul, 46
   *Sgt. Pepper's Lonely Hearts Club
      Band*, 46, 129
   and Pop Art, 98
Beck, Jeff, 100
Beckett, Samuel, 60
Belfast, 178
Belgium, 34, 65
Benn, Tony, 70, 76, 109, 110, 139, 181
   loses faith in Harold Wilson, 186
Bennett, Alan, 50
Bergonzi, Bernard, 61
Better Books, 127
Beyond the Fringe, 50
Biba, 93, 94
Bilk, Acker, 44
Birch, Nigel, 23
Birkin, Jane, 152
Birmingham Immigration Control
   Association, 114
Bishop of Woolwich, 54
Black, Cilla, 44, 45, 158
Black, Sir Cyril, 156
Black Dwarf, 126, 148, 159
Blackwell, Chris, 47
Blair, Tony, 138
Blake, Peter, 98, 101
Bloom, John, 30–1
Blow Up, 96–7
Blue Beat, 47, 169
Bob and Marcia, 47
Bogarde, Dirk, 86
Bomb Culture, 41
Bond, James, 84, 88–9
Booker, Christopher, 5, 50
Boothe, Ken, 47
Boshier, Derek, 103
Bottomley, Arthur, 107
Bowden, Herbert, 107
Bowie, David, 100
Braine, John, 25
Brando, Marlon, 27, 38, 86
Brian Poole and the Tremoloes, 44
British Board of Film Censors, 156
British Hospital Journal, 135
British National Party, 170

British Travel Association, 32
Broccoli, Albert, 89
Brockway, Fenner, 114
Brook, Peter, 154
Brown, Callum, 11–12, 53
Brown, George, 73, 106, 138, 139, 140
   National Plan, 108, 140
   resignation, 182
Burdon, Eric, 100
Burgess, Anthony, 62
Burns, Alan, 62
Burroughs, William, 26, 40, 118, 125
   The Naked Lunch, 118, 125
Burton, Richard, 86
Burton's, 23
Butler, Rab, 20, 64, 68, 70

Caine, Michael, 92, 96, 98
   Harry Palmer films, 89
Callaghan, James, 73, 106, 107, 181,
   186
   'backlash against permissiveness',
     154–5
   Chancellor 1964–5, 107–8
   and devaluation, 138–42
   Home Secretary, 146, 148, 150, 165,
     167, 183
   opposes *In Place of Strife*, 185
Cammell, Donald, 60
Campaign Against Racial Discrimination,
   170
Campaign for Nuclear Disarmament, 40,
   41, 56, 147, 175
Canada, 112
capitalism, 2, 13, 20, 23, 24, 29, 59, 144,
   189, 195
Carmarthen, 139, 172, 174
Carmichael, Stokeley, 129
Carnaby Street, 39, 94
Caro, Anthony, 102
   'New Generation' sculpture, 103
Carry On, 84, 87
cars, 23, 31
Carter, Angela, 62, 93
Cartoon Archetypal Slogan Theatre,
   127
Cassady, Neal, 125

Castle, Barbara, 105, 107, 109, 139, 163, 181
   opposes 1965 immigration White Paper, 113
   In Place of Strife, 185–6, 190
   trade union law reform, 184–6
Castro, Fidel, 5
Catholic Church, 54, 120
Cathy Come Home, 80, 137
Caulfield, Patrick, 101
censorship, 116, 122
Centre 42, 52
Centre for Contemporary Cultural Studies, 59
Chelsea Set, 93
Chichester-Clark, James, 178, 179
Child Poverty Action Group, 136, 137, 138, 196
China, 5, 124
Christianity, xii, xiii, 12, 53, 54, 155
Christie, Julie, 96
Churchill, Winston, 8, 17, 20, 21, 22, 61
cinema: *see* film
Clapton, Eric, 100
Cleland, John, 118
Cliff, Jimmy, 47
Coates, Ken, 134
Cocker, Joe, 46
Cohen, Leonard, 46
Cohn-Bendit, Daniel, 144, 146
Coldstream Report, 100
Cold War, xii, 16–17, 18, 24, 55, 175
Cole, Dorothy, 134
Collier, Graham, 99
Collinson, Peter, 87
Commonwealth, xiii, 1, 65, 66, 110, 112, 113, 171
Commonwealth Immigrants Act, 112–13
Commonwealth Immigration Act, 166–7
Communist Party of Great Britain, 55
Community Relations Commission, 169
Como, Perry, 26
Confederation of British Industry, 108
Congress for the Dialectics of Liberation, 129
Connery, Sean, 89
Conran, Terence, 95

conscription: *see* National Service
Conservative Party, 3, 17, 19, 24, 48, 75, 105, 110, 115, 140, 170, 171, 175
   Conservative government 1951–7, 20–2
   Conservative government 1959–64, 63–71, and 'modernisation', 67–8
   Conservative government 1970–4, 150, 194
   electoral recovery 1969–70, 186–9
   'Selsdon Man' policies, 188–9, 194
convenience foods, 32
Cook, Peter, 50
Cooper, William, 60
Coote, A. and Campbell, B., 162, 163
coronation, xii, 21
Coronation Street, 74, 81
Costa Brava, 32
Costa del Sol, 32
counter-culture, 3, 10, 14, 40, 41, 88, 97, 123–30, 155, 158
   legacy, 196
Cousins, Frank, 107, 109, 169
   resignation, 139
Crawford, Michael, 96
Cream, 46
Crick, Francis, 154
cricket, 29
Cripps, Stafford, 18
Crosby, John, 91
Crosland, Tony, 25, 71, 72, 99, 118, 139, 181, 186
   The Future of Socialism, 25, 71, 99, 118
Crossman Richard, 107, 109, 111, 114, 139, 181
   House of Lords reform, 183
Crowther Commission, 172, 173–4, 175
   Kilbrandon Report, 174, 175, 176
Cuba, 5
'cultural revolution', 9, 11, 29, 128
Cushing, Peter, 88

Dadaism, 101
Daily Mail, 148
Daily Mirror, 35, 150, 154, 180, 181

Daily Telegraph, 68, 91
Dalton, Hugh, 17, 18
Darling, 96
Dave Clark Five, 44, 96
Davenport, Nicholas, 49
David, Elizabeth, 33
Davies, Christie, 117
Davies, Ray, 100
Davies, S.O., 171
de Gaulle, Charles, 66, 67, 68, 90, 140, 143
Dean James, 27, 86
Dearden, Basil, 86
death penalty, 107, 117, 157
decolonisation, 65–6
Deep Purple, 126
Deighton, Len, 62
Dekker, Desmond, 47
Delaney, Shelagh, 86
Deneuve, Catherine, 92
Denning, Lord, 69
Department of Economic Affairs, 106, 108, 140
Derrida, Jacques, 11, 57, 127
Derry, 177, 178
Devlin, Bernadette, 177
Dimbleby, David, 154
Discrimination Against Women, 164
divorce, 53, 121–2,
    Divorce Reform Act, 121
dock strikes, 141
Doctor in the House, 27
Dodd, Coxsone, 47
Donnelly, Desmond, 109
Donovan, 46
Donovan, Lord, 184
    Donovan report, 184, 185
Donovan, Terence, 92, 96
Doors, 46, 129
Douglas-Home, Alec, 51, 70, 74, 75, 105, 110
Downing Street Declaration, 178
drugs, 6, 7, 38, 41, 125, 128, 151, 152, 153, 155, 169, 170
    Dangerous Drugs Acts, 151, 152
    Drug Squad, 153
    Legalise Pot Rally, 153

LSD, 30, 128, 152
    Misuse of Drugs Act, 154
Duffy, Brian, 92
Dunbar, John, 98
Dutschke, Rudi, 144
Dylan, Bob, 42, 46

earnings, 23, 37, 184
Eaton, Shirley, 89
Eccles, David, 21
Economist, The, 188
Eddy, Duane, 44
Eden, Anthony, 21, 22, 180
Edgar Broughton Band, 126
Edinburgh, Duke of, 49
Edinburgh Festival, 50
Egypt, 22
Eisenhower, Dwight, 68
Elizabeth II, Queen, 105, 161
Elliott, Tony, 126
EMI records, 45, 126
empire, 15, 30
Equal Pay Act, 163–4
'Establishment' the, xiii, 10, 25, 26, 49, 50, 105
European Economic Community, xiii, 66, 67, 69, 120, 140, 164, 194
Evening News, 154
Evening Standard, 77

Faith, Adam, 42
Faithfull, Mariannne, 98
Family Planning Association, 123
Farrell, Michael, 177
fashion, 23, 28, 35, 37, 42, 58, 93, 95, 97, 161
    men's fashion, 94–5
Ferguson, Marjorie, 161
Festival of Britain, 18–19
Festival of Light, 156
fiction writers, 60–2
film, 28, 35, 42, 48, 60, 83–90, 156, 158
    'New Wave', 26, 85–7, 95
Finney Albert, 86
Fisher, Seymour, 162
Fisher, Terence, 88
Fitt, Gerry, 179

Fleming, Ian, 89
Foley, Maurice, 114–15
Fonda, Peter, 90
Foot, Michael, 166, 183
Foot, Paul, 134
football, 28
    football hooligans, 39
    World Cup 1966, 69, 83, 91, 140
    World Cup 1970, 191
Ford Cortina, 31
Foucault, Michel, 11, 57, 127, 128
Fowles, John, 62
Fox, James, 60
Fox, William, 15
France, 2, 15, 22, 48, 65, 143, 146
Fraser, Robert, 98, 152, 153
Fraser, Ronald, 159
Fraser, Tom, 107
Frayn, Michael, 18–19
Freddie and the Dreamers, 44
Free Cinema Movement, 80, 85
Friedan, Betty, 160
Friends of the Earth, 196
Frost, David, 51
Fury, Billy, 44
Fyvel, T.R., 98

Gail Suzanne, 159–60
Gainsbourg, Serge, 152
Gaitskell, Hugh, 72, 73, 74, 108, 113
Galbraith, J.K., 25
gambling, 116
gardening, 34
Gay Liberation Front, 120, 196
Gay News, 156
general elections
    1959, 63, 72
    1964, 75–6, 104, 193
    1966, 110–11, 193
    1970, 170, 174, 175, 190–2, 193
generational divide, xiii, 1–2, 17, 27, 54
George VI, King, 19
Germany, 15
    West Germany, 48, 144
Gerry and the Pacemakers, 44
Ginsberg, Allen, 26, 41, 125, 128
Glasgow, 36

Godard, Jean-Luc, 86
Golding, William, 61
Gordon Walker, Patrick, 72, 106
    Smethwick, 106, 113
Gorer, Geoffrey, 120, 123
Graham-Dixon, Andrew, 20
Gramsci, Antonio, 55, 56, 129
'Grand Design for Housing', 21
Grateful Dead, 129
'Great Train Robbers', 7, 29
Green, Jonathon. 4, 129
Greenaway, Peter, 85
Greene, Hughie, 79, 82
Greenwood, Anthony, 107, 181
Greer, Germaine, 159
Griffiths, Peter, 113
Griffiths, Trevor, 80
Griffiths-Jones, Mervyn, 117
Groves Press, 117
Guardian, 188
Guevara, Che, 144
Gunter, Ray, 107

Habitat, 95
Hailsham, Lord: see Quentin Hogg
Hall, Stuart, 144, 149, 150, 155
Hamilton, Richard, 95, 98, 101
Hammer horror, 84, 88
Hampstead Set, 72
Harper, Gerald, 95
Harper's Bazaar, 33
Harper's and Queen, 30
Harris, Richard, 86
Harrord, Sir Roy, 49
Harvey, Audrey, 133, 134
Haynes, Jim, 126
    Paperback Book Shop, 126
    Traverse Theatre, 126
Healey, Denis, 107, 139, 181
Heath, Edward, 66, 70, 107, 110, 166, 181
    as Conservative leader, 186–8
    sacks Powell, 168
Heathcoat Amory, Derek, 24, 64
Hemmings, David, 96
Hendrix, Jimi, 46
Hewison, Robert, 13–14, 126, 147
higher education, 67, 144, 158, 160, 164

Hill, Lord, 156
hippies, 8, 28, 42, 124, 130, 148, 169
Hiroshima, 16, 59
Hitchens, Peter, 8
Hobsbawm, Eric, 1, 190
Hockney, David, 98, 101, 153
Hogg, Quentin, 70, 149
Hoggart, Richard, 51, 85
Holborn College of Law and Commerce, 145
holidays, 30, 32, 33
Holliday, Michael, 26
Hollywood, 20, 78, 84, 89, 90, 101
Home, Lord: *see* Douglas-Home, Alec
Homosexual Law Reform Society, 119
Honest to God, 54
Hornsey Art School, 145
Horsburgh, Florence, 21
Houghton, Douglas, 107
House of Lords, 183, 190
Hughes, Ted, 126
Hulanicki, Barbara, 93
Humperdinck, Englebert, 30
Hungary, 55
Hutchison, Robert, 99

immigration, xiii, 111–15, 157, 165, 166, 167, 168, 170, 171, 191, 196
    controls, 21, 109, 111–14, 145, 166, 170, 171, 189
    Immigration Act 1971, 170–1
    1965 White Paper, 113–14
ITV, 3, 26, 78, 79
Independent Television Authority, 78, 79
India, 111
Indica Gallery, 98
Industrial Reorganisation Corporation, 189–90
inflation, 23, 49, 64, 67, 191, 194
Ingrams, Richard, 50
International Federation for Internal Freedom, 128
International Marxist Group, 13, 124, 145
International Monetary Fund, 49
International Socialism, 145
International Socialist League, 13, 124
International Times, 118, 126, 158

Iraq, 141
Ireland, 171, 176
Ireland, Republic, 112, 176, 178
Irish Republican Army, 177, 178, 179
    Provisional IRA, 179, 193
iron and steel, 20, 107
Isle of Wight Festivals, 46, 129
Israel, 141
Italian Job, The, 88
Italy, 34, 144
Iwan, Dafydd, 173

Jagger, Mick, 60, 98, 125, 144
    arrest and drug charges, 152–3
Jamaica, 47
Japan, 48, 144
Jarman, Derek, 85
Jay, Douglas, 72, 107
Jefferson Airplane, 129
Jenkins, Roy, 72, 118, 139, 142, 181, 185
    Chancellor, 142, 182, 190, 191, 194
    The Labour Case, 118
    and liberal law reform, 119
    and race relations, 165–6
Jephcott, Pearl, 36
Johnman, Lewis, 192
Johnny and the Hurricanes, 44
Johnson, B.S., 62
Johnson, President, 109–10
Jones, Allen, 103
Jones, Brian, 125, 152, 153
'July measures' 1966, 140
juvenile crime, 36

Kane, Eden, 44
Keeler, Christine, 69
Kennedy, Bobby, 143
Kennedy, John, F., 68, 74
Kenya, 65, 166
    Kenyan Asians crisis, 166, 167
Kerouac, Jack, 26, 41, 125
Keynes, John Maynard, 16
Khrushchev, Nikita, 55, 68
King, Cecil, 180–1
King, Martin Luther, 143
King's Road, 28, 93, 194
Kinks The, 38, 46, 152

Kinnear, Roy, 51
Kinsey Report, 122
Kitaj, R.B., 101
Koedt, Anna, 162, 163
Koestler, Arthur, 75
Korean War, 19, 24
Kray twins, 7, 29, 98, 188
Kuwait, 141

'Labouchere amendment', 119
Labour government, xiii, 56, 195
    1964–6, 104–11
    1966–70, 136, 137, 138, 139, 140, 143,
        145, 150, 179, 180–6
    by-election record, 182
    criticised by left, 189–90
Labour in the Sixties, 72
Labour Party, 17, 18, 24, 27, 50, 63, 64,
    68, 171, 175
    Labour left, 55, 108–9, 184, 189–90
    political recovery 1959–64, 71–6
Lacan, Jacques, 11, 57, 127
Lady Chatterley's Lover, 53, 117, 118
Laing, R.D., 128, 129
Lane, Nicola, 130
Larkin, Philip, 126
Lawrence, D.H., 117
Lawrence, Stephen, 196
League of Empire Loyalists, 170
Leary, Timothy, 128
Le Carré, John, 62
Lee, Brenda, 44
Lee, Christopher, 88
Lee, Jennie, 98
Lennon, John, 46, 100
Lennox Boyd, Mark, 115
Lessing, Doris, 61
Lester, Richard, 84, 96
Lévi-Strauss, Claude, 11, 37, 56, 57, 127
Levin, Bernard, 7
Levy, Shawn, 9–10
Lewis, Saunders, 172
Leyton, John, 44
liberal law reforms, 7, 53, 116–17,
    119–23, 157, 196
Liberal Party, 68, 72, 75, 172
Littlewood, Joan, 25, 50, 126

Lloyd, Selwyn, 64, 68, 110
Loach, Ken, 86
London Film-Makers Co-op, 84
London School of Economics, 146, 150
long front of culture, 14, 62, 98
Longford, Lord, 105
Loog Oldham, Andrew, 93
Low Pay Unit, 137
Lukàcs, Georg, 55
Luxembourg, 34

MacCabe, Colin, 78
McCartney, Paul, 46, 100, 153
Maccioni, Alvaro, 33
MacDonald, Ian, 8, 25
McGoohan, Patrick, 81
MacGowan, Cathy, 93
MacInnes, Colin, 27, 170
    'Young England, Half English', 27
Macleod, Iain, 68, 70, 166
McLuhan, Marshall, 98
Macmillan, Harold, 21, 22, 23, 24, 26, 51,
    64, 65, 66, 69, 70, 74
    'Supermac', 68
MacPherson Report, 196
McRobbie, Angela, 94
Malik, Rex, 75
Mao, Chairman, 5, 124
Marcuse, Herbert, 11, 59, 81, 127, 129
    One Dimensional Man, 59, 127
marriage, xii, 123
Marwick, Arthur, 11, 116, 195
Marx, Karl, 55
Maschler, Tom, 25
Masters, Brian, 9, 10
Masters and Johnson, *Human Sexual
    Response*, 162
materialism, 6, 20, 28, 30, 40, 131, 195
Maudling, Reginald, 70
MC5 The, 46
Mellish, Bob, 185
Mercer, David, 80
Merseybeat sound, 44
MI5, 138, 148, 181
Miller, Jonathan, 50
Millie, 47
Mills, John, 85

Ministry of Defence, 40, 146
Ministry of Education, 21
Ministry of Labour, 20, 112, 131, 164
Mitchell, Joni, 46
Mitchell, Juliet, 159
Mitchell, Mitch, 46
Mods, 37, 38–9, 40, 41, 44, 46, 94
Monckton, Walter, 20
Moorcock, Michael, 62
Moore, Dudley, 50
Moore, Roger, 82
Moore-Gilbert, Bart, 10, 62
moral crusaders, 40
Morgan, Kenneth, 138, 174
Morrison, Herbert, 18
Morrison, Van, 46
motorcycles, 31
motorway network, 31
Mountbatten, Lord, 181
Movement for Colonial Freedom, 114
Muggeridge, Malcolm, 80, 156
Muldoon, Claire and Roland, 127
Murdoch, Iris, 62
Murdoch, Rupert, 116
Murray, Charles Shaar, 124
music press, 42, 45
    Melody Maker, 151, 155
    New Musical Express, 44
Myth of the Vaginal Orgasm, 162

Nagasaki, 16
Narizano, Silvio, 95
Nash Graham, 46
Nasser, Colonel, 22, 26
National Abortion Campaign, 121
National Assistance Act, 17, 134
National Committee for Commonwealth
    Immigrants, 165
National Economic Development
    Council, 67
National Front, 170
National Health Service, 17, 134, 142
National Incomes Commission, 67
National Insurance Act, 17, 134
National Joint Action Campaign for
    Women's Equal Rights, 163
National Organisation of Women, 160

National Plan, xiii, 75, 108, 140
National Service, 30, 35
National Union of Mineworkers, 194
National Union of Seamen, 138
National Union of Students, 145, 150
National Union of Teachers, 27
National Viewers' and Listeners'
    Association, 80, 155
Nationwide Petition for Public Decency,
    156
Neagle, Anna, 85
Neville, Richard, 59, 126
    Play Power, 59
'New Britain', 74, 75, 76, 104, 193
New Jerusalem, 17
New Left, 8, 55–6, 124, 161
New Left Review, 55, 56, 74, 127, 159
New Reasoner, The, 55
New Society, 93, 117, 123, 157, 168, 190
    survey of anti-war demonstrators, 145,
    149
New Zealand, 112
News of the World, 152
Nicholson, Viv, 28
Nigeria, 65
Night of the Long Knives, 68
Northern Ireland, 119, 150, 172, 176–9,
    194
    'Bloody Sunday', 194
    direct rule, 179
    Northern Ireland Civil Rights
        Association, 177, 178
    People's Democracy, 150, 177, 178
    Social and Democratic Labour Party,
    179
Notting Hill, 170
    Carnival, 170
    riots, 37
Nottingham, St Ann's, 134, 135
nuclear apocalypse, 17, 41
Nuttall, Jeff, 40, 41

Obermeier, Uschi, 116
Obscene Publications Act, 117, 118,
    156
O'Neill, Terence, 177, 178
Op Art, 103

Orange Order Apprentice Boys, 178
Osborne, John, 25, 50
Oz, 59, 126, 156, 158, 159
   trial, 118, 156

Paisley, Ian, 177
Pakistan, 111
Paolozzi, Eduardo, 101
Paris, 10, 41, 57, 93,
   May 1968, 143, 144, 146, 148
Passport Office, 32
pay pause 1961, 64
Peel, John, 129
Penguin books, 48, 117
People Show, 127
Percival, Lance, 51
Performance, 60
'permissive society', 116–17, 122, 123,
   151, 152, 155–6, 188
Phillips, Mike, 168
Pilkington Committee, 78–9, 80
Pill, contraceptive, 116, 123
Pimlott, Ben, 110, 140
Pink Floyd, 100, 126
Pinter, Harold, 34, 60
Plath, Sylvia, 126
Polaris, 67, 175
Policy for the Arts, 98–99
Political and Economic Planning Ltd,
   165, 169
Poor and the Poorest, 131, 133,
Pop Art, 14, 28, 58, 93, 95, 98, 101–2,
   193
   Independent Group, 101
pop music, xii, 28, 35, 41, 42–7, 53, 58,
   93, 100, 155
   charts, 43
post-modernism, 2, 11, 57–9
post-structuralism, 11, 56–7, 60, 127
Potter, Dennis, 80
poverty, 24, 99, 131–8, 138
   and children, 132, 135, 136
   definitions of poverty, 132–3
   and pensioners, 135–6
   Poverty and the Welfare State, 134
   *Poverty, Socialism and Labour in
      Power*, 136–7

Poverty: The Forgotten Englishmen,
   134
   rediscovery of poverty, 3, 92, 131–8
Powell, Anthony, 61
Powell, Enoch, 70, 146, 165, 167, 168,
   170, 171
   House of Lords reform, 183
   immigration issue, 112, 166, 192, 196
   more popular than Heath, 187
   'Powellism', 165–71
   resignation 1958, 23
   'rivers of blood' speech, 146, 167–8,
      170
Prague Spring, 144
prescription charges, 107, 142, 181, 182,
   189
Presley, Elvis, 26, 35, 44
Prices and Incomes Board, 109
Prince Buster, 47
Private Eye, 50, 70
Profumo affair, 69, 193
psychedelia, 29
   Psychedelic Review, 128
Public Libraries and Museums Act, 61
Punch, 77
Puttnam, David, 84

Quakers, 40, 136, 147
Quant, Mary, 93, 94, 95, 193

Race Relations Act 1965, 115, 165
Race Relations Act 1968, 167, 168–9
Race Relations Board, 115, 165, 169
Racial Adjustment Action Society, 170
racial discrimination, 112, 114, 165–6,
   169
Radio Caroline, 42, 152
Radio London, 42, 152
Radio Luxembourg, 38
Radio One, 42, 152
rastafari, 47
rationing, 23
Ready, Steady, Go!, 42, 82, 93
Rebel Without a Cause, 27
record players, 29–30, 35
Redding, Noel, 46
Rees-Mogg, William, 153

refrigerators, 23, 30, 33, 35, 77
reggae, 47
Reisz, Karel, 84, 85
Reith, John, 78
Rent Act 1965, 133
Resale Price Maintenance, 70
restaurants, 33
Rhodesia, 110, 145, 183, 189
    Ian Smith's regime, 110, 145, 146
Richard, Cliff, 44, 156
Richards, Jeffrey, 84, 87
Richards, Keith, 98, 100
    arrest and drugs charge, 152–3
Richardson gang, 29
Richardson, Tony, 84, 85, 86
Riley, Bridget, 103
road haulage, 20
Robbins Committee, 67
Roberts, Sonny, 47
rock music, 42, 45
Rockers, 38, 41
rocksteady, 47
Roeg, Nicholas, 60
Rolling Stones The, 3, 38, 44, 46, 98, 125,
    152, 153
Romantics, 2, 124–5
Ronan Point, 137
Round House, 52, 126, 129
Rowbotham, Sheila, 13, 130, 159, 168,
    195
Rowntree, Seebohm, 134
Royal Albert Hall poetry reading, 125
Royal College of Art, 101
Royal Court Theatre, 50, 126–7
Royal Festival Hall, 19
Runnymede Trust, 196
Rushton, William, 50
Russell, Ken, 84
Rycroft, Simon, 97

Sainsbury's, 31
Salinger, J.D., 27
Saltzman, Harry, 89
Sampson, Anthony, 34, 49, 52, 75
    Anatomy of Britain, 49
    New Anatomy of Britain, 34
Sandys, Duncan, 166

Sarstedt, Peter, 152
Sartre, Jean-Paul, 56
Sassoon, Vidal, 98
satire, 26, 50
Saussure, Ferdinand, 57
Schlesinger, John, 84
Schofield, Michael, 122
Schwartz, George, 133
scooters, 37
Scotland, xii, 31, 134, 171, 172, 175, 176
Scott, Paul, 61
Scottish National Party, 171, 172, 174,
    175, 176
Scottish nationalism, 171, 172, 174–6
Screen, 84
seamen's strikes, 138, 184
Second World War, xi–xii, xiii, 2, 8, 15,
    161
    pleasure culture of war, 2, 16
Seed, John, 10
Selby Junior, Hubert, 118
Selsdon Park, 188, 189, 191
Selvon, Samuel, 61
sexual attitudes, 122–3
sexual freedom, 93, 130, 162
Sexual Offences Act, 119–20, 156
Shadows, The, 44
Shanks, Michael, 49, 75
Shapiro, Helen, 44
Shaw, Sandie, 45
Shelter, 137, 196
shopping, 32
Shore, Peter, 73, 138
Short, Ted, 107
Shrimpton, Jean, 93, 98
Shulman, Milton, 77
Sight and Sound, 84
Signposts for the Sixties, 73
Silburn, Richard, 134
Sillitoe, Alan, 26
Six-Day War, 141
ska, 46–7, 169
Skatalites, 47
Skinheads, 39, 42, 47
Sly and the Family Stone, 46, 152
Small Faces, 46
Smith, Colin, 170

Smith, Richard, 101
Smithson, Alison and Peter, 101
Snow, C.P., 60
Socialist Labour League, 124, 145
Society for the Protection of the Unborn
    Child, 121
Soft Machine, 126
Sontag, Susan, 58
Soskice, Frank, 107, 115
Sound of Music
    film, 89
    soundtrack, 45
South Africa, 65, 189
Southall Residents' Association, 114
Soviet Union, 15, 16, 55, 144
Spain, 30, 144
Spark, Muriel, 62
Spearman, Diana, 168
Spectator, 167
Springfield, Dusty, 45, 158
Stamp, Terence, 92
Stalin, Joseph, 55
'state of the nation' literature, 49–50, 75,
    193
Steel, David, 120, 121
Steele, Tommy, 27, 42
Stephen, John, 39, 93, 94
sterling, 33, 105, 106–7, 109, 138, 139,
    140, 141, 174, 181, 184, 189, 193
    devaluation ruled out in 1964, 106
    devaluation, 138–42, 180
Stevenson, Randall, 61
Stewart, Michael, 140
Stoppard, Tom, 60
Storey, David, 26
structuralism, 56–7, 60, 127
students, 7, 30, 124, 127
    activists, 28, 144, 188
    movement, 6, 56, 129, 144–50, 155,
    177
    Revolutionary Socialist Students'
    Federation, 146
Suez crisis, 22, 25, 26, 65
'summer of love', 97, 125
Sun, 116, 123, 148
Sunday Express, 188
Sunday Times, 39, 123, 133

supermarkets, 31–2, 33
Supremes The, 45, 158
Sweden, 34
'swinging London', 6, 10, 69, 87, 91–7,
    121, 131, 193

Tanganyika, 65
Tebbit, Norman, 8
Teds, 37–8
teenagers, 26, 35, 36
    'teenage revolution', 27
television, 16, 23, 28, 30, 33–4, 35, 50,
    53, 77–83
    popular programmes, 81–3
That Was The Week That Was, 50–1, 70,
    82
Thatcher, Margaret, 8, 171
Thatcherism, 13, 193
Theatre Workshop, 25, 126
'This is Tomorrow', 101
Thompson, E.P., 56
Thomson, Roy, 78
Thorneycroft, Peter, 23
Thorpe, Jeremy, 172
Tilson, Joe, 101
Time, 92
Time Out, 126
Times, The, 68, 69, 132, 134, 148–9, 150,
    153, 166, 172
Tindall, Gillian, 123
Titmuss, Richard, 134
Top of the Pops, 42, 82, 152
Tornados The, 44
Townsend, Pete, 100
Townsend, Peter, 131, 132, 133, 134,
    136
trade unions, 20, 40, 52, 67, 107, 139,
    141, 184, 191
    In Place of Strife, 185–6, 190
    reject statutory incomes policy, 184
    Trades Union Congress, 52, 108, 184,
    185, 186
    trade union law, 20, 21, 107, 183, 184
Trafalgar Square, 22, 40, 91
Treaty of Rome, 66, 164
Tribune, 134
Trocchi, Alex, 118

Tushingham, Rita, 96
Twiggy, 93
Tynan, Kenneth, 117

Uganda, 65
Ulster Volunteer Force, 178
United Nations, 22
United States of America, 1, 15, 16, 22,
    23, 26, 27, 35, 42–3, 46, 48, 66,
    143, 144
  Federal Reserve, 109
  and sterling devaluation, 141
  US Embassy, 146, 147, 148, 149
Universities and Left Review, 55
university disturbances, 145–6, 150

vacuum cleaners, 30
Vatican II, 54
Velvet Underground The, 46
Victim, 86, 119
Vietnam Solidarity Campaign, 146, 147,
    148, 149, 150
Vietnam War, 30, 109, 124, 141, 143,
    145, 147, 150, 189
  bombing of Hanoi and Haiphong,
    110
  Saigon, 148

wages, 29, 137
  wage freeze 1966, 140, 189
  'wage-stop', 136, 137
Wailers, 47
Walden, Brian, 153
Wales, xii, 31, 171, 172, 173
Wales, Prince of, 174
Warhol, Andy, 58, 98
washing machines, 23, 29, 30, 31, 35
Waterhouse, Keith, 77
Waugh, Auberon, 167
Wednesday Play, The, 80
Weeks, Jeffrey, 155
Welch, Chris, 151, 151
welfare state, 21, 71, 131, 134, 135, 137
Welsh nationalism, 171, 172–4
  Plaid Cymru, 139, 171, 172, 173, 174,
    176
  Welsh Language Act, 173

Wesker, Arnold, 50, 52
West Ham Constituency Labour Party,
    113
West Indies, 111, 169
West Lothian, 36
'What's Wrong With Britain?', 48–53, 85,
    104, 193
Which?, 32
'white heat', 74, 108
Whitehouse Mary, 80, 155–6
  Clean Up TV Campaign, 155
Who The, 38, 46
Wigg, George, 182
Wild One, The, 27, 38
Williams, Marcia, 180
Williams, Raymond, 51, 190
  Communications, 51
  May Day Manifesto, 190
Wilmott, Peter, 36
Wilson, Angus, 60
Wilson, Colin, 25
Wilson, Harold, 17, 18, 51, 70, 72, 113,
    139, 140, 142, 172, 183, 186, 187,
    189, 193
  devaluation broadcast, 141
  general election 1970, 191–2
  leadership crisis, 180–1, 182
  In Place of Strife, 185–6, 190
  Prime Minister, 1964–6, 104–11
  trade union law reform, 184
  wins party leadership, 73–5
Wilson, Harriett, 134
Wimbledon tennis, 29
Windsor Borough Council, 151
Wisdom, Norman, 27
Wolfenden Committee, 86, 119
Women's Liberation Movement, xiii, 13,
    40, 53, 56, 130, 157–64, 196
  'consciousness-raising' groups, 159,
    160
  conference 1970, 160–1
  Ford car workers' strike, 163
women's magazines, 161
Women's National Co-ordination
    Committee, 158
Woodstock Festival, 46
Wootton Report, 154

Wyatt, Woodrow, 109
Wyndham, Francis, 98

X, Michael, 170

Yardbirds, 97
York, 134

York, Peter, 29, 30
'Young Contemporaries' exhibitions, 101
youth, 3, 34, 35, 45, *see also* teenagers
    Welsh youth, 173
    youth culture, 3, 34, 35–42, 54, 85, 95
    'youth question' 3, 26, 36
    youth subcultures, 36–42